Reading Hemingway's *Across the River and into the Trees*

READING HEMINGWAY SERIES
MARK CIRINO, EDITOR
ROBERT W. LEWIS, FOUNDING EDITOR

Reading Hemingway's *The Sun Also Rises*
    H. R. Stoneback

Reading Hemingway's *Men Without Women*
    Joseph M. Flora

Reading Hemingway's *Across the River and into the Trees*
    Mark Cirino

Reading Hemingway's *Across the River and into the Trees*

GLOSSARY AND COMMENTARY

Mark Cirino

The Kent State University Press
KENT, OHIO

© 2016 by The Kent State University Press, Kent, Ohio 44242
All rights reserved
Library of Congress Catalog Card Number 2015009892
ISBN 978-1-60635-239-7
Manufactured in the United States of America

Library of Congress Cataloging-in-Publication Data
Cirino, Mark, 1971–
  Reading Hemingway's Across the river and into the trees : glossary and commentary / Mark Cirino.
     pages cm. — (Reading Hemingway)
  Includes index.
  ISBN 978-1-60635-239-7 (pbk. : alk. paper) ∞
 1. Hemingway, Ernest, 1899–1961. Across the river and into the trees. 2. Hemingway, Ernest, 1899–1961—Criticism and interpretation. I. Title.
  PS3515.E37A734 2015
  813.'52—dc23
                    2015009892

20 19 18 17 16   5 4 3 2 1

But that before all my arrogant poems the real Me stands yet untouch'd, untold, altogether unreach'd.
—Walt Whitman, "As I Ebb'd with the Ocean of Life"

the bad poet is usually unconscious where he ought to be conscious, and conscious where he ought to be unconscious. Both errors tend to make him "personal."
—T. S. Eliot, "Tradition and the Individual Talent"

CONTENTS

Acknowledgments   ix

An Introduction to *Across the River and Into the Trees*   xi

Abbreviations for the Works of Ernest Hemingway Used in This Book   xix

Series Note   xxi

Reading *Across the River and Into the Trees*

Front Matter	3	Chapter 16	136	Chapter 31	179
Chapter 1	5	Chapter 17	139	Chapter 32	180
Chapter 2	11	Chapter 18	143	Chapter 33	181
Chapter 3	16	Chapter 19	145	Chapter 34	184
Chapter 4	26	Chapter 20	147	Chapter 35	185
Chapter 5	37	Chapter 21	149	Chapter 36	187
Chapter 6	43	Chapter 22	153	Chapter 37	189
Chapter 7	59	Chapter 23	156	Chapter 38	192
Chapter 8	71	Chapter 24	159	Chapter 39	195
Chapter 9	78	Chapter 25	160	Chapter 40	196
Chapter 10	100	Chapter 26	161	Chapter 41	199
Chapter 11	103	Chapter 27	163	Chapter 42	203
Chapter 12	109	Chapter 28	167	Chapter 43	204
Chapter 13	129	Chapter 29	169	Chapter 44	205
Chapter 14	133	Chapter 30	174	Chapter 45	206
Chapter 15	135				

Appendix 1   208

Appendix 2   210

Works Cited   212

Index   221

ACKNOWLEDGMENTS

I would like to thank generous, patient, and candid readers of previous versions of this book: Mark P. Ott, Kirk Curnutt, Rosella Mamoli Zorzi, and John Paul Russo. I thank all of them for their many suggestions, and for sharing their expertise.

Thanks to the many supportive friends in the Hemingway Society, particularly Carl P. Eby, Susan Beegel, James H. Meredith, Steve Paul, Sandra Spanier, and Robert Paul Lamb.

I appreciate the help of Stephen Plotkin, Susan Wrynn, and Jessica Green at the John F. Kennedy Library in Boston. Thanks to Carla Elia in Italy for her invaluable research help.

For their friendship and trusted counsel, I thank Anton Borst, Matt Blank, Caroline Hellman, and Matt Bolton.

Thanks to my helpful colleagues at the University of Evansville: Roger Pieroni, Bill Hemminger, Arthur Brown, Lesley Pleasant, and Larry Caldwell. Laura Summers and Meg Atwater-Singer did a superhuman job fulfilling my unreasonable number of interlibrary loan requests.

I am indebted to the Institute for Global Enterprise of Indiana for a generous Global Scholars award, which allowed me to complete this work.

Appreciation and admiration go to the intrepid and talented students of ENGL 399: Jenelle Clausen, Rachel Cochran, Nick Holder, Kevin Kay, Amanda Oaks, Natalie Updike, and Samantha Urban. Thanks to Susan Vandagriff for her magnificent editorial work.

Thanks to the supportive and professional team at The Kent State University Press, particularly Joyce Harrison, Will Underwood, and Mary Young. Thanks to Andras Bereznay for his work on the maps.

And of course, the biggest thanks of all go to the irrationally supportive Cirinos, Kristen and Luca and Noah, who are somehow on every page of this book. All my love.

IN MEMORIAM

Robert W. Lewis (1930–2013) died during the writing of this book. Lewis, the first general editor of this *Reading Hemingway* series, was a former Hemingway Society president and a legendary Hemingway scholar. Bob wrote *Hemingway on Love* (1965), *A Farewell to Arms: War of the Words* (1992), edited *Hemingway in Italy and Other Essays* (1990), and coedited the important posthumous Hemingway work, *Under Kilimanjaro*, published by the Kent State University Press in 2005.

Bob was an exacting critic with a colossal base of knowledge about literature, history, and psychology. He was also a generous and wonderful collaborator, quick to laughter. He was immensely proud of this series and his forthcoming work. I miss our conversations and I cherish the ones we had.

This and all future volumes in the *Reading Hemingway* series attempt to carry on Bob's high standards.

AN INTRODUCTION TO *ACROSS THE RIVER AND INTO THE TREES*

Although he is reflexively included among the greatest of all American novelists, Ernest Hemingway published only five full-length novels in his lifetime.[1] His career as a novelist spanned only from 1926 to 1950, from ages twenty-seven to fifty-one. Three are masterpieces: *The Sun Also Rises* (1926), *A Farewell to Arms* (1929), and *For Whom the Bell Tolls* (1940). The two others, *To Have and Have Not* (1937) and the concern of this book, *Across the River and into the Trees* (1950), are considered minor, flawed, or even failures. The generous or euphemistically inclined call them "transitional." To rail against this hierarchy of Hemingway's work strikes me as perverse and attention-seeking, ultimately unnecessary. In our effort to learn more about Hemingway's life and his art, scholars must not dismiss these inferior works any more than we can ignore a general's defeats, a president's botched decisions, or a scientist's failed experiments. "Do we really know the mountain," Victor Hugo asks in *Les Misérables*, "when we do not know the cavern?" (984). This book will never argue that *Across the River and into the Trees* belongs in the now trite and possibly imaginary category of the "neglected masterpiece" but rather that through some creative scrutiny and new information about the background of the writer and the novel, Hemingway readers will be able to enjoy or appreciate it in its own right, its historical context, and its relevance to Hemingway's life and other work.

To begin reading *Across the River and into the Trees*, it is necessary to recall that when Hemingway began writing the novel in the village of Cortina d'Ampezzo in northern Italy in March 1949, he was the most famous writer in the world. He had not published fiction since the epic *For Whom the Bell Tolls*, a full decade earlier. In the 1940s, Hemingway divorced his third wife and married his fourth, insinuated himself into the action of World War II, and traveled extensively throughout the world. Because of Hemingway's reputation and his long layoff, *Across the River and into the Trees* was met with higher expectations at its publication than anything comparable that might occur today, particularly since the death of J. D. Salinger means the impossibility of an antemortem sequel to *The Catcher in the Rye*. The reading world awaits no novel and demands excellence from no writer to the extent that it did of Hemingway. If Cormac McCarthy or Philip Roth writes a bad novel, it is a minor hiccup in an otherwise splendid career, not an international scandal. In that sense, the disappointment, wrath, and mockery that *Across the River and into the Trees* inspired in late 1950 demonstrates the importance of Hemingway in his time and perhaps to suggests that literature six and a half decades ago might have been treated with greater urgency than it does today.

Across the River and into the Trees is the story of Richard Cantwell, a dying fifty-year-old American colonel stationed in Trieste, Italy, who spends his weekend leave in Venice in order to hunt ducks; enjoy the city that he loves; spend time with his war buddies; and wine, dine, and romance an eighteen-year-old Italian contessa named Renata, the love of his life. Cantwell is a veteran of the Italian front in World War I, having defended the Veneto in 1918, and also World War II, having fought with the 4th Infantry Division in Normandy, the rat race through France, the Hürtgen Forest, and the Battle of the Bulge. Much to his bitterness, Cantwell has been scapegoated and "stars had been removed (13:15); he was demoted from brigadier general to colonel for following "other people's orders" (194:12, 222:18–19) and obeying the feckless, unrealistic expectations of the masters of war, the office-bound, no-fight generals that killed many good Americans. Cantwell takes enormous pride in his generalship, and despite the four or five years that have passed since his demotion, he is haunted by those mistakes and those events, even though the novel does not explicitly dramatize those past moments.

It may be apparent that this preceding summary does not really trace a plot or describe action that occurs but rather outlines a narrative situation and describes Cantwell's past. Indeed, most of *Across the River and into the Trees* is an extended fixation on memory; given Cantwell's heart condition, any nod to the future is ironic, a cruel punch line. As are Hemingway's other veterans, Cantwell is burdened by the past.

In William Faulkner's banquet speech upon receiving the Nobel Prize for Literature, delivered in Sweden just three months after the publication of *Across the River and into the Trees,* he identified the essence of enduring art as being the courageous depiction of "the human heart in conflict with itself" (649). In Cantwell's case, his internal conflict is to negotiate the competing demands of being a soldier who can successfully defend his country and being a gentle human being who can successfully love his girlfriend. Much of Cantwell's interiority is focused on maintaining a kind demeanor, particularly to the woman he so desperately loves. From the first moment to the last, Cantwell finds it a constant demand of his effort to remind himself not to act like a soldier but rather to be a gentleman worthy of a wonderful woman. In early stories like "Soldier's Home" and "Big Two-Hearted River" from his first collection, *In Our Time* (1925), Hemingway investigated a soldier's emotional state once war is over, an often traumatized, scarred individual who does not find reintegration into society to be without tremendous frustration and difficulty.

One of the pleasures of reading narrative of any kind is its invitation to the reader to experience vicariously the growth, development, and lessons of the protagonist.

What to do, then, with a novel like *Across the River and into the Trees,* which almost had the swaggering title *The Things That I Know,* and in which the protagonist sometimes seems like he has known everything from the beginning? Unlike Hemingway's earlier protagonists, Cantwell experiences no insight, no epiphany or moment of change during the action of the novel—this novel is his song of experience, with the innocence already lost in the wars.

Cantwell's only lesson, then, is not to gain knowledge but to lose it. His is not a story of growth but of recession. He need not learn; he must unlearn his years of military training that taught him how to kill but left him wanting some of the softer qualities that make for an ideal husband. In this respect, Cantwell's effort is determined, his success limited. In the final breakfast with Renata (193–94), he is kinder and more easily so than earlier in the novel—this is all thanks to Renata, his unlikely muse and mentor. Later in the same scene, however, he imagines "with anticipation" the hanging of his ex-wife (197:11), before her memory is eradicated through Renata's gentle guidance.

THE COMPOSITION AND PUBLICATION OF *ACROSS THE RIVER AND INTO THE TREES*

When Hemingway began *Across the River and into the Trees* in early March 1949 in Cortina d'Ampezzo, a town in the Veneto in Italy, it was originally entitled "A Short Story," until, over the next nine months, it grew into a novel. The Hemingways left Italy at the end of April, and Hemingway continued writing the novel in Cuba and then finished it at the Ritz Hotel in Paris in late November. Hemingway had a habit of including in his correspondence of September, October, and November the word count for that day or that week, to convince his friends (and possibly himself) that he was making impressive progress.

For example, his unpublished letters reveal that in a given week, Hemingway reported his production as follows:

WORD COUNT	DATE
1,174	14 September 1949
901	15 September
474	16 September
664	17 September
"the servant rested"[2]	18 September
1077 and then 564	19 September
1224	20 September

The novel in slightly more primitive form was serialized in *Cosmopolitan* over five issues from February through June 1950. Hemingway was paid $85,000 for the serial rights. Although he had elsewhere disingenuously asserted that he did not negotiate for serial rights during the composition of a novel, on 10 June 1949 he wrote A. E. Hotchner, then a member of the *Cosmopolitan* staff, committing to the magazine's rights to his novel: "I can tell you personally that I will not give the novel to anyone else. You can count on this the same as you could count on a contract" (JFK Outgoing Correspondence).[3]

Across the River and into the Trees was published on 7 September 1950. Scribner's first printing was a run of seventy-five thousand. The novel appeared on the *New York Times*'s best-seller list for twenty-one weeks, including first place for seven of those (Hanneman 62, 63).

"CRITICAL REACTION HYSTERICAL BOTH WAYS":
THE RECEPTION OF *ACROSS THE RIVER AND INTO THE TREES*

Although a novel's reviews are not always relevant and rarely even interesting, the contemporary reception of *Across the River and into the Trees* has created such a legacy that readers would gain insight through the often incendiary reactions, many of which have gained traction over the past sixty-five years.[4] One of the associations of *Across the River and into the Trees* is the intensity of the negative judgments it received.

Although the ferocity of the reviews is something to behold, it is a fallacy that the novel met with unanimous condemnation. Tennessee Williams called the novel "the best and most honest work that Hemingway has done . . . the finest thing Hemingway has done" (35). *Newsweek* judged it "Hemingway's best and most carefully thought out book. The colonel who is its hero is his subtlest characterization" (92), just as Malcolm Cowley called Cantwell the "most fully realized of Hemingway's heroes" (1). Fanny Butcher, Kate Simon, and the reviewer for *Saturday Night* all use the word "magic" to describe the writing in *Across the River and into the Trees* (3, 21, 24). Novelist John O'Hara's explosive *New York Times* review—which along the way occasionally lampoons the novel—dubs Hemingway the "most important author living today, the outstanding author since the death of Shakespeare" (1). As Hemingway lamented, O'Hara set the expectations so impossibly high that the novel was attacked with still more glee; subsequent reviewers commonly referred to the O'Hara review with derision.[5] Most critics, seizing on the first opportunity to review Hemingway since 1940, declared it his swan song, never entertaining the possibility that in two years he might publish a work of the quality of *The Old Man and the Sea*.

Those inclined to compliment *Across the River and into the Trees* always mention first that the novel is not Hemingway's "important" epic they were awaiting, so it should be put in perspective; second, Hemingway is always Hemingway, with his innate power of description and ear for dialogue; third, the duck hunt that frames the novel is beautifully written; and, finally, the writer's love for Venice is unmistakable and effectively conveyed.

Likewise, the novel's weak points were also a matter of general agreement: first, Cantwell is too much like Hemingway (they share experiences, opinions, a vocabulary, and attitude) and it is impossible to separate the writer and his protagonist; second, Renata is not a believable creation, she is dreamlike, a wish-fulfillment; third nothing happens—the novel is too talky; fourth, Cantwell is excessively self-pitying; and, last, Hemingway's prose style is self-parodic.

The reader of *Across the River and into the Trees* will find some substance in these five fairly major criticisms. In the negative perception surrounding this novel that has endured to date, three preeminent intellectuals led the vanguard: Maxwell Geismar, Philip Rahv, and Alfred Kazin. Their level of vitriol forced many subsequent reviewers to review the reviews as well as the novel, creating kind of a self-feeding maelstrom of negativity towards Hemingway among the literati.

To Geismar, writing in the *Saturday Review* of 9 September 1950, *Across the River and into the Trees* is "an unfortunate novel and unpleasant to review . . . Hemingway's worst novel . . . a synthesis of everything that is bad in his previous work and it throws a doubtful light on the future." The novel is "so dreadful," Geismar continues, "that it begins to have its own morbid fascination" (18). Specifically, he complains about the characterization of Renata ("a fantasy of the completely docile, pliant child bride" [18]) and Cantwell ("overwhelming narcissism" [18]). The gleam of hope in *Across the River and into the Trees* is that it will clear the way for a more important work, "an emotional release for an intricate and tormented talent" (19).[6]

Kazin's *New Yorker* review expresses "pity" and "embarrassment" for Hemingway, who he believes has made "a travesty of himself" (378). As Geismar and Rahv do, Kazin finds the dialogue "remarkably false" (379), with Hemingway "just sounding off" on his "pettiest, most irrelevant opinions" (381). Kazin, whose breadth of knowledge on American literature was unmatched in the middle of the century, deems *Across the River and into the Trees* "one of the most confused and vituperatively revealing self-portrayals by an American I have ever seen" (379).

Echoing Kazin, Philip Rahv, writing for *Commentary*, dismissed *Across the River and into the Trees* as "so egregiously bad as to render all comment on it positively embarrassing," remarking on the "disappointment" and "demoralization" he felt after reading the novel. Rahv considered the novel a "parody . . . of his own manner" to the extent that "the legend suffers irremediable damage." As do other critics, Rahv found that the novel invited a consideration of Hemingway "the man, rather than to Hemingway the artist . . . the artist appears to have been entirely displaced by the man." Like Geismar, Rahv judges Renata "not a recognizable human being at all but a narcissistically constructed love-object" (400).

These three major voices in American letters created such a disturbance that subsequent reviews had to factor in the condemnations that were a matter of public record.

Although no Hemingway critic has suggested that *Across the River and into the Trees* is his best novel, it is widely acknowledged that the novel more than any of his others requires the kind of intensive explication and commentary which is this book's goal. As Hemingway scholar Ben Stoltzfus writes of the novel, "We need to incorporate analyses of the historical, literary, and artistic references as they resonate throughout the novel like bells from the church towers" (24). Hemingway biographer Michael S. Reynolds finds "more allusions and arcane references" in this novel than any other (*Final Years* 211). James H. Meredith has cautioned that the failure of literary critics to mine the novel and "decipher its allusions" will risk the novel "remaining in comparative obscurity" (60). Charles Poore writes: "It is a short novel, but if you follow all its forays and judgments and allusions it will last you a long time" (29). The French critic Fernand C. Danchin laments the "obscure allusions which tomorrow no one will understand" (qtd. in Smith and Miner). As Renata herself says in the novel: "I do not understand the local allusions. But you can explain them when you care to. Please keep on telling me" (214:21–23).

Those allusions, however, are the easy part. Hemingway's cultural, military, and personal references, no matter how well disguised, can usually be tracked down. The more difficult work is in assimilating this novel with his greater accomplishments. The first-time reader of *Across the River and into the Trees* will discover, then, that Hemingway presents a version of his traditional themes: love tempered by the exigencies of danger and disease and complicated by notions of immorality. The reader will also find a meditation on the conduct of men at war and veterans in society. As this volume demonstrates, the novel exists in conversation with *The Sun Also Rises, A Farewell to Arms,* "The Snows of Kilimanjaro," *The Old Man and the Sea,* and his more canonical works. An understanding of *Across the River and into the Trees* enriches our understanding of those enduring masterpieces.

Across the River and into the Trees enters into two quintessential Hemingway themes: the soldier after the war, and the function of love at the exact center point of a bloody and bellicose twentieth century. Hemingway handles this familiar material more brutally, sometimes less subtly than in his more celebrated works, but in his depiction of Cantwell, we receive laid bare Hemingway's statement on the divided self's struggle to remain human during and after the battle.

I have always believed that the most exciting efforts in literary criticism end in ellipses or question marks, not exclamation points. I view the critic not as fascistic or sententious but as someone interesting in provoking conversation and consideration about the topic at hand. By this, I mean that I hope that this first book about *Across the River and into the Trees* inspires further work on the novel that will keep peeling layers to get us closer to Hemingway's alchemy, only to realize that we are ever further from it.

NOTES

1. I consider *Torrents of Spring* (1926) and *The Old Man and the Sea* (1952) novellas. Novels are typically about sixty thousand words; *The Old Man and the Sea*, for instance, is less than half that length, at about twenty-six thousand.
2. 18 September 1949 was a Sunday, so Hemingway invokes the Bible: "the seventh day is a Sabbath to the Lord your God; in it you shall not do any work . . . and your maidservant may rest as well as you" (Deuteronomy 5:14).
3. Six weeks later, Hemingway wrote *Ladies Home Journal* that while he is doing no negotiations about the novel during its drafting, he would keep the door open for the possibility of an agreement (17 July 1949, Outgoing Correspondence).
4. "Critical reaction hysterical both ways" is Hemingway's phrase, from a 13 October 1950 letter to A. E. Hotchner (*Dear Papa* 82).
5. Hemingway responded to his publisher, Charles Scribner, "Naturally the thing about Shakespeare, the undisputed champion, is ridiculous. . . . Why did he have to say such a thing? . . . I am very grateful to O'Hara. But I would have been 100 times happier if he had understood the book" (*SL* 713). Of the O'Hara review, Hemingway lamented wryly to his friend General Charles "Buck" Lanham—the main inspiration for *Across the River and into the Trees*'s protagonist—that it "will make me plenty of friends" (*SL* 715).
6. Hemingway's personal history with Geismar was volatile. After meeting the critic and discussing books in spring 1944 (*SL* 625), in September 1947 he requested an autographed copy of Geismar's *Last of the Provincials*, a study of the American novel from 1921 to 1925. Two years later, Hemingway reported that Geismar's writings on Fitzgerald "made me sick," and he concluded that Geismar "is through" and has "menopause of the brain" (*SL* 657, 696). Geismar's chapter devoted to Hemingway in his 1947 study *Writers in Crisis: The American Novel, 1925–1940* expresses reservation at the thinness of Hemingway's understanding of sociopolitics displayed in *For Whom the Bell Tolls* yet holds out hope that he might develop this vision in the future.

WORKS CITED

Butcher, Fanny. "The Old Black Magic That Is Hemingway's." *Chicago Sunday Tribune Magazine of Books* (17 September 1950): 3, 14.

Cowley, Malcolm. "Hemingway: Portrait of an Old Soldier Preparing to Die." *New York Herald Tribune* (10 September 1950): 1, 16.

Faulkner, William. "Address upon Receiving the Nobel Prize for Literature." *The Portable Faulkner*. Ed. Malcolm Cowley. New York: Penguin, 2003. 649–50.

Geismar, Maxwell. "To Have and to Have and to Have." *Saturday Review* 33 (9 September 1950): 18–19.

Hanneman, Audre. *Ernest Hemingway: A Comprehensive Bibliography*. Princeton: Princeton UP, 1967.

Hemingway, Ernest. *Across the River and into the Trees*. 1950. New York: Scribner, 1996.

———. *Ernest Hemingway: Selected Letters, 1917–1961*. Ed. Carlos Baker. New York: Scribner, 1981.

Hugo, Victor. *Les Misérables*. 1862. Trans. Lee Fahnestock, Norman MacAfee, and C. E. Wilbour. New York: Signet, 1987.

Kazin, Alfred. Review of *Across the River and into the Trees*. *New Yorker* (9 September 1950): 101–03. Rpt. in *Hemingway: The Critical Heritage*. Ed. Jeffrey Meyers. London: Routledge & Kegan Paul, 1982. 378–81.

M.B. "Afterglow." *Saturday Night* 65 (3 October 1950): 24.

Meredith, James H. "The Rapido River and the Hürtgen Forest in *Across the River and into the Trees*." *Hemingway Review* 14.1 (Fall 1994): 60–66.

"The New Hemingway." *Newsweek* 36 (11 September 1950): 90–95.

O'Hara, John. "The Author's Name Is Hemingway." *New York Times Book Review*, 10 September 1950: 1, 30–31.

Poore, Charles. "Books of the Times." Review of *Across the River and into the Trees*. *New York Times*, 7 September 1950: 29.

Rahv, Philip. *Commentary* 10 (October 1950): 400–02

Reynolds, Michael S. *Hemingway: The Final Years*. New York: Norton, 1999.

Simon, Kate. "Old Age of a Hero." *New Republic* 123 (18 September 1950): 20–21.

Smith, Thelma M. and Ward L. Miner. *Transatlantic Migration: The Contemporary American Novel in France*. Durham, N.C.: Duke UP, 1955.

Stoltzfus, Ben. "The Stones of Venice, Time, and Remembrance: Calculus and Proust in *Across the River and into the Trees*." *Hemingway Review* 22.2 (Spring 2003): 19–29.

Williams, Tennessee. "A Writer's Quest for a Parnassus." *New York Times Magazine*, 13 August 1950: 16, 35.

ABBREVIATIONS FOR THE WORKS OF ERNEST HEMINGWAY USED IN THIS BOOK

ARIT	*Across the River and into the Trees.* New York: Scribner, 1950.
BL	*By-line Ernest Hemingway: Selected Articles and Dispatches of Four Decades.* Edited by William White. New York: Scribner, 1967.
CSS	*The Complete Short Stories of Ernest Hemingway: The Finca Vigía Edition.* New York: Scribner, 1987.
DLT	*Dateline: Toronto: The Complete* Toronto Star *Dispatches, 1920–1924.* Edited by William White. New York: Scribner, 1985.
DIA	*Death in the Afternoon.* New York: Scribner, 1932.
DS	*The Dangerous Summer.* New York: Scribner, 1985.
FTA	*A Farewell to Arms.* New York: Scribner, 1929.
FWBT	*For Whom the Bell Tolls.* New York: Scribner, 1940.
GOE	*The Garden of Eden.* New York: Scribner, 1986.
GHOA	*Green Hills of Africa.* New York: Scribner, 1935.
IOT	*In Our Time.* New York: Boni and Liveright, 1925. Rev. ed., New York: Scribner, 1930.
IIS	*Islands in the Stream.* New York: Scribner, 1970.
JFK	Ernest Hemingway Collection, John F. Kennedy Presidential Library and Museum, Boston, Massachusetts.
Letters 1	*The Letters of Ernest Hemingway.* Vol. 1. *1907–1922.* Ed. Sandra Spanier and Robert W. Trogdon. Cambridge: Cambridge University Press, 2011.
Letters 2	*The Letters of Ernest Hemingway.* Vol. 2. *1923–1925.* Ed. Sandra Spanier, Albert J. DeFazio III, and Robert W. Trogdon. Cambridge: Cambridge University Press, 2013.
MAW	*Men at War.* New York: Crown Publishers, 1942.
MF	*A Moveable Feast.* New York: Scribner, 1964.
MF-RE	*A Moveable Feast: The Restored Edition.* Edited by Seán Hemingway. New York: Scribner, 2009.
OMS	*The Old Man and the Sea.* New York: Scribner, 1952.
Poems	*Complete Poems.* Edited, with an introduction and notes by Nicholas Gerogiannis. Rev. ed. Lincoln: University of Nebraska Press, 1992.
SAR	*The Sun Also Rises.* New York: Scribner, 1926.

SL   *Ernest Hemingway: Selected Letters, 1917–1961.* Edited by Carlos Baker. New York: Scribner, 1981.
TAFL   *True at First Light.* Edited by Patrick Hemingway. New York: Scribner, 1999.
THHN   *To Have and Have Not.* New York: Scribner, 1937.
 TOS   *The Torrents of Spring.* New York: Scribner, 1926.

SERIES NOTE

All page references in this volume are keyed to the First Scribner Paperback Fiction edition of *Across the River and into the Trees* (1996), which begins on page 11 and ends on page 283.

Annotations are given a page and line number, separated by a colon. A reference to the third line of page 17, for instance, would be 17:3. A reference to the first three lines of page 40 would be 40:1–3.

When citing, I have appropriated the standard abbreviations for Hemingway texts used by the *Hemingway Review,* in concert with the Hemingway Letters Project (see xix–xx).

Reading *Across the River and into the Trees*

FRONT MATTER

Title: The title for *Across the River and into the Trees* is explained in its last chapter, when Colonel Richard Cantwell tells his driver (also named Jackson) of Stonewall Jackson's last words: "let us cross over the river and rest under the shade of the trees" (282:4–6). At the same point in the manuscript, Hemingway wrote a note to himself: "Put in entire and correct quotation from book by KIDD entitled 'I Rode with Stonewall'" (JFK 1). The book to which Hemingway refers was written by Henry Kyd Douglas, a member of Jackson's staff. Douglas describes "the light of the eternal future" shining onto the dying Jackson, who then says, as Cantwell correctly recalls, "let us cross over the river and rest under the shade of the trees" (221). This moment is also invoked by the Sidney Lanier poem "The Dying Words of Stonewall Jackson," the epigraph of which reads:

> "Order A. P. Hill to prepare for battle."
> "Tell Major Hawks to advance the Commissary train."
> "Let us cross the river and rest in the shade." (238)

According to biographer Carlos Baker, Hemingway also considered the titles "The Things That I Know" and "A New-Slain Knight" (*Life Story* 474). Michael Reynolds reports that Hemingway considered "A New Slain Knight," "Our One and Only Life," and "Over the River and into the Trees" (*Final Years* 207). The "Across the River and into the Trees" manuscript contains another note to himself: "Title for Memoirs" and beneath that heading "The Things That I Know." The novel also uses the phrase "moveable feast" twice (69:21, 250:16), suggesting that his memoirs and their eventual title were very much on his mind in 1949 when he wrote the novel.

Baker points out that the inclusion of Stonewall Jackson's line emphasizes Cantwell's hand that has been ruined in a war injury (*Writer as Artist* 268), an injury that, like Jackson had, Cantwell received from friendly fire. The majesty and poetry of Jackson's last line will stand out when compared to Cantwell's own (282:16–17). In a novel littered with references, allusions, and surreptitious quotations both mangled and accurate, it is fitting that Cantwell cannot utter his own dying words without first referring to someone else's. Like Stonewall Jackson, he also gives a practical deathbed instruction, an order to an underling, rather than a metaphysical revelation.

Dedication: In 1944, following Hemingway's first lunch with Mary Welsh (1908–1986), who would become his fourth wife, he vowed to marry her and dedicate a book to her. Mary asked, "With love?" And Hemingway said he would. Mary recalls in her memoir, *How It Was*, "Six years later he did in what I thought his poorest book" (103). Mary found it "comic that of all his dedications the only one he made 'with love' was the one to me which I least admired" (272). In a 1944 letter to her, Hemingway writes, "Hope to write a very fine, good, grown-up novel of which all I have so far is the dedication / To Mary Welsh / If you don't like novel you can dedicate it to anybody you want as it is your property. . . . But I will write a good novel, win, lose, or draw" (*SL* 568).

Hemingway's dedication also contains an unmistakable irony, since he absolutely viewed Adriana Ivancich (1930–1983), the model for Renata, the novel's heroine, as his muse and inspiration, just as he did for *The Old Man and the Sea* (1952). *The Old Man and the Sea* is dedicated to his editor and publisher, respectively, Maxwell Perkins and Charles Scribner. Hemingway inscribed the copy of *Across the River and into the Trees* he gave to Adriana as a gift: "To Adriana who inspired all that is good in this book and nothing which is not." As Adriana recalls in her autobiography, "A beautiful dedication, I thought. A really beautiful dedication" (*La torre bianca* 136–37, my translation).

Note: As Hemingway's career developed, he commonly included explanatory notes that either clarified the lines between fact and fiction or blurred them and sometimes did both simultaneously. In the note to *Across the River and into the Trees*, he is stressing the complete fictitiousness of this novel. In *Green Hills of Africa* (1935), his foreword describes his attempt "to write an absolutely true book" to determine whether it "if truly presented, can compete with a work of the imagination." In the preface to *A Moveable Feast* (1964), Hemingway invites the reader to consider his memoirs as fiction but then suggests "there is always the chance that such a book of fiction may throw some light on what has been written as fact."

Hemingway's insistence on *Across the River and into the Trees* as fiction did not dissuade readers from associating the fifty-year-old colonel with the fifty-year-old writer, nor the teenaged contessa Renata with the teenaged contessa Adriana.

CHAPTER 1

1:1 They started two hours before daylight: The novel begins before dawn on Sunday in the winter of 1948–49 in the Veneto. "They" refers to the hunting party in the six boats, which includes the "shooter," who is the protagonist, Colonel Richard Cantwell and the "poler," a surly boatman.

It is fitting that the first sentence of the novel introduces the theme of time, since its treatment in the novel has bedeviled so many readers. The action of the novel takes place over the last four days (Thursday–Sunday) of Cantwell's life and is framed by this duck-hunting sequence in chapter 1 and chapters 40–45. Cantwell sees his doctor for a checkup on Thursday, drives down from Trieste to Venice on Friday, spends Friday and Saturday with Renata, and then hunts ducks on Sunday before he dies on his way back to Trieste in the evening. For the essential study of temporality and narrative structure in this novel, see Peter Lisca's important article, "The Structure of Hemingway's *Across the River and into the Trees*."

See Time Chart Appendix 1.

1:4 the poler: As has been noted by previous critics (e.g., Lisca 242, Stoltzfus 25, Young, *Reconsideration* 115, Russo 396), this character is a clear allusion to Charon, the ferryman of the underworld in Greek mythology. In a novel where Dante will become such a conspicuous counterpoint to the protagonist, Hemingway invites us to recall Canto III of the *Inferno,* in which Charon rounds up all the souls destined for hell, "beating with his oar those whoever lingers" (l. 111). Dante fittingly takes this negative characterization from Virgil; in the *Aeneid,* Charon is a "figure of fright . . . foul and terrible" (ll. 408–09). The *Inferno*'s other angry boatman is Phlegyas in Canto VIII, the boatman of the fifth circle and the river Styx. Therefore, Hemingway introduces this novel at once as both classic literature and a journey that courts death and hell.

In Thomas Mann's *Death in Venice* (1912), another constant literary counterpoint to this novel, the protagonist Gustav von Aschenbach is transported by an unpleasant gondolier, "a man of disagreeable, even brutal features," with a "surly, arrogant . . . strangely uncompliant, weirdly stubborn" attitude (17), an exact match for this poler.[1]

The poler's unappealing manner is ultimately redeemed when Barone Alvarito, a young friend, explains to Cantwell that his sullenness originates from when his wife and daughter were raped by Moroccans during World War II (277:30–31). These mass rapes, called *marocchinate,* occurred in 1944 by French Goumier soldiers in southern Italy. We then reexamine the behavior of the poler in this first chapter, during which he casts off decoys "in a hatred" (15:20–21), "as though he were ridding himself of something obscene" (14:11–12). The poler becomes another Hemingway character displaying the sometimes ugly effects of wartime trauma.

In an echo scene, chapter 21 begins with Cantwell taking a gondola across the Grand Canal "and standing with the crowd of those condemned to early rising" (172:2–3).

11:5 **The shooter:** This epithet introduces Colonel Richard Cantwell, who is not referred to as a colonel until 17:1, not referred to as "Cantwell" until 75:11, and not referred to as "Richard" until 81:26, although his doctor refers to him as "Dick" at 17:9. One of the most common reactions and criticisms of this novel is that Cantwell is such a transparent representation of Hemingway's self-image—the gruff, intelligent, worldly, epicurean, veteran, literary, cultured, lothario. In an 11 October 1949 letter to World War II friend Colonel Buck Lanham, Hemingway claimed that Cantwell was based on Major General Charlie Sweeny (1882–1963), Lanham (1902–1978), and himself.[2]

Hemingway also modeled Cantwell's character after that of his friend Chink Dorman-Smith (1895–1969), who shared many of the colonel's experiences.

12:21 **the shooting barrel:** These barrels, submerged into the marsh, are the blinds in which the shooter will stay during the hunt. The hunter typically sits on a pail in this barrel. Cantwell sits on a "shell box" (13:10). As Adriana Ivancich recalls in her memoirs of a hunting trip she shared with Hemingway, and as Hemingway recounts in innumerable letters from the period, Hemingway and his party used this method of hunting in the Veneto. This reference is the same "oaken staved hogshead sunk in the bottom of the lagoon" (13:4–5), "sunken oak hogshead" (256:1), "wooden barrel" (258:1), "barrel in a marsh" (268:2), and "sunken barrel" referred to throughout the text (271:2). The colonel also mentions the "*botte*" (75:21), Italian for "barrel," in which they will hunt ducks.

12:31 **jerk:** The reader will note the conspicuous use of this word, beginning here and recurring fourteen more times. "Jerk" refers to this boatman (12:31, 13:1); his driver Jackson (45:32); the writer and soldier Gabriele D'Annunzio (55:15); the pockmarked American writer (93:27); the French general Jacque Philippe Leclerc (126:23, 200:22); the Fascist hall porter at the Gritti (164:1); a hypothetical contractor who profited by making bad raincoats for the military (172:13); two young, possibly ex-Fascist men who trail Cantwell (175:29); the unnamed commander who gave catastrophic orders to Cantwell, leading to the loss of his division (214:24); and those who hold rank while never fighting (230:13). Cantwell explains to Renata that a "jerk" refers to "a man who has never worked at his trade (*oficio*) truly, and is presumptuous in some annoying way" (93:30–31). This definition recalls Dante's eighth circle of hell, reserved for the fraudulent. Renata defines the word as a snob or someone with "new money" (241:1), who has presumably profited ignobly from war. Finally, Cantwell turns it on himself right before his death, hoping he is not "the type of jerk" (281:24) who will worry about dying when there is nothing to be done about it.

13:1, 2 **in English . . . in Italian:** Cantwell joins a Hemingway tradition, in which his American protagonists are typically multilingual: Jake Barnes in *The Sun Also Rises* (1926) knows French and Spanish, *A Farewell to Arms*'s (1929) Frederic Henry knows Italian, Robert Jordan of *For Whom the Bell Tolls* knows Spanish, Thomas Hudson of *Islands in the Stream* (1970) knows French and Spanish, David Bourne in *The Garden of Eden* (1986) knows French, and Cantwell speaks Italian, Spanish, French, and German. He communicates with Renata in a mixture of these languages. It is not always specified, but "in Italian" is denoted here and six other times (43:10–11, 103:19, 110:20, 183:6–7, 189:33, 263:27), and "in English" is denoted here and at 181:16.

In this situation, Cantwell uses English simultaneously to hide and exorcise his disdain for the boatman, without arousing a confrontation.

13:4 **daylight:** Per the first sentence of the novel, two hours have elapsed since the opening of the narrative.

13:13 **patch on the left shoulder:** Cantwell is wearing his combat jacket that displays his colonel's shoulder patch, a silver eagle with outstretched wings. Later in the novel, he will reveal a memory of when the patch incited a street fight between him and two sailors (260:21–22), which Cantwell wins. During that anecdote, he describes himself as wearing such a patch on each shoulder.

13:14–15 **where stars had been removed:** The mostly unspoken backstory of the novel is the Colonel's bitterness over being demoted from a general to a colonel. Although we will never get the complete details, this incident is the simmering tension with which Cantwell must come to terms in the last weekend of his life. We do learn that he had been a general, but "Not for too damn long" (136:21). His driver Jackson thinks, "Just because he was a B.G. [brigadier general] once he knows everything. If he was any good as a B.G. why didn't he hold it?" (34:31–32). This demotion is such an indignity to Cantwell that as he reminisces and recounts war stories, he occasionally lapses into the mindset of being a general (64:10, 161:8, 184:23). During an anecdote in chapter 41 (268:32–270:8), Cantwell reveals that he was a general during the Ardennes engagement. The Battle of the Bulge took place in

December 1944, which suggests that his infraction, or at least the judgment against him, took place following this episode of the war.

One of Hemingway's friends from World War I, Chink Dorman-Smith, suffered a similar demotion, but for the opposite reason. As Jeffrey Meyers points out, while Cantwell was demoted for following impossible orders, Churchill demoted Dorman-Smith for—however justly—disobeying orders ("Chink Dorman-Smith" 321).

See also the extraordinary meditation in *For Whom the Bell Tolls*:

> But should a man carry out impossible orders knowing what they lead to? Even though they come from Golz, who is the party as well as the army? Yes. He should carry them out because it is only in the performing of them that they can prove to be impossible. How do you know they are impossible until you have tried them? If every one said orders were impossible to carry out when they were received where would you be? Where would we all be if you just said, "Impossible," when orders came?
>
> He had seen enough of commanders to whom all orders were impossible. That swine Gomez in Estremadura. He had seen enough attacks when the flanks did not advance because it was impossible. No, he would carry out the orders and it was bad luck that you liked the people you must do it with. (162)

14:3 **trade:** This word, referring to the boatman's occupation as a hunting aid, carries tremendous thematic weight throughout the novel. Cantwell incessantly refers to soldiering as a "trade," and his means of defining this trade is revealing. What, to Cantwell then, is his trade? "[K]illing armed men" (65:21); "making things clear" (138:32); the dispensing of death (202:26); "Figuring things out . . . Figuring things out when they were shooting at you" (267:27–29).

His trade of soldiering is also his explanation for why he occasionally acts in a brutal, cruel, vulgar, rude, brusque, and insensitive way (66:17–19). This tendency will also mark a crucial tension in the novel: his wish to be gentle to Renata and humane to others but also his instinct toward the trade of soldiering. When he glares at Renata, for instance, he apologizes for having "slipped into my trade unconsciously" (81:31–32). During an affectionate moment soon after, Cantwell says, "I love you and my trade can gently leave" (82:9–10). This schizophrenia between being a lover and being a soldier is the internal crisis Cantwell must perpetually negotiate. He tells Renata, "you are not supposed to have a heart in this trade" (127:24–25) and that it involves the constant proximity with death, "love's opposite number" (202:24–25). Renata refers to Cantwell's "sad trade" (91:6), just as Cantwell mentions the "*triste métier* of war" (231:3). "Loving and leaving" is, according to Cantwell, a "Very rough trade" (265:18).

This attitude carries some biographical resonance. Hemingway's fourth wife, Mary, once said, "I've finally figured out why Papa sometimes gets mean now that the war is over. . . . It's because there's no occasion for him to be valorous in peacetime (Ross 57).

The word "trade" is important enough that it is translated into Spanish as "*oficio*" twice (89:30, 93:31).

Cantwell also refers to the treacherous duck's "trade" of warning other ducks (265).

In "The Snows of Kilimanjaro," the writer's trade depends on his ability to "think about some one else" (*CSS* 40).

15:3 shot exactly as he should have shot: As in elsewhere in Hemingway's work, we see a meticulous focus on the propriety, execution, technique, and efficiency of Cantwell's behavior. Such description has been disparaged as Hemingway imitating Hemingway. However, we must remember that Cantwell's time and health are waning. He has an injured hand, he is sick and dying, and he therefore puts a premium on executing actions economically and competently. Such qualities would also be naturally valued by military officers.

15:8 I'll be a sad son of a bitch: Cantwell uses this phrase of disbelief over the poler's reprimand, which Cantwell then repeats in reaction to Renata declaring that she likes to feel the pressure of the Colonel's buttons during intimate moments (201:19) and then later, when he wonders how Renata could love someone like him (266:2).

15:18 **dekes:** That is, the decoys.

15:18 The hell with him: In this first chapter, which takes place in Italy and with a Charon-like boatman, Hemingway continues to establish Dante as a thematic touchstone. Critics have glibly referred to this novel as Hemingway's *Inferno*, in which he is able to cast his foes or perceived foes into hell. In addition to the poler, he sentences other people, things, words, and concepts to hell: his doctor, in a joke (19:30); notions of the picturesque (40:3); a too-expensive vaporetto ride (47:16); himself (65:12, 107:21, 149:18–19); being mean (89:2); feeling his fragile health (89:21); the decisions he made at war (91:7); a petty linguistic dispute with Renata (134:28–29); things being too hard to explain (138:32–33); restraint due to his poor health (147:16); talking to the portrait of Renata (154:6, 164:21); taking pills (155:4–5, 212:20); Renata's portrait (161:21), which in turn tells Cantwell to go to hell himself (161:24); anything American except Cantwell himself (165:11); sorrows (208:11); SHAEF (Supreme Headquarters Allied Expeditionary Forces) (212:21); his bad hand (224:16); death and consequences (232:6); memories of war (234:10); the road to Trieste (280:5). Clearly, as more than an idiomatic quirk, Cantwell does take the liberty of consigning to hell anything that rubs him the wrong way.

15:22 Don't let him spoil it: Part of Cantwell's challenge in the last days and moments of his life is to cherish the things he loves the most, which are Venice and its sights and culture, Renata and his other friends from the Veneto, and duck hunting. He knows it may well be the last time he can enjoy these passions, and he must coach himself not to allow his temper, his bad memories, his mood, and his bad habits to ruin these pleasures. Chapter 1 ends with Cantwell reminding himself: "I must not let him ruin it. . . . Keep your temper" (16:19, 16:22). It becomes one of the dramas of the novel.

Even in this brief paragraph of only four sentences, Cantwell reminds himself not to let the poler or anything else "spoil it" three times (15:22, 15:25, 15:26–27).

15:25–26 You don't know how many more times: Directly after he coaches himself not to let the surly boatman spoil his fun, we get our first indication that Cantwell's future will be short. As he will soon say, "Every time you shoot now can be the last shoot" (16:20–21).

15:30–31 snow-covered mountains a long way off: Cantwell is looking at the southern Alps (Dolomites), which also would evoke his experiences at the Italian front during World War I, which staged a murderous series of battles between Italy and the Austro-Hungarian Empire.

16:17–18 the shooter did not know it: Although this detail is relatively unimportant, we must remember that during strategic moments in the novel, the narrator remains outside Cantwell's perspective. The narrator knows more than Cantwell. Cantwell's voice is the dominant perspective but not the exclusive one.

NOTES

1. All references to *Death in Venice* are to the Appelbaum translation, except the entry for 41:5, which refers to the Lowe-Porter translation published by Vintage.
2. According to the editors of the second volume of Hemingway's *Letters*, Sweeny is "the likely prototype for Colonel Boyle" in *The Garden of Eden* and was one of Hemingway's honorary pallbearers (382n2).

CHAPTER 2

17:1 But he was not a boy: In a novel where aging and dying and the memory of youth are central to the plot, the word "boy" is conspicuous and recurrent. In addition to addressing himself or referring to himself as a "boy" over a dozen times, part of the challenge is to be a "good boy" (154:9). Cantwell at one point is at a loss when talking to himself, wondering which of his four identities he really wants to address: "So don't be gloomy, boy, or man, or Colonel, or busted General" (176:16-17). In other words, is he referring to himself as a World War I soldier, an adult, the colonel he is, or the general he was? A reference to when Cantwell was a "boy" connotes his World War I activities in northern Italy, 1918 (see 257:20).

Likewise, Renata later is ambiguous about her identity as a girl or a woman (145:4-5).

17:1 He was fifty: Although he is fifty at this point, he is later said to be "fifty plus one" (74:32). Renata refers to Cantwell as "over fifty years old" (88:28-29). He includes himself in a group of "fifty year old Colonels" (175:8-9). On four occasions, he refers to himself as "half a hundred" (33:27, 65:13, 168:12, 200:11), and he describes a smile that he has used for fifty years (89:23). Renata asks Cantwell, "Do you think it is true that men make their own faces after fifty?" (120:23-24). Hemingway turned fifty during the writing of *Across the River and into the Trees,* 21 July 1949; by his count, he wrote 573 words of the novel that day.

See entry at 62:23-24.

17:5 mannitol hexanitrate: This chemical, also mentioned at 18:8 and 39:16, would provide positive readings on Cantwell's heart exam, which the "quite skeptical" surgeon who has known Cantwell "a long time" understands (17:16). Cantwell is determined to pass the physical so that he might be allowed to hunt one last time. The text describes Cantwell taking more than sixteen pills throughout the last weekend of his life. According to Michael Reynolds, Hemingway was taking mannitol in 1949 to control his blood pressure (*Final Years* 202).

The Colonel's Pill-Taking Chart

PAGE	NUMBER OF PILLS
39:16	two
89:17	takes "medicine"
139:13	takes "medicine"
183:11–12	four
207:31	two
244:32	two
258:29–30	two
270:21	two
272:17	two

17:10–11 increased intra-ocular and intra-cranial pressure: The surgeon is suggesting that with more fluid behind the eyes and pressure in the cranium, an improved heart reading is incongruous. Cantwell, of course, professes innocence.

17:15 reduced from being a general officer: See entry at 13:14–15: this reduction is always at the forefront of Cantwell's consciousness, particularly in these final days of his life, as he reviews his life and military experiences.

17:19 We sound like song writers: The surgeon makes a reference to "It's Been a Long, Long Time," written by Jule Styne (1905–1994) and Sammy Cahn (1913–1993). This song has been recorded many times, but at the time of the novel's composition, it had been a No. 1 hit by Harry James (1916–1983) in 1945 and also by Bing Crosby (1903–1977) and the Les Paul Trio later that year. The song, with its appropriate timing after World War II, takes on significant thematic importance, as the speaker and his long-lost love are reunited.

18:1 nitroglycerin: This explosive liquid is used to combat angina and chest pain. To defer to a medical explanation: "Nitroglycerin works by dilating (widening) the body's veins and small arteries. This vasodilation reduces both the volume of blood returning to the heart and the pressure against which the heart must pump blood. These effects decrease the work the heart has to do and reduce the amount of nutrients, including oxygen, that the heart requires. Nitroglycerin also dilates the coronary arteries and may help to improve the delivery of oxygen to the heart muscle. When the drug works, the angina symptoms should disappear—or at least diminish markedly—within 1 to 5 minutes" ("Nitroglycerin"). As Cantwell will go on to say, nausea is a common side effect of this treatment.

18:2 drag a chain like a high-octane truck: This chain is attached to the chassis of a motor vehicle (such as a gasoline tank truck) and drags on the roadway to ground the chassis and prevent accumulation of static electricity ("drag chain").

18:11 **seconal:** Seconal, the brand name for secobarbital, is a barbiturate. According to Reynolds, Hemingway took Seconal to sleep during the late 1940s (*Final Years* 137, 202). Hemingway's protagonist in *Islands in the Stream,* Thomas Hudson, also takes a double Seconal "that would put him to sleep again and let him wake in the morning without a hangover" (212). The Seconal in that novel is the subject of an unusual conversation between Hudson and his cat. As Hemingway told Lillian Ross for her 13 May 1950 *New Yorker* profile, his cat thought Hemingway was "holding out on him" because he wouldn't give him blood-pressure tablets or Seconal as sleeping pills (65). In Hemingway's extraordinary article following his 1954 African plane crashes, "The Christmas Gift," he lists "a full bottle of Seconal" as one of the many easy places to find death (*BL* 460).

18:11–12 **minor tactics for the heavy pressure platoon:** The "heavy pressure" Cantwell mentions goes back to the diminishing of pressure in the head and eyes to which the surgeon referred earlier.

18:16 **hit in the head:** When Cantwell identifies "ten. . . . Give or take three" concussions, it invites a comparison with Hemingway's own history. In Jeffrey Meyers's harrowing list of Hemingway's lifetime of "Accidents and Illnesses" (*Hemingway* 573–75), he includes five separate concussions, which would be a conservative estimate.

18:18 **in my 201:** In the military, each service member has a 201 file, containing personal information, including evaluation documents.

18:20 **Then he said.** The period should be a comma preceding the subsequent quotation mark.

18:22–23 **try to wind your clock:** The surgeon insists he would not try to get Cantwell to retire prematurely.

18:24 **Wes:** This only mention of the surgeon's name might be a reference to the surgeon in Hemingway's childhood, Dr. Wesley Peck, who removed Hemingway's tonsils in 1919 without anesthetic (Meyers, *Hemingway* 48).

18:30 **Counting polo:** In a bit of a surprise, Cantwell emerges as a former polo player (see 241:4).

18:32 poor old son of a bitch: This epithet is reminiscent of Owl Eyes's indelible remark in F. Scott Fitzgerald's *The Great Gatsby* (1925); he summarizes Gatsby's funeral by saying, "The poor son-of-a-bitch" (175).

19:4–5 in the marshes at the mouth of the Tagliamento: The mouth of the Tagliamento River in northeast Italy is the Adriatic Sea, between Marano and Caorle. Hemingway and Cantwell were both wounded on the banks of the Tagliamento in 1918.

19:5–6 some nice Italian kids I met up at Cortina: In December 1948, Hemingway went on a duck hunt in the Caorle lagoon on the property of Baron Nanuk Franchetti (Moriani 23). Also present on the trip were Carlo Kechler, Count Carlo Robilant, and Adriana Ivancich. Cortina d'Ampezzo is a town in the Veneto which houses a rest center that Cantwell calls "a fine place. Good chow. Well run. Nobody bothers you" (23:13–14). Hemingway, too, fled to the Villa Aprile in Cortina in 1949 to be away from the city and begin work on what would become *Across the River and into the Trees*. Cortina is also the rest stop at which another driver, Burnham, is stationed. Cantwell recalls fighting Rommel "from Cortina to the Grappa" (116:15), a reference to the twelve Battles of the Isonzo, from 23 June 1915 to 7 November 1917.

To Renata, Cantwell describes Cortina as being "in a high valley in the mountains" (243:10–11), the southern (Dolomitic) Alps. In the "Hunger Was Good Discipline" chapter in *A Moveable Feast*, Hemingway recalls that he wrote "Out of Season" in Cortina d'Ampezzo during a skiing vacation with Hadley, which was spring 1923 (75). Frederic Henry recalls a lovely sojourn he made in Cortina in *A Farewell to Arms* (253). In a 1925 letter, Hemingway refers to Cortina as "the swellest country on earth . . . the loveliest country I've ever known" (*Letters 2*, 390)

19:9–10 ducks . . . Mallard . . . pin-tail . . . widgeon . . . geese: In letters of late 1948 and 1949, Hemingway wrote similar catalogues for friends, closely echoing Cantwell's description.

In *Islands in the Stream*, Thomas Hudson remembers of Hong Kong: "You could see pin-tails, teal, widgeon, both males and females in winter plumage, and there were wild ducks that I had never seen with plumage as delicate and complicated as our wood ducks" (282), similar to Cantwell's description.

19:10 Just as good as at home when we were kids: As Cantwell looks back on his life, his focus is primarily on his military experience rather than his family or his childhood. As he and Renata converse—with Renata usually taking the role of questioner and Cantwell the responder—her questions are more about war than his personal background, except the wife he has divorced. Therefore, any information we get about Cantwell's childhood is crucial. Here, he compares hunting "at home" to hunting ducks in the Veneto, just as he will recollect walking through cow dung as a boy (227:27–29). Renata asks about the linguistic nuances "out West when you were a boy" (191:27), and Cantwell later refers to his participation in the Montana National Guard (208:17). If he is indeed from Montana as it appears, then he joins *For Whom the Bell Tolls*'s Robert Jordan as a Montana native, along with *Islands in the Stream*'s Thomas Hudson, who owns a ranch in Montana. Hemingway told journalist Lillian Ross in 1950, "Where I like it is out West in Wyoming, Montana, and Idaho, and I like Cuba and Paris and around Venice" (35–36).

19:11 **I was kids in twenty-nine and thirty:** The surgeon, then, might be ten years younger than Cantwell, a notion that would particularly gall the Colonel, given his awareness of his own mortality.

19:32 **Longchamps on Madison Avenue:** The surgeon is wryly saying that he can order duck at a fancy restaurant, rather than go through the trouble of hunting it. The original Longchamps, which became a chain of French restaurants, opened in 1920 in New York and was owned and operated by Henry and Allen Lustig (O'Neill 132).

CHAPTER 3

21:1 That was day before yesterday: In what is possibly the most confusing sentence in the novel, "That" refers to Cantwell's appointment with his doctor, which takes place on Thursday. The drive south from Trieste to Venice takes place on Friday. He meets Renata on Friday, sees her again and says goodbye to her on Saturday, then hunts on Sunday before he dies. Therefore, since the action of chapter 3 and following picks up on Friday, this reference to the day before yesterday—that is, Wednesday—is erroneous. In his important article about the narrative structure of the novel, Peter Lisca refers to this moment as "an oversight on the part of Hemingway or the Colonel" (235). See Appendix 1 on page 208 for issues of time.

21:2–3 from Trieste to Venice along the old road that ran from Monfalcone to Latisana and across the flat country: This trip is about one hundred miles: Trieste to Monfalcone is eighteen miles. Monfalcone to Latisana is another thirty miles. Latisana to Venice is about sixty. This mention of Monfalcone is the only one in the novel; Alvarito later asks Cantwell for transportation to "Latisana or just above" (276:25). Trieste, the former home of James Joyce, is the capital of the Trieste province and the Friuli-Venezia Giulia region. Monfalcone—also in the Friuli—is in the province of Gorizia. Latisana is in the province of Udine, also in the Friuli-Venezia Giulia region of the Veneto. One of Italy's motivations for declaring war on the Austro-Hungarian Empire was to reclaim Trieste for Italy, which it did on 3 November 1918. Cantwell and Jackson will begin to return to Trieste in the last pages of the novel. Cantwell dies on the road during his return to Trieste (282).

21:8 the distances are all changed: One of the central themes in this novel and all of Hemingway's work is the impossibility of actualizing a nostalgic impulse. The memory of war and the reality of war never match, and Hemingway is inviting the reader to consider whether the protagonist is privileging the subjective memory or the objective truth. In *Death in the Afternoon* (1932), Hemingway writes that "memory, of course, is never true" (100). In its sequel, *The Dangerous Summer* (1960), he describes taking his traveling companion to a war site, in which "I was sure I remembered incorrectly due to haste or stress or the distortions of vision that being under fire bring" (120). When Cantwell mentions everything being "much smaller when you are older" (21:8–9), it echoes the telescoping of time described in "The Snows of Kilimanjaro."

21:11 camion: A camion is a "truck or wagon formerly used for transporting cannon" (*OED*).

21:16–17 made a curve and crossed the Tagliamento on a temporary bridge: Jackson and Cantwell are around Latisana, roughly at the halfway point of their trip.

22:1–2 ruined country house once built by Longhena: Baldassarre Longhena (1598–1692) was a Baroque architect who worked mainly in Venice. He has been described as Venice's "greatest native architect" (Howard 211), someone "gifted with that particular combination of intelligence, ingenuity, technical skill, artistic sensibility and visual imagination, which made his works stand out above those of all his contemporaries in the whole of northern Italy" (212). Hemingway is referring to the Villa Mocenigo, which became Villa Ivancich in San Michele al Tagliamento, which was designed by Longhena and destroyed during World War II. Adriana's brother, Gianfranco (1920–2013), suggested that Hemingway include Longhena's name in the description (Ivancich-Biaggini 221). In fact, in the manuscript, Hemingway leaves a wide gap after "built by" to fill in later. Longhena's Santa Maria della Salute, visible entering Piazza San Marco by water, was designed as a commemoration of the plague infesting Europe in 1630.

22:8–9 Giotto to paint you any frescoes: Giotto di Bondone (1266 or 1267–1337) is generally considered the father of the Italian Renaissance. In 1958 Hemingway included Giotto among the thirty artists from whom he had "learned the most" (Plimpton, "Art of Fiction" 118). The most famous anecdote regarding Giotto is that to convince the Pope of his worthiness to receive a commission he simply drew a perfect circle, a theme that resonates in this novel. See entry at 57:3, 4 for the full anecdote of Giotto's circle. Early in chapter 7, during an interior monologue, Cantwell wonders, "Didn't Giotto describe a circle . . . ?" (57:3–4). Giotto's "perfect" circle echoes Cantwell's allusion to Dante's circles of hell, in which Cantwell assumes a position of adjuticator, and he "drew all the circles" (225:30). Dante's *Divine Comedy* contains nine circles: limbo, the lustful, the gluttonous, the hoarders and spendthrifts, the wrathful, the heretics, the violent, the fraudulent, and the treacherous.

The reference to Giotto's frescoes brings to mind the famous frescoes of the Virgin Mary that Giotto painted for the Scrovegni Chapel in Padua in 1305. He also painted a fresco of Dante.

22:14 mulberry trees: Hemingway's most famous evocation of mulberry trees appears in the beginning of "Now I Lay Me," a short story from *Men Without Women*

(1927), which begins with an insomniac Nick Adams listening to silkworms munching incessantly on mulberry leaves (*CSS* 276).

22:17 **heavies:** Cantwell and Jackson are distinguishing between the heavy bombers of World War II and the mediums, mentioned earlier (22:2–3).

22:29 **Piero della Francesca:** Like Giotto, Piero della Francesca (1420?–1492), was an Italian Renaissance painter known for a cycle of frescoes, in his case *The Legend of the True Cross* in Arezzo. Piero della Francesca also is thematically important because of the connection between his art and geometry, which Hemingway stressed in the composition of this novel. Piero wrote "On Perspective in Painting," in which he used the language of mathematics and geometry to convey the correct method for rendering perspective. In an early Hemingway story, "The Revolutionist" from *In Our Time* (1925), the young man buys reproductions of Giotto, Masaccio, and Piero della Francesca (*CSS* 119).

22:30 **Mantegna:** Andrea Mantegna (1431–1506) was an Italian Renaissance painter also renowned for his work in frescoes. His *St. Sebastian* (1490) is at the Ca d'Oro in Venice, a palace on the Grand Canal. His work at the Prado is, for Robert Jordan in *For Whom the Bell Tolls*, the equivalent of the holiness he feels, the "consecration to a duty" as part of his sacrifice to "all of the oppressed of the world" (235). To Frederic Henry in *A Farewell to Arms*, Mantegna is "Very bitter . . . Lots of nail holes" (280).

For a fuller discussion of the connection between Hemingway and Mantegna, see Johnston.

22:30 **Michelangelo:** Michelangelo di Lodovico Buonarroti Simoni (1475–1564), synonymous with Italian Renaissance art, painted the frescoes on the Sistine Chapel of St. Peter's Cathedral in the Vatican City in Rome (1508–12).

22:31 **Do you know a lot about painters, sir?** This question brings two things to the surface. First, it establishes the Socratic nature of the dialogue in this novel, about which many critics have commented and complained. At this point in Hemingway's life, it is obvious that people were generally asking him questions, soliciting his opinions, more so than at any other point. As Philip Young phrases it, "the unintentional delusion under which Hemingway labored throughout the novel is that he was being interviewed" (*Reconsideration* 117). Kenneth E. Bidle remarks on Cantwell's "obsessive desire to conduct every conversation—even those with his sweetheart—as an interview" (260). Jeffrey Meyers finds that the questions "provide an excuse for a series of smug disquisitions" (*Hemingway* 461). Likewise, Cantwell, particularly when he speaks with Renata and Jackson, is speaking with younger, less experienced, willing listeners who question more than they are questioned. Second, the theme of knowledge—what Cantwell knows and has learned and can impart to others—dominates the text, his expertise of painting, writing, warfare, food and drink, geography, history, politics, and so on.

23:5 **Brueghel:** Pieter Brueghel the Elder (1525–1569), unlike most of the other painters mentioned, was Flemish and not Italian, and favored the depiction of landscape rather than frescoes. Hemingway was unstinting in his praise of Brueghel in *For Whom the Bell Tolls;* he mentions him in the same sentence as Mantegna (235), just as he mentions him in the same sentence as Giotto when listing his many influences (Plimpton, "Art of Fiction" 118). In a famous scene in Lillian Ross's *New Yorker* profile of Hemingway, which coincided with the publication of *Across the River and into the Trees,* they attend the Metropolitan Museum of Art, and much to Hemingway's disappointment, the Brueghel room is closed for repairs. Hemingway mentions the Brueghel painting *The Harvesters,* which impresses him by the way Brueghel "uses the grain geometrically, to make an emotion that is so strong for me that I can hardly take it" (Ross 85).

Cantwell's point is that the flatness and lack of geometry of the land would have been uninspirational to Brueghel.

23:9 **Burnham:** In the first of the novel's many references to Shakespeare and his works, Cantwell's misidentification of his driver refers to *Macbeth,* in which the third apparition, a child crowned with a tree in his hand, assures Macbeth that he "shall never vanquished be until / Great Birnam Wood to high Dunsinane Hill / Shall come against him." Macbeth, eager to believe this prophecy, responds, "That will never be" (4.1.108–10).

This misidentification also is meant to convey another crucial Hemingway theme. In "The Killers" (1927), the owner of Henry's diner is unseen, unlike George, who works there, just as Nick addressed Mrs. Bell as Mrs. Hirsch, confusing the owner with the worker. In a novel where the killers are the unseen masters of war as opposed to (or perhaps in addition to) the actual soldier who pulls the trigger, this confusion is notable and intentional.

23:10 **Jackson:** Ronald Jackson emphasizes the title of the novel, from Stonewall Jackson. As a character, he also serves as a benign interlocutor with Cantwell, as well as someone whose attitude is distinct from the Colonel's. We see Cantwell reflect on Jackson's behavior—mostly unfavorably and condescendingly, the reasons for which he will enumerate. See next entry, 23:18.

23:18 **Uffizi . . . Pitti:** Cantwell makes two excellent guesses about what Jackson obtusely refers to as "that big place in Florence" (23:17). Jackson's character is slowly revealed: while he took the time to visit a place of high culture in a foreign land, he cannot be bothered to remember its name. Unlike the savvy of Hemingway protagonists,

Jackson's behavior is a quintessential sign of an ugly American, a born tourist, like Robert Cohn in *The Sun Also Rises*. It reflects poorly on Jackson, for instance, that he does not accept Cantwell's offer of a drink, which makes him "a prissy jerk" (45:32). Jackson is later characterized as one of those "*sad* Americans" (61:9) by the *Gran Maestro* and Cantwell describes him as emblematic of a generation that is "Sad, self-righteous, over-fed and under-trained" (61:11–12). Jackson also sleeps while Cantwell is hunting (275:20), just as he sleeps while Cantwell makes his symbolic trip to the site of his wounding (27:21). Jackson also favors comic books, not Dante, Shakespeare, Byron, D'Annunzio, or even Red Smith as does Cantwell.

The Palazzo Pitti, near the Ponte Vecchio, was owned by the Medici family in the late sixteenth century. It has been open as an art museum since 1919. The Uffizi, synonymous with Italian masterpieces, holds many works from the artists mentioned in this novel, including Michelangelo, Giotto, Titian, and Piero della Francesca. Renata is compared to Botticelli's *The Birth of Venus,* which is also housed in the Uffizi. In a letter to Mary in 1948 as she traveled to Florence without him, Hemingway wrote that he predicted the Uffizi would make her weary, recalling that he used to think, "show me one more goddamn Madonna and see how you like it gentlemen" (JFK, Outgoing Correspondence), sounding very much like Jackson as an art critic.

24:12 **Titian:** Tiziano Vecelli (1488 or 1490–1576) was the most important painter in sixteenth-century Italian art. In Ross's *New Yorker* profile, she recounts Hemingway stopping to look at Titian's *Portrait of a Man,* which the museum attributes to Titian and Giorgione. "They were old Venice boys, too," Hemingway says (83), in a phrase his protagonist might also use.

Titian was born in a small cottage in Pieve di Cadore, a town in the Veneto. Giorgione, incidentally, was from Castelfranco Veneto, also in the region.

24:20 ***Campaniles:*** In this early evocation of Cantwell's multilingualism, the word for "bell tower" is, indeed, "*campanile,*" but its plural form in Italian would be "*campanili.*"

24:21 **Ceggia:** a town in the province of Venice, north of the city. If Cantwell is referring to a campanile he and Jackson see from the car "ahead at Ceggia," then they have traveled about sixty miles from Venice, or two-thirds of the total trip. The campanile that Cantwell mentions is of the Chiesa Parrocchiale di San Vitale Martire.

24:29 **Rawlins to Buffalo:** Jackson's wife, to be clear, would not run him across the entire United States of America, from Rawlins, Wyoming, to Buffalo, New York; Buffalo, Wyoming, is about 225 miles south of Rawlins. Jackson owns a garage in Rawlins (30:9), which is about 275 miles south of Sheridan, Wyoming, where Hemingway spent time in the summer of 1928 finishing the first draft of *A Farewell* *to Arms* (Reynolds, *Homecoming* xiii). The hero of Hemingway's only published play, *The Fifth Column* (1938), is named Philip Rawlings.

25:1 **Liver Eating Johnston [*sic*]:** a reference to John "Liver-Eating" Johnson (1824–1900), a mountain man from the old West who was said to have hunted down the Black Crow tribe of Native Americans who killed his wife and then eaten the liver from the deceased. Robert Redford starred in a film about Johnson directed by Sidney Pollock, *Jeremiah Johnson* (1972).

Jackson's reference to the local museum might be to the Carbon County Museum in Red Lodge, Montana, which has materials related to Johnson (Nelson).

25:10, 14 **Trieste . . . Florence . . . Rome:** As Cantwell explains, Trieste was part of the Austro-Hungarian Empire until after World War I when Italy annexed it as part of its claim to Italian-speaking lands that had been controlled by Austria. See entry at 21:2–3.

25:19 **Thirty-sixth Division:** Jackson's 36th Division would have worn a shoulder patch with a blue arrowhead with a green "T" superimposed over it, symbolizing a confluence of Oklahoma and Texas. As James H. Meredith points out, the 36th was "actually a Texas National Guard unit" ("Rapido" 61). This division served as part of the 5th Army in the Rapido River action, from 20 to 22 January 1944, as Jackson tells Cantwell. Meredith explains that the failed attempt to cross the Rapido and establish a bridgehead "ended as one of the Army's most decisive disasters in World War II" (62). Two regiments (the 141st and 143rd) of the division were lost. One of the reasons Cantwell responds so sympathetically to Jackson's show of temper is that the men of the 36th understood that the orders to cross the river were suicidal. Other men's orders, as the novel demonstrates, represent Cantwell's greatest sorrow (194:12). When Jackson sees the Piave in chapter 4, he does not think it looks anything like the Rapido (29:20).

Given the novel's title, the crossing of the Rapido River, like the final words spoken by Stonewall Jackson, lends thematic resonance to Jackson's memory.

25:28–29, 31 **San Dona di Piave . . . Fossalta:** It is about six miles from Ceggia to San Donà di Piave, from which it is about twenty-five more miles to Venice. As Cantwell sees the sights from the road, he thinks aloud to Jackson. Fossalta di Piave, roughly five miles from San Donà di Piave, was the site of Hemingway's World War I wounding on 8 July 1918. Fossalta is also the town where, a few weeks earlier, Cantwell defecated on the site of his own wounding and buried money, thus attaining a measure of closure about his war injury (26:16–18). This wounding seems to have taken place in the aftermath of Caporetto, during the Battle of Vittorio Veneto, in which the Italian army essentially saved Venice and the Veneto from the Central Powers.

26:1–2 **big fifteenth of June offensive in eighteen:** This date refers to a central World War I memory to which Cantwell will return many times, the Battle of the Piave, from 15 to 23 June 1918. The Austrians attacked the Italian lines early in the morning on 15 June 1918, and the Allied counteroffensive—"Monastier" (Monastier di Treviso; 26:3–4) and "Fornace" (Fornaci) (26:4)—refer to the Allied counteroffensive on 19 and 20 June 1918. In the counteroffensive, 118,000 Habsburg soldiers were killed, wounded, sick, captured, and missing (Thompson 346–47). The aftermath of the battle, which continued into early July, was where Hemingway and presumably Cantwell were wounded.

This counteroffensive prevented the Habsburg Empire from reaching the Veneto, so Cantwell's assertion that he defended Venice as a young man stems from this episode in the war.

After his 1918 wounding, Hemingway was treated at a field hospital in Fornaci. "A Way You'll Never Be," a Nick Adams story from Hemingway's collection *Winner Take Nothing* (1933), ends with Nick saying to himself, "I don't want to lose the way to Fornaci" (*CSS* 315).

26:6 **A few weeks ago:** Rather than divulge the content of the memory—the text states that "he remembered" twice in a single sentence—the anecdote from thirty years later replaces the World War I scene. In present time, a few weeks ago is the earliest moment in the current action, the winter of 1948–49. When he "relieved himself" (26:16), it is not only a physical relief but more so an emotional catharsis. According to Carlos Baker, this incident has its autobiographical parallel. When visiting the site of his own wounding in late October 1948—which also would have been thirty years and a few months after his wounding (26:18)—Hemingway "would have liked to accomplish a ceremonious defecation. Finding this impossible, he dug a small hole with a stick and inserted a 1,000 lire note. This homemade symbolism was meant to indicate that he had contributed both blood and money to the Italian soil" (*Life Story* 468). Reynolds, incidentally, has Hemingway burying 10,000 lire (*Final Years* 180).

For a second scene of Cantwell defecating, see 156:14–158:31.

26:17 **triangulation:** This reference brings to mind Hemingway's notion of the writing of this novel as calculus, transcending simple mathematics. It also speaks to the Colonel's wherewithal and knowledge of terrain, tactics, and problem solving.

26:19, 21 **A poor effort. . . . But my own:** In Miriam Mandel's *Reading Hemingway* (335), she identifies an allusion to Touchstone in Shakespeare's *As You Like It*: "A poor virgin, sir, an ill-favoured thing, sir, but mine own" (5.4.55–56). "Effort" is "shit" in the manuscript.

26:20 **heavy with autumn quiet:** The memory has an autumnal quality, but the present action is "on this winter day" (26:4) earlier on the page. We can assume that this weekend takes place in the early winter, just as Hemingway's own Venice trip did in 1948 and 1949. Therefore, the suggestion by some critics that the theme of rebirth in this novel literally places the action of the Colonel's death on Easter weekend is seductive but erroneous (e.g., P. Miller 137–38; Lisca 248; Meyers, *Hemingway* 337). Cantwell's journey might be associated with rebirth, but Easter has nothing to do with it. Further, the *Gran Maestro* tells Cantwell that fresh asparagus comes from Bassano in April, not "in these months" (66:2). In chapter 11, the *Gran Maestro* remarks of the bar's emptiness: "There is no one here now in the winter time" (103:1–2). See also when there are no leaves on the trees because they "had fallen early, that year, and been swept up long ago" (253:31–32). On the last day, Sunday, Alvarito tells Cantwell that the ducks "will be on their way south tonight" (276:32). Cantwell plans to release the wing-tipped duck "in the Spring" (273:29), obviously a future consideration. We also see that in a description of the wind off of the canal, Cantwell feels it to be "as clear and sharp as on a winter day, which, of course, it was" (51:28–29). Likewise, Cantwell observes the "late afternoon winter light on the wind-swept water" as he looks out the window of the Gritti (57:14–15).

Dante's pilgrimage takes place on Easter weekend 1300.

26:26 **Sollingen clasp knife:** Solingen, Germany, is the knife-making capital of the world. Hemingway misspells the name of the city.

26:30 **ten thousand lira note:** Note that Cantwell donated ten times what Hemingway did, according to Baker. In 1948, the conversion rate for the devalued Italian lira was 541.56 per $1 U.S. Therefore, Cantwell buries about $18.50, which would have bought six copies of *Across the River and into the Trees,* the buying power of $178.13 in 2012. Hemingway's actual gesture was with a 1,000 lire note, but perhaps one reason for the brown 10,000 lire note is that beginning in 1947, Italy honored Dante with his image on this bill. In the manuscript, clearly going by memory, Hemingway is unsure whether the bank note was green or brown; he made a note to himself to verify it.

26:33–27:1 **Medaglia d'Argento al Valore Militare:** Literally the Silver Medal for Military Valor, Hemingway received this award for his service in World War I, which was given at a banquet in Chicago in November 1921 (Meyers, *Hemingway* 61). In a sort of interview with *Time* magazine as *Across the River and into the Trees* was published, Hemingway explains: "For technicalities, the decorations that Hemingstein the writer holds, and the only ones that he respects, are the *Medaglia d'Argento al Valore Militare* and three *Croce al Merito di Guerra* ("Hemingway Is Bitter about Nobody" 110). In a 1927 letter to editor Maxwell Perkins, Hemingway writes that he received the military awards "not for valourous deeds but simply because I was an American attached to the Italian army" (*SL* 247). Adriana Ivancich recalls that Hemingway used a tablecloth after dinner to show a group of people how to fight a bull, using Mary as the bull. "'Bravo toro,' he said with a smile, 'Here is the *medaglia al valore militare*'" ("I Am Hemingway's Renata" 260).

After Frederic Henry's wounding in *A Farewell to Arms,* his friend Rinaldi tells him: "You will be decorated. They want to get you the medaglia d'argento but perhaps they can get only the bronze" (63).

27:1 **V.C.** The Victoria Cross is the British equivalent of the military medal for valor.

27:2 **D.S.C.** Distinguished Service Cross. Besides the Medal of Honor, it is the highest military honor that can be given to a member of the United States Army.

27:6 **Gino's leg:** In *A Farewell to Arms*, a character named Gino also appears during the confusion of the retreat from Caporetto.

27:6 **both of Randolfo's legs:** Randolfo is the first name of Randolfo Pacciardi, who will become an important figure in chapters 6 through 8 (see entry at 44:24).

27:6–7 **my right kneecap:** This injury recalls Hemingway's actual wounding. As he writes in a letter to his parents six weeks after his wounding, "In the right knee the bullet went under the knee cap from the left side and didnt smash it a bit" (*Letters 1*, 118). In his 1950 *Time* interview, Hemingway refers to the explosion that "blew off the right knee cap" ("Hemingway Is Bitter about Nobody" 110).

27:8, 9 **Fertility, money, blood and iron:** Picking up on the "merde, money, blood" theme from 27:4, Cantwell invokes the "blood and iron" phrase from the first German chancellor, Otto von Bismarck's (1815–1898) 1862 speech, which promoted military preparedness.

27:14 **spat in the river:** The shitting and spitting continues the ceremony of atonement for Cantwell. Later, he will take his tablets without drinking because "he had always been able to spit since 1918" (39:16–17). He tells Renata that he would be able to join her in a tumbril and "still be able to spit" (238:3–4).

27:22 **son:** Cantwell calls Jackson "son," just as he will later call Renata "daughter," thus introducing a conspicuous motif.

27:22 **he had said:** The past perfect tense is a reminder that this anecdote of the symbolic defecation takes place in the past, a flashback within a flashback. In other words, his drive with Jackson, which takes place "Yesterday" (21:1)—that is, Friday—inspires a memory of weeks before, when he buried the money along with his feces. The defecation anecdote spans from 26:6 to the end of chapter 3, 27:24.

27:23 Treviso: The direction from Fossalta di Piave to Treviso is west. Treviso is also mentioned as the place near where Alvarito's mother stays (52:3–4) and where the *Gran Maestro* has a "small house" (64:16). Directly preceding Renata and Cantwell's gondola ride in chapter 13, the second waiter at Harry's informs Cantwell that his wife and children were killed when his house in Treviso was bombed (141:21–22). Treviso was the victim of Allied carpet-bombing on 7 April 1944, which led to the death of more than one thousand people.

CHAPTER 4

28:1 **Now:** The flashback from a few weeks previously that ended chapter 3 is over and Hemingway is explicit about putting the action back to the trip into Venice, which takes place on Friday. Unlike an author like Joyce, Faulkner, or Virginia Woolf, when Hemingway manipulates time, he usually guides the reader. See "The Snows of Kilimanjaro," in which he uses italics and explanatory phrases such as "now, in Africa" (*CSS* 43) and *"Now in his mind"* (42, emphasis in original) to distinguish between temporal perspectives.

28:1 **Venice:** Critic John Paul Russo has argued: "The key to this novel is Venice" (394). In a novel that is sometimes a love song to the city he has defended and of which he claims ownership, Cantwell's attachment to Venice is never forgotten. Venice is mentioned in the first paragraph of chapters 2, 3, and 4 and never in between. Cantwell regales Jackson with the history of the establishment of Venice (35:9–36:2). He refers to Venice as "my town" (36:27). Renata calls it the "best town" (134:17). Alvarito acknowledges that Cantwell may love Venice "the best of all" (277:10).

In March 1950 Hemingway wrote Leonard Lyons of the *New York Post:* "Am a boy with five home towns now—Paris, Venice, Ketchum (Idaho), Key West and Havana" (qtd. in Lyons 30). In a 1950 *Time* interview, Hemingway described *Across the River and into the Trees* as being "about the city of Venice and the Veneto, which Hemingway has known and loved since he was a young boy" ("Hemingway Is Bitter about Nobody" 110). Reynolds points out that Hemingway had never set foot in Venice until late October 1948 (*Final Years* 180). As early as 1923, however, he wrote to Ezra Pound that he and his first wife, Hadley, hoped to travel through Italy, avoiding "cultural centers . . . with the Veneto has the final objective" because, he writes, "Hadley as never seen Venetzia [sic] except with her family and the last time we were at Mestre we didn't have the fare across the viaduct" (*Letters* 2, 9).

28:2 **the big Buick:** Hemingway drove a Buick Roadmaster in the Veneto during this period. According to Gianni Moriani, the car was "an impressive old Buick convertible in metallic blue which earned him the admiration of the locals and which children in Caorle called 'the car with the wings'" (21). In her 1965 article in *Epoca* magazine, likewise, Adriana Ivancich refers to Hemingway's car as "that big blue Buick" ("I Am Hemingway's Renata" 259). Later, Cantwell will offer Renata the use of the car (241:16). His claim that the engine has 150 horsepower, or "One hundred and fifty ponies" (31:26), is completely accurate.

28:3–4 cleared the last of San Dona and came up onto the bridge over the Piave: Cantwell and Jackson are traveling on via 24 maggio, a road named to honor the day in 1915 that Italy entered World War I. The bridge they are crossing is the Ponte della Vittoria, named for Italy's victory at Vittorio Veneto. In its only other mention in the novel, San Donà is referred to as a "cheerful town" (see entry at 25:28–29, 31).

28:11–12 a great killing at the last of the offensive: The offensive to which Cantwell refers is the Italian response to the Battle of Caporetto, known as the Battle of the Solstice, in which Austro-Hungarian losses are placed at 118,000 men (Thompson 346).

28:20 attained colossal proportions: Hemingway's most eloquent and gruesome statement about this phenomenon appears in his short story "A Natural History of the Dead," from *Winner Take Nothing,* in which he describes the same aftermath of the Battle of the Solstice. "The dead grow larger each day," Hemingway writes, "until sometimes they become quite too big for their uniforms, filling these until they seem blown tight enough to burst. The individual members may increase in girth to an unbelievable extent and faces fill as taut and globular as balloons" (*CSS* 337).

29:7 *ossario* up by Nervesa: "*Ossario*" is Italian for "ossuary," a place to bury the remains of the dead ("*osso*" is Italian for "bone"). Nervesa della Battaglia is a small town in the region of Treviso that was ravaged during World War I. The Military Sanctuary in Nervesa houses the remains of 9,325 soldiers who died during the war. In an 11 December 1918 letter, Hemingway recounts to his family a trip to Nervesa della Battaglia, where he saw "the old Austrian front line trenches and the mined houses of Nervesa by moonlight and searchlight. It was a great trip" (*Letters 1,* 161).

29:18 like Normandy only flatter: Here Cantwell compares two of his four major war memories: the Battle of the Piave, the Battle of Normandy, the liberation of Paris, and later Hürtgen Forest and the Battle of the Bulge. Hemingway covered the 6 June 1944 invasion of Normandy at Omaha Beach as a journalist. According to William E. Coté, Hemingway "witnessed hellish sights" but never touched land himself (95). In Hemingway's journalistic account of the Normandy invasion for *Collier's,* he refers to when "we took Fox Green beach and Easy Red beach" (*BL* 355). Donald Beistle has compiled a chronology of Hemingway's European Theater of Operation activities, and he refers to the *Collier's* article—"Voyage to Victory"—as "bombastic." Hemingway's notes of the June 6 invasion, according to Donald Beistle, "bear no resemblance" to the 20 July article (3).

29:22–23 **hydro-electric projects:** Cantwell also mentions these hydroelectric projects in a discussion with Arnaldo, the glass-eyed waiter, in chapter 8 (71:3).

These hydro-electric projects are described in detail in an ecological case study of the region:

> The Piave River basin is characterised by an artificial system of water resources built between 1920 and 1960. It is, in fact, an artificial hydrographic network placed over the natural system for the use of hydroelectric power. There are in the Piave basin 22 hydroelectric power plants. There is the natural river which no longer shows signs of life and an artificial river which, on the other hand, is hydraulically very lively, composed of reservoirs, 6 big dams, 17 penstocks, tunnels, sluice gates, line canals, etc. The artificial system has radically changed the hydrologic form of the river, modifying the fluvial dynamic, the transport of solid materials and the landscape of the riverbed. (Euro-Mediterranean)

29:24 **shingle:** Cantwell is using the word to mean loose, small stones.

29:25 **Grave di Papadopoli:** This island is three miles long and one mile wide and lies in the middle of the Piave River and was used as an Austrian advance post. It was captured on 23–26 October 1918, with aid from the British army (Cassar 188, 190–91). The "main attack on the Piave," writes David Raab, "was October 26, 1918, with Lord Cavan's infantry crossing from the Grave di Papadopoli to the eastern bank of the Piave" (83).

29:27 **He knew how boring any man's war is to any other man:** One of the novel's rhetorical tics is Cantwell's incessant awareness of his audience, of either his certainty that he is boring his listener, usually Jackson or Renata, or his ironic emphasis on the contrary. "Everything about war," Cantwell tells Renata, "bores those who have not made it" (131:16). When Renata asks him to tell her about World War II, his odd reply is, "It was not very interesting" (125:19). For this reason, he constantly seeks affirmation of the listener's interest. One cannot help but assume Hemingway was having similar misgivings about his own material, much of which is structured as an interview; a confessional; or as lengthy reveries, monologues, and anecdotes. One is reminded of the loquacious grandfather in John Steinbeck's *The Red Pony* (1937), who is finally called on his habit of repeating stories of fighting native Americans on the drive to the west. Although shaken, the grandfather realizes: "I tell those old stories, but they're not what I want to tell. I only know how I want people to feel when I tell them" (93). As Shakespeare's Othello says, "little of this great world can I speak / More than pertains to feats of broils and battle. And therefore little shall I grace my cause / In speaking for myself" (1.3.86–89).

Renata says she wants to know about Cantwell's three decisions, and he replies,

"They'd bore you" (90:30). During his account of the invasion of Normandy, he says, "Does this bore you? It bores the hell out of me" (126:4). He asks Renata, "What can I tell you that won't bore you?" (128:17), and he suggests some topics but then adds that they "would bore you" (128:25, 128:27). While discussing the liberation of Paris, he wonders if his discourse is "too technical and does it bore you?" (132:3). He goes on to discuss the breakthrough and says, "Please tell me if this bores you" (204:19); "not to bore you" (206:3); "Do I bore you?" (214:20). When he says, "I hope I am not boring you," Renata's response is exactly what he wants to hear: "You never bore me" (216:14). He then says, "Do I bore you? . . . I bore myself" (219:28, 219:30), to which Renata objects. She knows he is not bored by his experiences, and she encourages him to be honest about that reality. He also asks his driver, "Am I boring you, Jackson?" during his lectures about the origins of Venice (35:24).

He tells Renata after a particularly feverish daydream, "I am very dull" (92:6–7), to which she responds, "You are never dull" (92:8). In chapter 31, when Cantwell rehearses the military fighting orders, he calls it "dull but . . . informative" and he doubts if "anyone is ever interested" (221:10, 221:11).

See also "Go on" (132:6, 132:14, 204:17, 214:22–23)—Renata says "go on" seven times (e.g., 132:6, 132:114, 204:17), almost as if she believes it's good for him to confess, to talk it out. She begs him to talk to her about it (215:25, 216:1). She continually urges him: "You never bore me" (216:14); "tell me some more" (218:15–16, 220:9); "Please tell me about combat without being too brutal" (224:19–20). She also, in turn, disingenuously apologizes to Cantwell for boring him about the artifices of a woman (113:2–8).

The apotheosis of this strain occurs during Cantwell's massive hotel-room anecdote, when he says, "I bore myself, Daughter" (219:30). Renata, like the readers, quickly calls him on his remark. Renata responds emphatically: "I don't think you do, Richard, you would not have done something all your life if you were bored by it. Don't lie to me please, darling, when we have so little time" (219:32–33). Cantwell fascinates himself and fascinates Hemingway, who indulges his character's memories at great length and to the occasional detriment of the plot.

30:4 **combat infantryman badge:** This badge, fairly new at the time of the novel's action, is a horizontal rectangle depicting a service rifle surrounded by a wreath. All infantry who were engaged in combat received this badge.

30:4 **Purple Heart:** This award, instituted in 1917, is given to those wounded or killed in battle.

30:5 **was in no sense a soldier:** Cantwell distinguishes between himself and Jackson, who is technically a soldier but does not have the spirit or makeup of one. Cantwell can tell that he is boring Jackson, which indicates to him that the driver does not have a love of combat. Imagine what Cantwell thinks when Jackson confesses that he is "not much of a shot" (32:32) and that he would rather sleep than hunt, as is evidenced on 275:20, to say nothing of his reading comic books (277:18). Here, Jackson recalls *Othello*'s Michael Cassio, who "never set a squadron in the field / Nor the division of a battle knows / More than a spinster" (1.1.21–23).

30:20–21 **waiting for; but he was impatient:** Hemingway uses a semicolon idiosyncratically here, as he does elsewhere (e.g., 34:10, 34:11, 34:12, 38:15, 46:3, 47:8, 152:8, 200:32).

30:28 **I don't trust those side roads:** Another distinction arises between Cantwell and Jackson: Jackson distrusts anything to do with spontaneity, self-reliance, disorder, instinct. This fear will set up the last scene of the novel. When Cantwell asks Jackson if he knows the way to Trieste, Jackson response is telling: yes, because he has a map (282:15).

This comment also brings to mind a similar, far more grave moment in *A Farewell to Arms*, during which Frederic Henry is leading an ambulance unit that becomes stuck during the retreat from Caporetto. "I knew there were many sideroads," Frederic recalls, "but did not want one that would lead to nothing" (198).

31:23–24 **like the Indians do in Oklahoma:** Cantwell credits as a Native American trick the technique of modifying one's cars to go off road.

31:34 **He was not:** *He* was not; the Colonel was not.

32:1 **a sail moving:** This epiphanic vision of the big red sail slowly moving along seems like it would set up a powerful motif throughout the novel, but it does not persist. When Cantwell receives the portrait of Renata, the concierge who presents it to him "came into the room with the portrait, carrying it in its big frame, much as a ship moves when she is carrying too much sail" (136:33–137:2).

This passage (32:1–8) correlates to a similar moment in D'Annunzio's *Notturno*: "A painted cart moves along the shore, drawn by a pair of white oxen. Is it not filled with my rustic childhood as with fragrant hay? The yoked animals stand out against the blue-green sea, glowing like the sirocco-filled sails in the distance" (100). Cantwell also links the sails with oxen (32:6).

According to Frederick Douglass's slave narrative, he was moved to escape when he saw sails on the Chesapeake Bay. Douglass describes seeing the many sails on the bay, and then he transcribes his "apostrophe to the moving multitude of ships" (74). The vision is one of the most moving sequences in Douglass's narrative. Zora Neale Hurston alludes to the moment in the first line of her novel, *Their Eyes Were Watching God*: "Ships at a distance have every man's wish on board" (1).

32:22 **Sile canal:** According to historian Peter Ackroyd, the debris from the Alps upon which Venice was founded came from three main rivers, the Sile, the Brenta, and the Piave (4). See also 35:13–16, in which Venice's origins with respect to the Sile are further discussed.

32:29–30 **Nebraska along the Platte:** The Platte River has a Northern Platte tributary, which enters Wyoming and a Southern Platte tributary, which enters Colorado.

33:5 **K rations:** The K-ration was invented in 1942 for World War II and included three meals. Cantwell later declares, "They weren't bad" (221:8). The breakfast unit of the K-ration had a fruit bar, which may be what Cantwell is referring to when he describes to Renata the inedible "osage-orange" fruit (221:3; see Streeter).

33:5 **Ten in One:** According to Stephen C. McGeorge, the ten-in-one ration was named for the number of soldiers each unit would feed. It weighed forty-five pounds and required a stove and "basic mess gear" to prepare. McGeorge calls it the most popular of all World War II rations (468). Later, Cantwell will declare these ten-in-ones "good" (221:9).

33:14 **Pilot Town:** This refers to Pilottown, in southeast Louisiana, which is, as Cantwell suggests, near the mouth of the Mississippi. Pilottown incurred serious damage during Hurricane Katrina in late August 2005. The town of Venice, Louisiana, is fittingly only about ten miles from Pilottown.

33:15–16 **squared tower of the church at Torcello:** This cathedral, dedicated to Santa Maria Assunta, dates from the seventh century. Torcello figures prominently in Cantwell's explanation of the history of Venice and his description of the surroundings to Jackson (35:8–36:25). In chapter 6, the Colonel is compared to the old church in Torcello (44:9–11), and the same church is mentioned as a potential place to stage an homage to the Brusadelli (63:8–9). Renata refers to Cantwell as a "Torcello boy" (151:8).

Hemingway stayed in Torcello in 1948 at the Locanda Cipriani, where he also hunted duck and visited the local museum and church. For beautiful pictures of this stay in Torcello, see Moriani (107–23).

33:16 *campanile* **of Burano:** Burano, an island in the Venetian lagoon, is known for the "Campanile Storto" (crooked bell tower) atop its Church of San Martino. See 36:13.

33:20–21 **Dese River above Noghera:** Ca' Noghera, about two miles northeast of Venice's Marco Polo Airport, is, as Cantwell asserts, south of the Fiume Dese, which runs about thirty miles east-west across the Veneto and flows into the Venice lagoon.

33:22–23 **that winter:** In other words, this would be the aftermath of Caporetto, the winter of 1917–18, which predates Hemingway's own involvement in World War I. Allied forces, particularly France and England, supported Italy following the defeat at Caporetto to defend against the Austro-Hungarian army crossing the Piave River.

33:32 **chicken colonel:** This term signifies that Cantwell has earned the rank of full colonel. This nickname might derive from the "screaming eagle" on his shoulder patch (see 13:13, 260:21–23).

34:5–6, 7 *Vive la France et les pommes de terre frites. Liberté, Venalité, et Stupidité . . . clarté:* "Long live France and the French fries. Liberty, venality, and stupidity . . . clarity." Cantwell is sending up the national motto of France: "liberté, égalité, fraternité," or "liberty, equality, fraternity."

34:8 **du Picq:** This praise of military acumen refers to Charles Jean Jacques Joseph Ardant du Picq (1821–1870), a French army officer whose writings influenced French military theory. At the time of writing *Across the River and into the Trees*, Hemingway owned an English translation copy of du Picq's *Battle Studies: Ancient and Modern Battle* (Brasch and Sigman 54). Miriam Mandel points out that Cantwell's approves of du Picq's realistic attitude about war, one concerned with "the infantry, the troops, and not the reputations of their leaders." Du Picq, Mandel writes, "was the first French military thinker to value the infantry soldier and to downplay the grandiose leader" ("Reading the Names Right" 134).

In a 27 July 1949 letter to Buck Lanham, Hemingway wrote that a du Picq book Lanham sent him "is one of the best books on the [sad] science I have ever read. I've found, when reading it, that I read it in Italy when I was a kid but reading it in Italian I associated it with the name of the translator. This was a very dumb thing to do but I was very dumb at the time. Also found that several of the ideas which I thought I invented myself were much better expressed by Dr. DuPicq" (JFK, Outgoing Correspondence, 1949).

34:9 *Mangin, Maginot,* **and** *Gamelin:* The three schools of thought to which Cantwell refers describe World War I French general Charles Mangin's (1866–1925)—nicknamed "The Butcher"—preferred style of attack, which was *la guerre à outrance,* or a war to the death, which would be Cantwell's "hit them on the nose" (34:10–11). France constructed the Maginot line to protect itself from the borders to Italy and Germany. Although the Maginot Line prevented a direct attack, it did, as Cantwell suggests, leave the "left flank" open (34:12); Germany attacked through the Ardennes Forest in Belgium. Maurice Gamelin (1872–1958) also was a French general during World War II; Cantwell accuses him of hiding his head in the sand. Gamelin did not appropriate troops to defend the Ardennes Forest, believing it impenetrable, and stated that he would "await events" (Shirer 562). Four days after the attack on Pearl Harbor, Hemingway wrote Maxwell Perkins, saying, "the myth of our matchless navy has been exploded as badly as the myth of Gamelin the great general" (*SL* 531).

34:18 Foch: Ferdinand Foch (1851–1929) was a main figure in the French victory at the Marne in World War I. He was named marshal of France and then supreme commander of the Allied troops in 1918. In Hemingway's early journalism, Foch is mentioned as an example of the French mindset of complete loyalty to the government. Foch, Hemingway reports, "was opposed to the Ruhr occupation. He washed his hands of it absolutely. But once it was launched, he did not come out against it" (*DLT* 268). In *Across the River and into the Trees,* Foch is used to counterbalance Cantwell's negativity; he is an example of one of "the fine ones" (34:17). Hemingway owned several books concerning Foch, including *The Principles of War,* translated by Hillaire Belloc (Brasch and Sigman 147). Foch is mentioned in Hemingway's satire, *The Torrents of Spring* (1926), described as "praying for victory" (37).

34:21–22 Don't be a bitter: In addition to Renata spending much of the novel coaching Cantwell not to be bitter, brutal, bad, et cetera, Cantwell often must coach himself. In this paragraph, Cantwell instructs himself to "remember" six times, and then tells himself, "Don't be a bitter . . ." and "Cut it out"—this metacognition, evaluating the value of his own thoughts, is a constant theme in Hemingway's work, seen prominently throughout *The Old Man and the Sea* and to spectacular effect during the final sequence of *For Whom the Bell Tolls.*

However, the notion that this trip is "to have fun" (34:24) seems reductive. This trip is meant to reconcile with his war wound, to allow him to die in a happy state in a place he loves after having seen the woman he loves. Later, he cannot recall ever walking in Venice "that it wasn't fun" (49:13). He tells Jackson that he doesn't like seeing him because he is a worrier and "you don't have fun" (60:22–23). He then commands Jackson to go and have fun. After contemplating the affection he feels for all those who have been wounded in battle, he thinks: "I'd rather not love anyone. . . . I'd rather have fun" (71:32–33). Renata later accepts Cantwell's refusal to discuss some unpleasant military experiences with "let's have fun" (91:12). During subsequent conversation, Cantwell says, "we are having fun again, aren't we?" (95:10–11). If Cantwell's main objective was to have fun, the mission was accomplished. Despite the surly boatman, Cantwell ultimately admits: "I have had as much fun shooting here as I ever had in my life" (258:26–27).

See also Cantwell's bathroom meditation in chapter 16, when he says to himself, "Don't be bitter, boy" (157:25). Renata will later tell him: "Don't you see you need to tell me things to purge your bitterness?" (220:2–3), but then she will invite him to be "just as bitter as you want" (220:9–10).

Cantwell's bitterness was captured as the headline of the *Time* magazine interview-by-correspondence when *Across the River and into the Trees* was published: "Hemingway Is Bitter about Nobody—But His Colonel Is," in which Hemingway writes in the third person, "Hemingway is bitter about nobody. But the colonel in his book is. Do you know any non-bitter fighting soldiers or any one who was in the Hürtgen [Forest] to the end who can love the authors of that national catastrophe which killed off the flower of our fighting men in a stupid frontal attack?" (110). Cantwell asks a version of this rhetorical question during Renata's nap: "How can I remember if I am not bitter?" to which he responds, "Be as bitter as you want" (230:22–23). Renata has earlier asked him if he is bitter about everything, and Cantwell says, "No. It is just that I am half a hundred years old and I know things" (200:11–12).[1] He tries to think of his ex-wife "as unbitterly as he could" (195:31–32), although that proves to be not possible. Cantwell will also refer to himself aptly as the "unjust bitter criticizer" (210:7–8).

34:30 **I wonder what he's riding me for now:** Here is a rare moment from Jackson's perspective. Cantwell is such a strong presence in the novel that it can be difficult to remember that we are reading this novel from a third-person omniscient narrator, who knows more than Cantwell (see entry at 16:17–18). Jackson's brief interior monologue (34:30–33) reveals that he is wondering why Cantwell is needling him, he thinks Cantwell is a know-it-all because he used to be a general, he wonders why Cantwell was demoted, and then he concludes that Cantwell has been mentally compromised from all his battle experiences.

34:31 **he was a B.G. once:** That is, Cantwell was a brigadier general. See the entry at 13:14–15 for a discussion of the crucial theme of Cantwell's demotion.

35:7 **geometrically clear:** Just as Cantwell determined the site of his wounding by "triangulation" (26:17) and Piero della Francesca (22:29) and Brueghel (23:5) are noted for the geometry in their art, Hemingway viewed his composition of *Across the River and into the Trees* in mathematical terms, as "calculus" rather than algebra or simple mathematics. Hemingway claimed in 1950, "In writing I am through arithmetic, through plane geometry and algebra, and now I am in calculus. If they don't understand that, to hell with them" (Breit 62). Although robust critical debate has since been ongoing about how literally to take Hemingway's metaphor, James H. Meredith argues that Hemingway "was not being facetious in making this claim" ("Calculating the Complexity" 96). See entry at 64:25–27.

35:28 **Caorle:** This town is on the coast of Italy, north of Venice and east of San Donà di Piave. Hemingway traveled to Caorle in 1948 to hunt in the Valle San Gaetano with Nanuk Franchetti and Mary, Hemingway's fourth wife. For photos of this hunting trip, see Moriani (125–43). See also entry at 19:5–6.

35:32 **smuggled it out under a load of fresh pork:** This anecdote appears in William Carew Hazlitt's epic history of Venice: "Two Venetian merchants, named Buono and Rustico, the former of Malamocco, the latter of Torcello . . . resolved, in a fit of pious ardour, to attempt the rescue of the Saint from the peril by which he was threatened" (88). These enterprising men, smuggling the body from the Muslim Alexandria back to Venice, "then placed in a deep basket, where it was cunningly ensconced beneath a thick layer of herbs and savoury joints of pork" (89). This event occurred in 828 A.D. The Tintoretto painting *The Stealing of St. Mark's Body* is housed at the Galleria dell'Accademia and is also referenced later in the novel (49:7). Renata also makes a reference to this pork anecdote (151:5–6).

36:4 **pretty Byzantine:** Byzantine, referring to antiquity or the Roman empire during the late middle ages, is contrasted with the figures of the Italian Renaissance, most of whom Cantwell reveres. Cantwell is correct in saying that Venice's trade with the East facilitated Byzantine influence in art and architecture. As scholar Deborah Howard writes, "It was in the Byzantine period that the foundations of Venetian architecture were laid, both literally and conceptually" (7).

36:7 **It was, indeed:** Another instance where the narrator is a separate entity from Cantwell. Here, the narrator is perhaps gratuitously affirming the veracity of one of Cantwell's observations.

36:13 **Burano:** As Cantwell mentions, in addition to its fishing, Burano is famous for its lace and brightly colored homes. The Tower of Pisa leans about four meters, following its recent correction; the campanile in Burano is about two meters off perpendicular.

36:18 **Murano:** Murano is the glass-making capital of Italy. Later, Renata suggests to Cantwell that he buy some good glass: "We could go to Murano together" (133:16). Cantwell confesses that he doesn't know anything about glass, a rare admission that he lacks knowledge about something.

36:20 **vaporetto:** A vaporetto is a small canal water boat. See also 47:15.

36:21 **bambinis:** As with "campanile" (24:20), Cantwell is incorrectly using the English plural form to an Italian word. The Italian word for babies is "bambini."

36:22–23 **punt guns:** A punt gun is an enormous shotgun used in the nineteenth and early twentieth centuries for shooting waterfowl. This weapon is so named for its use on a "punt," a small, narrow boat used for fishing and hunting. See also 268:18 for another reference. In an unpublished fragment, entitled "Torcello Piece," Hemingway describes hearing punt gunners in the night, going to the window, seeing Venice in the moonlit mist, and feeling "both humble and proud" (JFK #773).

NOTE

1. In "Hills Like White Elephants," the American man, trying to comfort Jig, says, "You mustn't feel that way." Jig tells him: "I don't feel any way . . . I just know things" (*CSS* 214), anticipating Cantwell's disavowal of his emotions.

CHAPTER 5

37:1 **But he continued to look:** Just as chapters 2 and 3 begin by responding to the conclusion of the previous chapter (17:1), the opening of chapter 5 refutes Cantwell's "Let's roll" command (36:32).

37:2 **when he was eighteen years old:** Cantwell is referring to the Battle of the Piave, which took place on 15–23 June 1918, when Hemingway, like Cantwell, was eighteen years old. However, Hemingway was not in action during the battle. Another of his fictional protagonists in Italy, Frederic Henry of *A Farewell to Arms,* is also wounded in the Battle of the Piave and takes part in the subsequent retreat at Caporetto. If we assume that Hemingway and Cantwell share a birthdate or at least a birth year, then the action of *Across the River and into the Trees* takes place during the winter of 1948 and early 1949.

37:4–5 **The winter had come very cold that year:** The reference to "That winter" (37:15–16) invokes the Battle of Vittorio Veneto, from 24 October to 3 November 1918, Italy and the Allies' response to Caporetto that led to the fall of the Habsburg Empire.

37:19 **sore throat:** This condition resonates autobiographically; biographer James Mellow refers to a Hemingway sore throat in 1922 as his "old complaint" (182). "All his life," Michael Reynolds confirms, Hemingway "was prone to sore, inflamed throats" (*Paris Years* 19). See also 38:21.

38:1 **The Austrian attacks:** This paragraph (38:1–9) demonstrates the novel's most powerful use of second person, which Hemingway typically employs more frequently than he does in this novel, a technique of inclusion that disassociates the speaker from an intense experience just as it allows the reader to participate in the action. This technique is not common in this novel, but the six examples of "you" and the single "your" in this paragraph are conspicuous and striking.

38:22 **stick bombs:** A stick bomb, a World War I innovation, was "a large spherical bomb fitted with a steel or wooden rod, or stick. The stick was placed in a barrel at the bottom of which lay a propellant charge that, when ignited, propelled the bomb toward its target. The stick bomb had a range of between 200 and 500 yards" (*History of World War I* 834). Some of Hemingway's other World War I fiction include stick bombs, such as his short story "A Way You'll Never Be," from *Winner Take Nothing*, in which they are part of the "much material" that is "scattered over the road" following the attack (*CSS* 306). In *A Farewell to Arms*, too, Frederic sees a Germany bicycle troop and notes: "Stick bombs hung handle down from their belts" (211). The fifth and final flashback of "The Snows of Kilimanjaro" contains just one memory, of "Williamson, the bombing officer" who is "hit by a stick bomb some one in a German patrol had thrown as he was coming in through the wire that night" (*CSS* 53).

38:25 **But he never hated them:** Although this may seem a startling declaration, it is a fundamental one to Cantwell's ethos. Cantwell will come to realize that he really loves people "who had fought or been mutilated" (71:22–23). Cantwell reserves his hatred for the feckless, the presumptuous, the cowardly, the murderous, the incompetent, rather than someone who is of a different nationality or fighting honestly and bravely for a different side. This theme is also fundamental to many of Hemingway's narratives, from Pedro Romero's identification with the bulls he kills, even though he regards them as "best friends" (*SAR* 189), to Santiago's notion in *The Old Man and the Sea* of the marlin that he is battling to the death as his brother (e.g., 59). As Cantwell will later muse aloud to the portrait of Renata, must he hate the Germans because his job is to kill them? Must he hate them as people? It "seems too easy a solution" (164:12); see also his feelings about the Russians (70:30–31).

In *Islands in the Stream*, Thomas Hudson's kindness to a dying German prisoner earns him the epithet "Kraut-lover" (353).

39:3 **hit three times:** In addition to these three times being hit, Cantwell also tells Renata that he made three bad decisions (90:27–28), lost three battalions (91:25), lost three women in his life (91:20–21, 160:12), and had to fight three times seriously when liberating Paris (132). The description of the heart attack that ends Cantwell's life reads: "The Colonel started to speak but he stopped while it hit him the third time and gripped him so he knew he could not live" (282:9–11). Renata and Cantwell also have three disparate sexual episodes in the gondola (143–47).

39:5–6 **his personal immortality:** Unlike other Hemingway protagonists, such as Frederic Henry and Nick Adams, we never witness Cantwell actually lose his sense of personal immortality but only see him recall the moment thirty years later. As Cantwell will wryly surmise of surrendering this illusion, "Well, in a way, that is quite a lot to lose" (39:11–12).

In Hemingway's introduction to *Men at War*, a volume of war writing he selected and edited in 1942, he writes: "When you go to war as a boy you have a great illusion of immortality. Other people get killed; not you. It can happen to other people; but not to you. Then when you are badly wounded the first time you lose that illusion and you know it can happen to you" (xii). In a letter to Mary from Hürtgen Forest, he wrote of his emotion during battle: "I get the old feeling of immortality back I used to have when I was 19—right in the middle of a *really* bad shelling . . . the pure old thing we used to operate on" (qtd. in Reynolds, *Final Years* 120). In a 1948 letter describing his emotion following action during World War II, Hemingway wrote, "I think there is a steady renewal of immortality through storms, attacks, landings on beaches where landing is opposed, flying, when there are problems and many other things which are all awful and horrible and hateful to those who are not suited to them" (qtd. in Meyers, *Hemingway* 400).

39:21 left outside road when we hit the fork for Mestre: Mestre is one of the six boroughs of Venice: Murano-Burano, Lido-Pellestrina, Favaro Veneto, Mestre-Carpenedo, Chirignago-Zelarino, and Marghera. The two mentions of Mestre on this page and the one on the next, the only three in the novel, identify an important town in Hemingway's life. Hemingway stayed in Mestre in 1918 the night before he was transferred to the Italian front (Griffin 72). After Frederic Henry's desertion in *A Farewell to Arms,* he hides on the train to Mestre in the gun car. In "A Way You'll Never Be," too, Nick Adams mentions riding drunk from Mestre to Portogrande (*CSS* 309). In chapter 7 of *In Our Time,* the unnamed soldier makes a promise of chastity to Jesus during a bombardment but then breaks it and goes to a whorehouse in Mestre once the danger abates (*CSS* 109). In a related poem, "Riparto d'Assalto," Hemingway writes, "Lieutenants thought of a Mestre whore— / Warm and soft and sleepy whore, / Cozy, warm and lovely whore" (*Poems* 46).

39:29–30 I stole that, he thought: This confession of literary theft has inspired some debate, since Cantwell's memory of the original line is inexact. Stephen L. Tanner and Scott Donaldson each link Cantwell's description of New York as "shining, white and beautiful" with F. Scott Fitzgerald's "My Lost City," in which the city is described as being "glittering and white," a "shining edifice" (*The Crack-Up* 33, 32). Hemingway is mentioned in the essay, which not only evokes Fitzgerald's constant theme of recalling the past luminescence of a city (see, for example, the 1931 short story "Babylon Revisited") but also fits in nicely with Cantwell's own project of reexperiencing his love of Venice. Tanner argues, "It is highly implausible that Cantwell would have read, much less remembered, Fitzgerald's essay. It is Hemingway who is speaking in this allusion" (214). Tanner's source for the allusion originates with Matthew J. Bruccoli, who maintains that Hemingway "probably" is referring to "My Lost City" ("Hemingway 'Theft' Identified" [4]); Donaldson is less equivocal (188). In Fitzgerald's *The Great Gatsby,* too, the entry into New York enters mythical terms: "The city seen from the Queensboro Bridge is always the city seen for the first time, in its first

CHAPTER 5 · 39

wild promise of all the mystery and beauty in the world" (68). George Wickes, in a response to Bruccoli's point, argues for *Gatsby* as Cantwell's inspiration ([3]). Joseph Warren Beach refers to this passage more broadly as "a trifle cliché" (231).

See Mark Twain's "Eve's Diary," in which Eve remarks about her reflection in the lake: "there she was again, white and shining and beautiful" (*Complete Short Stories* 287).

In a description of the liberation of Paris, Cantwell ironically describes the attacking planes: "Shining, bright and beautiful" (205:4).

Hemingway might also be accusing himself of self-plagiarization: in one of Robert Jordan's final visions, he describes Madrid as "rising white and beautiful" (*FWBT* 467).

40:6 the Brenta: The Brenta River runs 108 miles from Trentino to the Adriatic Sea, just below the Venetian lagoon. The Brenta River takes on greater importance when Renata later recalls that Germans "killed my father and burned our villa on the Brenta" (116). After signing the armistice with Italy in September 1943, German troops invaded Italy and imprisoned and killed many citizens.

40:12 I'll ask Alberto: This, the first and only mention of an "Alberto" in the novel, obviously refers to a wealthy friend in the Veneto, one who owns a plot of land that might house Cantwell's remains. This reference might be a nod to Hemingway's Italian publisher and friend, Alberto Mondadori (1914–1976).

40:28 ugly Breda works: Società Italiana Ernesto Breda was a mechanical manufacturing company founded by Ernesto Breda in Milan in 1886. As Cantwell will inform Jackson (40:31–33), the firm specialized in locomotives and railway machinery but branched out into other products. One would see the Breda works, now called Fincantieri, before arriving at the Piazzale Roma, the site of the Fiat garage (Zorzi and Moriani 39).

40:28–29 Hammond, Indiana: Located in the extreme northwest of the state, Hammond was historically a gateway for commerce in the west and was itself a famous industrial town, specializing in meatpacking. Hemingway also mentions Hammond in his 1926 satire, *The Torrents of Spring* (53).

41:5 queen of the seas: This phrase is traditionally associated with Venice and is used as the title of Thomas F. Madden's history of Venice. In Thomas Mann's *Death in Venice*, von Aschenbach travels through Venetian canals, realizing that "the charm of this bizarre passage through the heart of Venice, even while it played upon his spirit, yet was sensibly cooled by the predatory commercial spirit of the fallen queen of the seas" (*Death in Venice and Seven Other Stories* 36).

In Canto IV of Byron's *Childe Harold's Pilgrimage,* Venice is described similarly: "She looks a sea Cybele, fresh from ocean / Rising with her tiara of proud towers / At airy distance, with majestic motion, / A ruler of waters and their powers" (4.2.1–2). Later, Venice becomes "a queen with an unequall'd dower" (4.11.9).

41:8 **Cheyenne:** Hemingway spent much of his later years in Cheyenne, the capital and most populous city in Wyoming. He married his third wife, Martha Gellhorn, there on 21 November 1940.

41:11 **Casper:** Casper, the second largest city in Wyoming, is nicknamed "The Oil City," much as Cantwell suggests. In a 2011 *New York Times* essay, A. E. Hotchner recalls that Hemingway, on a break from Mayo Clinic treatments for depression, attempted to commit suicide by walking into a plane propeller in Casper ("Hounded by Feds" A19). In 1949, Hemingway called Casper "an oil town where Mary lost our kid" (*Dear Papa* 48), a reference to her ectopic pregnancy on 19 August 1946.

41:18 **Cooke City, Montana:** This riff cataloguing the relative toughness of various cities in the United States anticipates Hemingway's 26 January 1954 article about his African safari that appeared in *Look* magazine: "Nairobi for a foreigner with no one with a grudge against him is safer than New York, five times safer than parts of Memphis, West Memphis or Jacksonville, infinitely safer than many parts of Chicago and most certainly safer than Brooklyn, the Bronx, Central Park at night, or Cooke City, Montana, on the date of the celebration of the Old Timers Fish Fry" ("Safari" 20). Hemingway gives an example of this toughness when he describes "boys" who were jailed because they tried to drag a truck driver to death "the night of the Old Timers' Fish Fry" over the alleged assault of a lady with a poker (*BL* 153). In the early 1930s, Hemingway spent a summer on a dude ranch owned by Lawrence and Olive Nordquist in Clark's Fork Valley, Wyoming, twelve miles from Cooke City, Montana (*SL* 328). To Bernard Berenson in 1953, Hemingway, sounding very much like Cantwell, wrote, "I come from the Barco de Avila, Cooke City, Montana, Oak Park, Illinois, Key West, Florida, here [Cuba], the Veneto, Mantova, Madrid. Too many places. But you are a local boy in all of them. This has its advantages and disadvantages" (*SL* 815). In Hemingway's preface to his short story collection *The First Forty-Nine Stories,* he recalls Cooke City as one of his favorite places to write.

In *For Whom the Bell Tolls,* Robert Jordan disposes of his grandfather's gun, which his father used to kill himself, by riding his horse to Red Lodge, Montana, "where they had built the road to Cooke City now over the pass and across the Bear Tooth plateau" (337), and dropping it off the cliffs into the lake. Jordan is referring to the Beartooth highway, also known as U.S. Route 212.

Cantwell later explicates his definition of toughness: "I suppose it is a man who will make his play and then backs it up. Or just a man who backs his play" (52:19–21).

41:20, 21, 25 **Memphis . . . Chicago . . . Bologna:** This bizarre cataloguing of cities continues, ending with Bologna. Memphis and Chicago state the claim Hemingway will later make in his *Look* magazine article (see entry at 41:18). Cantwell mentions Bologna as an example of a "good town" (88:4), in contrast with Florence.

41:33 **They don't steal here:** This debate about the safety of Cantwell's possessions recalls *Othello:* "What tells't thou me of robbing? This is Venice" (1.1.107).

42:7 **with the old deadliness:** This novel is framed not only by episodes of a duck hunt but also by examples of Cantwell's explosive temper toward Jackson, to be repeated at 280:9–11. Cantwell will even use this malocchio, his evil eye or death glare, at Renata (81:30), for which he apologizes, blaming his tendency to slip unconsciously into his soldiering trade. When Renata later instructs Cantwell to tell him stories, and uses the phrase "have to" (134:20), Cantwell snaps back at her, "and the cruelty and resolution showed in his strange eyes as clearly as when the hooded muzzle of the gun of a tank swings toward you" (134:21–23). This forcefulness actually reduces Renata to tears toward the end of chapter 12 (135:5), a moment prefigured when she tells him that she loves his "strange eyes that frighten me when they become wicked" (133:11). When confronting two fascists in the streets, he "smiled his old and worn death smile" (174:25), which does serve as an effective deterrent. Thinking of his ex-wife, "his eyes were bad and remembering" (197:6), causing Renata to ask him, "please never look at me nor think of me like that" (197:9–10).

As Desdemona prophetically says to Othello of his malocchio, "And yet I fear you, for you're fatal then / When your eyes roll so" (5.2.39–40).

42:8–9 **a mean son of a bitch . . . God-damn nice:** Jackson, by characterizing Cantwell with both of these phrases articulates well the two sides of the Colonel's character and his constant struggle to be a human being rather than a brute. In the novel, the word "damn" is used 68 times; "God" 31 times, and "hell" 105 times.

CHAPTER 6

43:2 **post-war rich from Milan:** Another consistent theme in Hemingway's work is his disdain for those who profit from war, the so-called *pescecani* (43:16, 48:6, 103:14, 188:10, 188:15), whom he despises. One of the central tenets of the Order to which Cantwell belongs is "a true, good hatred of all those who profited by war" (61:27–28). When buying sausage for Bobby, the hunting dog, Cantwell keeps his motive to himself, not wanting to behave with the boorishness of one who has profited from the war (178:19–22). In *A Farewell to Arms,* Gino, the head of the ambulance unit during Frederic's absence, informs Frederic that "dogfish" are selling food supplies (184). "Dogfish" is a literal translation of "*pescecani.*" Hemingway introduced *A Farewell to Arms* in 1948, the same period of the composition of *Across the River and into the Trees,* by writing, "I believe that all the people who stand to profit by a war and who help provoke it should be shot on the first day it starts" (*FTA,* Hemingway Library ix).

See "A Veteran Visits the Old Front" for an early reference to "evil-smelling Italian profiteers going to Venice for vacations" (*DLT* 178). Later in this chapter, Cantwell will turn "to look at the Milan profiteers; but they were gone" (46:3). In Shakespeare's *1 Henry VI,* Lord Talbot will use this epithet: "Frenchmen, I'll be a Salisbury to you. / *Pucelle* or pucelle, Dauphin or dog-fish, / Your hearts I'll stamp out with my horse's heels / And make a quagmire of your mingled brains" (1.6.84–87). For more on this topic, see Cirino, "You Don't Know the Italian Language Well Enough" (52, 60n9).

43:4 *negronis:* Somewhat different than Cantwell explains it—cocktail authority Philip Greene asserts that the Colonel "somewhat botches the recipe" (176)—the Negroni cocktail is made of one part gin, one part vermouth rosso (red, semi-sweet), and one part bitters, traditionally Campari. In Hemingway's fable "The Good Lion," the titular lion would "ask politely if he might have a Negroni or an Americano and he always drank that instead of the blood of the Hindu traders" (*CSS* 482). Later in the short story, Mr. Cipriani asks the lion, "A Negroni, Signor Barone?" (484). This was Hemingway's cocktail of choice while in Venice. An Americano is a similar drink, except it contains seltzer instead of gin.

43:17 **Commendatore:** The Italian president awards the chivalric title of commendatore to those in the Ordine al Merito della Repubblica. This designation is superior to the ufficiale or the cavaliere.

44:14–15 **Gordon's gin and Campari:** The bartender has ordered these for the Negroni (see 43:4).

44:24 **the Honorable Pacciardi:** Randolfo Pacciardi (1899–1991) was an Italian politician who also fought during World War I and the Spanish Civil War. As the text indicates, Pacciardi was the minister of defense in the Italian Republic. He is the "same age" as Cantwell (44:27), and almost seven months older than Hemingway. Pacciardi is a running reference during chapters 6, 7, and 8 in this bar, including Cantwell referring to Pacciardi defending the now-dry Piave from the Russians (70:33–71:4). In chapter 6, Cantwell wryly suggests that he is getting just slow enough that perhaps even Pacciardi could outsmart or defeat him (46:4–6). In fact, this moment has perhaps the novel's most extended passage of exposition, where the narrator clarifies and amplifies Cantwell's behavior. From 44:25 to 45:3, the narrator explains the reference and what it means to Cantwell and the bartender. According to Elisabetta Zingoni Nuti, Hemingway met Pacciardi during the filming of *The Spanish Earth* in Spain in 1936 (56).

44:30 **he, himself, was an observer:** Amid the joking, we do get the valuable piece of background information that Cantwell was "an observer" in Spain. Pacciardi fought during the Spanish Civil War in 1936 and 1937 as part of the Italian Antifascist Legion, which he formed. If Cantwell were an "observer" during the Spanish Civil War, then his experiences mirror Hemingway's own, even beyond the two world wars.

45:11 **anthrax:** In 1927 Hemingway contracted an anthrax infection at the Grau-du-Roi from cutting his foot on the rocks while swimming (Mellow 350). Hemingway was also concerned that in addition to contracting erysipelas in the Veneto in 1949, he had also been infected with anthrax. See entries at 184:8 and 184:10.

45:13–14 **Better to live one day as a lion than a hundred years as a sheep:** According to historian R. J. B. Bosworth, this is one of Mussolini's "quiver of slogans" (315), which were also emblazoned on the walls of Italian towns (La Bianca 197). The ossuary at Fagaré della Battaglia in Treviso has preserved a segment from an Italian wall with this motto in Italian—"*È meglio vivere un giorno da leone che cent'anni da pecora*" on it.

A rejected title for Hemingway's classic short story, "The Short, Happy Life of Francis Macomber" was "Than a Dead Lion," alluding to Ecclesiastes 9:4, "a living dog is better than a dead lion" (Smith 330). See also Psalms 84:10: "For a day in thy courts is better than a thousand elsewhere."

45:15 Better to die on our feet than to live on our knees: Emiliano Zapata popularized this motto during the Mexican revolution. This quotation is also variously ascribed to La Pasionaria (Andrews 788), Che Guevara, and Albert Camus, in *The Rebel: An Essay on Man in Revolt* (15). During El Sordo's last stand in *For Whom the Bell Tolls,* Joaquín refers to La Pasionaria's coining of this cliché (309) and then, ironically, begins to repeat it before he segues into the Hail Mary right before he is killed by fascist planes (321).

45:20–21 A million men will spring to arms overnight: Cantwell and the bartender continue the game of parroting jingoistic, empty wartime clichés. In this case, Cantwell quotes William Jennings Bryan (1860–1925), the ambassador to France, secretary of state, and Democratic presidential candidate who believed that if the country were threatened, there would be sufficient troops. Bryan is also mentioned during the Burguete episode of *The Sun Also Rises,* when amid a lively, allusive exchange between Jake and Bill Gorton on their pastoral fishing excursion, Jake informs Bill that the previous day's paper announced Bryan's death. Bryan died on 26 July 1925.

45:24 Big Picture: This "big picture" is alluded to by Northrop Frye who, in reviewing *Across the River and into the Trees,* remarks upon Cantwell's resistance to "the hideous 'big picture' in which strategy is based on politics and publicity stunts instead of on fighting" (611). In a 1958 interview, Hemingway claimed to be "embarrassed by nearly all big pictures—like big questions—except for Tintoretto's 'Crucifixion of Our Lord,' in Venice. From it I learned principally how to crucify, and how wonderfully the thief on the right behaved. On the right when you look at it. Actually on the left of our Lord" (Plimpton, "Art of Fiction" 60). Tintoretto's masterpiece, actually called *Crucifixion* (1565) is, literally, a big picture, about twenty feet high and forty-five feet wide.

Cantwell makes fun of Harry Butcher (1901–1985)—without naming him—who had written a book about "the truly Big Picture" after commanding without knowing anything about combat (129:28). During World War II, Butcher served as the Naval Aide to Eisenhower. Focused on this same strain, Cantwell also mocks "the Big Picture the Semi-Big Picture and the Super-Big-Picture" (217:13–14). Rather than having this ineffectual, impractical outlook, he explains to the sleeping Renata: "you have to throw away the Big Picture and be a division" (227:15–16).

45:33 he corrected: These incessant corrections continue the central motif of the novel, which is Cantwell's negotiation between being a civilian (i.e., a civil man) and a soldier. Here, he reprimands himself for brutality and the reflexive insulting of Jackson, which he actually just thinks and never says aloud.

46:12 I hope there is nothing wrong with him: This moment is another rare instance where we hear from the direct perspective of a character other than Cantwell. Here, the bartender expresses concern about Cantwell's health.

46:15 my Colonel: This phrase becomes something of a refrain in the novel, demonstrative of the affection with which the Venetians—generally workers in the service industry—view Cantwell. This phrase is evoked forty-eight times: by the bartender; the boatman; the porter; the barman; the *Gran Maestro;* the elevator boy; the waiter, Arnaldo; Ettore; Alvarito; the second waiter; the night porter; and the concierge.

46:24 *imbarcadero*: Italian for "pier" or "wharf." See 140:1–2.

46:30 the Gritti: The Gritti Palace, at Campo Santa Maria del Giglio 2467, joins Harry's Bar as one of the two primary interior locations of the novel. Hemingway stayed at this hotel when he was in Venice during the writing and editing of *Across the River and into the Trees,* and also on 23 March 1954, arriving from Africa following his plane crashes, when he arrived "with 87 bags" (Zorzi and Moriani 29). The Gritti Palace, long considered Venice's preeminent hotel, occupies the Palazzo Pisani and was purchased by Count Camillo Gritti in 1814 (29). Hemingway's opulent room overlooking the Grand Canal was, at the time, the best room in the best hotel in Venice.

46:34 Three thousand five hundred: The 3,500 lire Cantwell is being charged would equate to $2.88 USD in 1950, or slightly less than the cost of a new hardcover edition of *Across the River and into the Trees* when it was published. Cantwell soon realizes the idiocy of haggling over a buck or two on the last weekend of his life. The sixty lire that the vaporetto would cost equates to about fifty cents at that time (47:1). In the manuscript, the boatman names 1,500 lire as the fee.

47:4–5 they will stop at the imbarcadero past Harry's: From Harry's Bar at Calle Vallaresso, 1323 to the Gritti is about one-third of a mile, less than a ten-minute walk. But to walk anywhere in Venice, as Cantwell will soon muse, is like doing a crossword puzzle (49:16–17). Or, as Marcel Proust (1871–1922) puts it: "an interlacement of alleys, like those palaces in oriental tales whither mysterious agents convey by night a person who, brought back home before daybreak, can never find his way back to the magic dwelling which he ends by believing that he visited only in a dream" (882).

Also see Appendix 2 on pp. 210–211 for the transcript of the nine-minute sound recording that Hemingway made, called "In Harry's Bar in Venice," in which he describes the bar as "a small place, but, in effect, a microcosm of all of that great and beautiful city which has been so well described by those writers Ruskin, Sinclair Lewis, Byron, and others."

47:18 *Con piacere:* Italian for "With pleasure."

47:30 **T.D.** An abbreviation for "tank destroyer."

47:34–48:1 **the smallest model Universal puts out:** According to an archivist at Westerbeke Corporation, which acquired Universal Motors in 1990, the smallest model Universal produced in the late 1940s was a twelve-horsepower gasoline propulsion engine called Blue Jacket (message to author, 2 April 2013).

48:7 **Lido:** The rich *pescecani* are described as gambling at the Lido here as well as on 103:15. The Lido is also the site where a pederast is attacked (92:21–24). The site of the Venice Film Festival, the Lido is also the home of the Venice Casino. The Lido is a beach that has attracted tourists and is also the site of many hotels, including the Grand Hotel Excelsior, where von Aschenbach stayed in Mann's *Death in Venice*.

48:9 **gondola:** In this first mention in the novel, the boatman references the sailing craft that automatically conjures up Venice.

48:11 **I might get you a jeep engine:** Although this minuscule aspect to the plot is only mentioned four more times, it is nevertheless a strand to the web of *Across the River and into the Trees* to which readers must remain attentive. Hemingway's inclusion of recurrent motifs allows the novel to transcend a linear narrative and become self-referential, circular, and self-sustaining, the calculus with which he envisioned its creation. Not only does this show Cantwell's generosity and his concern for the less fortunate, but it also creates a kind of textual memory so that Cantwell's comments are not simply random asides but things that he remembers, and readers must, too. In fact, after Cantwell vows that he'll "get you the God-damned jeep complete with handles" (51:10–11), he promises that he'll "not forget about the overage jeep engine" (56:9). Almost two hundred pages later, "he had not forgotten about the jeep engine" (253:23), even though readers very well might have. In the waning pages of the novel, Cantwell thinks: "But how do I get that condemned jeep engine to that old man?" (267:25–26). He never does. Nevertheless, this is one of the strands of the novel that compel us to move forward, as opposed to the memories which are forcing us and the characters to look backward.

48:22, 24 **the Regime:** In the manuscript, "Fascism" replaces "the Regime" in both instances on this page (JFK 1).

48:29–30 **the canal that runs from Piazzale Roma to Ca' Foscari:** Piazzale Roma is the square that houses the main bus station in Venice and is the entry point to the city. Ca' Foscari is a beautiful Gothic building modified by Doge Francesco Foscari

(1373–1457), on the Grand Canal, now the site of the Università di Venezia Ca' Foscari. There is about a half mile in between these two locations. Zorzi and Moriani refer to Piazzale Roma as "the most unexciting place you can see" (39).

49:3 On retirement pay: Cantwell's monthly retirement salary would have been $619.88, or 75 percent of his active monthly rate, $826.50.

49:7 Tintorettos at the Accademia: Tintoretto (1518–1594), named Jacopo Comin, was a Venetian Renaissance painter. Cantwell is certainly referring to *The Stealing of St. Mark's Body,* which is referred to in the novel (35:30–36:2). Later, the portrait of Renata is described as the way Tintoretto would have done it (137:14). Tintoretto is named as one of Hemingway's many influences in various artistic media (Plimpton, "Art of Fiction" 118). Tintoretto's series on the story of Genesis is also in the Accademia. The Galleria dell'Accademia (also mentioned 50:15, 178:30), a museum gallery of pre-nineteenth-century art, sits on the south bank of the Grand Canal in Venice; it houses fourteen Tintorettos.

49:7–8 Scuola San Rocco: The Scuola Grande di San Rocco is a fifteenth-century building in Venice that houses paintings depicting biblical scenes, most of which were done by Tintoretto or his assistants, including the *Crucifixion,* which was so important to Hemingway (see entry at 45:24). In John Ruskin's view, this building is one of the three most important of its kind in Italy, along with the Sistine Chapel and the Campo Santo in Pisa. Ruskin urges "unembarrassed attention and unbroken time" to the visitor of the San Rocco (316), and he does likewise in his painstaking description of the paintings in the San Rocco (317–43). Of the *Crucifixion,* Ruskin confesses that he "must leave this picture to work its will on the spectator; for it is beyond all analysis, and above all praise" (343).

49:20–21 insufficient command of the language: As the first complete volume of Hemingway's letters prove, from his first stay in Italy in 1918—as in the moment referenced here in Cantwell's life—the young Hemingway was an enthusiastic and unembarrassable, even if flawed speaker of Italian. This theme does not go unnoticed in his Italian fiction, such as "In Another Country" and *A Farewell to Arms.* For a broader discussion of this theme, see Cirino, "You Don't Know."

49:23 rising from the sea: This refers to Titian's painting, *Venus Rising from the Sea* (circa 1520), which is housed in the National Gallery of Scotland in Edinburgh. In his history of Venice, Peter Ackroyd remarks on Venice being compared with a woman, or Venus, and depicted in art as rising from the sea (268). Hemingway also uses the same phrase in *The Old Man and the Sea,* when Santiago "went on dreaming to see the white peaks of the Islands rising from the sea" (25). Renata says that the portrait that was painted of her makes her look like "as though I were rising from the sea without the head wet" (93:13–14).

49:24 Merde: The Italian word for "shit" is "*merda*," not to be confused with the French "*merde*" (see also 27:4, 246:12). With "merde," Cantwell is paying tribute to the French legend that at Waterloo, the general Count Pierre Jacques Étienne Cambronne (1770–1842) responded to a demand to surrender with that single French expletive, to which Victor Hugo in *Les Misérables* refers as "the finest word, perhaps, that a Frenchman ever uttered" (341). "Merde" is also for this reason known as "the word of Cambronne." Hemingway often referred to Cambronne's use of this word in letters, usually to defend his own use of the same word, either in his work or the letter itself (see, e.g., *SL* 297, 647, 810). He also praises Cambronne's audacity as he repeats the story in his introduction to *Men at War* (xix).

49:24–25 that winter up at the juncture: This refers to the winter of 1918, the response to the Battle of Caporetto, when the Austro-Hungarian army was finally repelled in the Battle of Vittorio Veneto, fought between 24 October and 3 November 1918 (see entry at 37:4–5).

49:26–27 Knowing what I know now: Cantwell's epistemology is a forceful theme in the novel, along with this example, the impossibility of applying the experience of age to the events of youth. According to Carlos Baker, an alternate title for the novel was "The Things That I Know" (*Life Story* 474), which is demonstrably in a list of Hemingway's potential titles for *A Moveable Feast*. Recall also the moment in *The Sun Also Rises* when Robert Cohn is invited to think of what he'd like to do most, and—falling right into Harvey Stone's trap—suggests that he'd like to play football knowing what he knows now, proving himself to be a classic case of "arrested development" (51).

See also an interesting occasion of plotting Cantwell's knowledge, with respect to the narrator's (266:3–8), or for the plotting of Cantwell's knowledge in relation to the surly boatman's and the narrator's (16:16–18). While contemplating the portrait of Renata at the beginning of chapter 19, he will wonder how girls like the portrait and Renata "know so much so damn young" (166:10–11).

49:30 And all this time: This interior monologue that begins with "He looked to the right" (48:33) is a good example of the presentation of Cantwell's thoughts in the novel, particularly the way Venice and its sights excite his imagination and memory and stimulate his consciousness in a Proustian manner. In this one-page interior monologue, for example, he has taken the reader through the present view of a building, the possibility of relocating to Venice and going to the museums, the places he would eat, the potential of going on long walks, the way he felt about the city as a young soldier in 1918, and his willingness to fight for Venice again.

50:5 **Rio Nuovo:** Cantwell takes the path to the Gritti by way of the Rio Nuovo, the entrance into the Grand Canal.

50:5 **two stakes:** Hemingway negates the force of the objective correlative of the two stakes, chained but never touching, by explicating it himself: "like us" and "that's us" (50:6, 50:9). However, this "us" is the first explicit reference in the novel to our main concern, Cantwell's relationship with Renata. She will be referenced again on 69:16 before she physically enters the narrative on 78:23. Carlos Baker explicates this passage in an interesting—yet ultimately unconvincing—reading which argues that the various bridges are "symbolic reminders of certain milestones in his youthful experience" (*Writer as Artist* 278) and that the two stakes represent his former and current self.

50:11–12 **the great lantern that was on the right of the entrance to the Grand Canal:** This great lantern rests at the corner of Rio Nuovo and Canal Grande, on the building of the Università di Venezia Ca' Foscari, which recently restored it.

50:26 **Bassano:** Bassano del Grappa, located in the foothills of the Grappa mountains, is mentioned twice, on this page and at 66:3, as the place where good asparagus can be found. It is the town in the Veneto where the aperitif grappa was invented.

50:26 **on the other side of the Grappa:** The boatman refers to Monte Grappa, the mountains in the Veneto, part of the Venetian Prealps. Renata and Cantwell later speculate that the colonel should be buried on the Grappa (209:13–15).

50:29 **the big ossario:** The boatman is referring to the Tempio Ossario di Bassano del Grappa. This ossuary is on the outskirts of the historic centre, on Piazzale Cadorna. More than 5,400 fallen soldiers are at rest in the Tempio Ossario.

50:29 **Feltre:** Feltre is a town in the commune of Belluno in the Veneto, located on the Stizzon River.

51:2 **nineteen-eighteen:** If the boatman's brother was killed on the Grappa in 1918, he might have served during the Austrian offensive in the summer of 1918 during the second Battle of Monte Grappa. During the Battle of Vittorio Veneto, "brutal fighting" took place on 24 October when the Monte Grappa front was bombarded (Raab 83).

51:2–3 **inflamed by hearing d'Annunzio talk:** One of D'Annunzio's roles during the war was to travel to Italian troops and inspire them with jingoistic rhetoric. According to Zorzi and Moriani, Hemingway actually could have heard D'Annunzio speak to the Arditi troops on 29 June 1918 in Roncade (50), although no certain evidence exists to verify this claim. This adjective—"inflamed"—is a wink at D'Annunzio's novel *Il Fuoco* (1900), literally "The Fire," but officially translated as *The Flame of Life*. Many critics have commented on the theme of D'Annunzio in this novel, as well as his presence as an iconic figure during Hemingway's life. According to Carlos Baker, Hemingway read *The Flame of Life* as early as 1920 in Toronto (*SL* 114). In 1918, Hemingway announced plans to see D'Annunzio's drama, *La Nave* (*The Ship*) at La Scala in Milan (*Letters 1*, 160–61; Mellow 80–81).

Hemingway had read Tommaso Antongini's 1938 biography, *D'Annunzio* (Brasch and Sigman 53), as well as, after writing *Across the River and into the Trees*, Frances Winwar's *Wingless Victory: A Biography of Gabriele D'Annunzio and Eleonora Duse* (Brasch and Sigman 379). Brasch and Sigman do not have Hemingway holding any of D'Annunzio's writings. Reynolds, per Baker, lists Hemingway as having read *The Flame* (Reynolds, *Hemingway's Reading* 115).

D'Annunzio has been discussed at great length as a possible perverse role model for the young Hemingway. For particularly shrewd commentaries, see Comley ("Italian Education" 45–48), Russo (particularly 415–32), and Tintner.

51:7–8 **Isonzo ... Bainsizza ... Carso:** The boatman's reference to his family members who were lost "beyond the Isonzo" indicates the devastating Battles of the Isonzo, a series of twelve clashes between Italy and the Austro-Hungarian Empire, in which 689,000 Italian soldiers were killed (Thompson 381). These battles, which took place from June 1915 to November 1917, led to the Battle of Caporetto and then finally to Italy's victory at the Battle of Vittorio Veneto in October and November 1918. The Isonzo River is located in present-day Slovenia, although it was inside Austria and Hungary during World War I. In August and September 1917, the eleventh battle of the Isonzo was fought to capture the Bainsizza Plateau in Gorizia, overlooking the Isonzo River, which Italy did claim. According to the definitive historian of the Italian front, Mark Thompson, the Bainsizza "was almost a trackless wilderness—there were no proper roads and very few paths. And it was almost waterless" (250). The Carso is just south of the Bainsizza Plateau, separated by the Selva di Ternova. The series of battles began there in 1915 and the carnage continued during 1915 and 1916.

Later, it is mentioned that Cantwell and the *Gran Maestro* fought together "on the three key points, Pasubio, Grappa, and the Piave, where it all made sense," but also "the earlier stupid butchery on the Isonzo and the Carso" (62:10–11, 62:12–13). When surmising about the origins of D'Annunzio's eye injury, Cantwell mentions the speculation that it occurred "beyond the Carso where everyone died, or was incapacitated, that you knew" (53:15–16). Hemingway mentions the Pasubio during one of the italicized flashbacks in "The Snows of Kilimanjaro" (*CSS* 42).

51:15 Contessa Dandolo: Cantwell is referring to no actual person, but instead Hemingway is drawing from a rich historical association. The Dandolos were a ruling family of Venice, most notably Enrico Dandolo, a doge who led Venice from 1192 to 1205, including during the Fourth Crusade. Giovanni Dandolo ruled from 1280 to 1289 and Francesco Dandolo from 1329 to 1339.

In the manuscript, Hemingway had written "Contessa Reale," a reference to Contessa Amelia de Reali, whom Mary Hemingway once called "enduring" and "endearing" ("Harry's Bar" 62). However, Gianfranco Ivancich, Adriana's brother, suggested that he change the name to Dandolo, for its historical authenticity (Ivancich-Biaggini 221).

51:17 He did not say, but thought: Indeed, this begins a lengthy, wildly allusive interior monologue that lasts until 54:29, stimulated by the water, the familiar and evocative houses, and the memories. This rhetoric matches the Proustian mode introduced on 49:30.

51:29 winter day, which, of course, it was: The exact month is never identified, but the novel takes place during winter. However, one of the duck hunts that inspired the novel, during which Hemingway met Adriana Ivancich, took place in early December 1948, which would technically have still been autumn. The Italian victory over the Austro-Hungarian Empire took place in November 1918 and the Battle of the Bulge occurred in December 1944 and January 1945, all events central to Cantwell's memory. The placement of this novel in winter negates some critics' suggestions that the action of the novel takes place during Easter weekend (as does, for example, Dante's *Divine Comedy,* Faulkner's *The Sound and the Fury,* and D'Annunzio's *Notturno*). See the entry for 26:20.

51:31, 32 knowing. . . . knowing: This paragraph is critical to an understanding of the conceit of this novel, the mixture of memory to the present scene. Each house Cantwell sees during the present scene, for instance, is informed and colored by the people he has known and thought about, in some cases for thirty years. For this reason, the disproportionate attention spent on a car ride from Trieste to the port and then the boat ride into Venice actually provides the reader a panoramic view of Cantwell's history of the region, as well as his present associations, a tour through Cantwell's Veneto through space and time, distance and memory. See entries at 49:30 and 51:17 for further discussion of this issue.

51:32 palazzos: This Italian word for "palace" should be italicized, as earlier (51:21), and the plural form is *"palazzi."*

52:1 Alvarito's mother's house: As will be demonstrated in subsequent entries (e.g., 122:18, 124:22, 133:27, 185:16–17, and 275:15 and following), a convincing argument can be made for Alvarito as the third most important character in the novel, less present but more important to the plot than Jackson, the *Gran Maestro,* or anyone else besides Cantwell or Renata. Hemingway used Baron Nanuk Franchetti (1926–1997) as the inspiration for this character. He is referred to as the "Baron Alvarito" only once (56:27); usually it's Barone.

Nanuk Franchetti's father, Raimondo (1889–1935), died in a plane crash in Egypt. His sister, Afdera (1931–), married the actor Henry Fonda (1905–1982), and was a friend of Adriana Ivancich.

52:7–8 George Gordon, Lord Byron: Although the only three explicit mentions of Byron (1788–1824) are on this page, he nevertheless serves as the antithesis of hack or opportunistic writers that exploit Venice without understanding it or earning it. Hemingway was often aligned with Byron, with his perceived equal interests in art and action. Reynolds points to figures such as Theodore Roosevelt, D'Annunzio, and Byron as historical prototypes for this twentieth-century man of action, man of thought figure (*Young Hemingway* 211). In a 1933 article for the *Nation,* Clifton Fadiman introduced Hemingway as "an American Byron."

Byron is distinguished from Robert Browning (1812–1889) and Elizabeth Barrett Browning (1806–1861), both of whom wrote about Venice, but are not, according to Cantwell, well loved by the natives. Byron is mentioned favorably along with John Ruskin and Sinclair Lewis in "In Harry's Bar in Venice" as worthy writers who made Venice the subject of their work. In an unpublished letter to John Dos Passos, Hemingway asserts of Venetians: "Mr. Byron is their writer" (JFK, Outgoing Correspondence, 29 May 1949).

Byron stayed in the Palazzo Mocenigo; a plaque honors the site on the Grand Canal. One wonders why Cantwell mentions Byron's palace after they pass under the Accademia bridge, as it is located before the bridge.

52:16 Robert Browning . . . Mrs. Robert Browning: Robert Browning was a British poet and dramatic monologist, the author of "My Last Duchess." His book of poetry, *Men and Women* (1855), might have inspired Hemingway's modernist response, *Men Without Women* in 1927. Elizabeth Barrett Browning was also an accomplished poet. They moved to Italy for Elizabeth's health in 1846. Hemingway also considered appropriating a phrase from Elizabeth Barrett Browning—"If you must love"—as a title for the novel that became *A Farewell to Arms* (Reynolds, *Hemingway's First War* 297).

Although Cantwell holds that Browning was not well loved, it should be mentioned that the pioneering Italian-American immigrant novelist Constantine Maria Panunzio (1884–1964) uses Browning—even as a Victorian writer—as a symbolic touchtone, in which Browning's poem "Paracelsus" (1835) provides for him a key to American life, "an inexhaustible spring of vigor, power, and optimism" (284).

"It was Browning," Panunzio writes, "who first penetrated my being with the rays of *radiant optimism*" (292, emphasis in original). Browning died at his son's home Ca' Rezzonico in Venice.

52:25 Havre or Cherbourg: These are two cities on the western coast of France, off the English Channel, which Cantwell analogizes to his current boat trip. The 4th Infantry Division battled from Normandy to Cherbourg after D-Day. Hemingway flew into Cherbourg in July 1944 and stayed there for a week with other war correspondents (Beistle 3).

52:25–26 banlieue: French for "suburbs."

52:28 There *he* lived: The "*he*" refers again to D'Annunzio. Contrary to Cantwell's assertion, D'Annunzio did not live in such a villa on the Grand Canal with Eleonora Duse (1854–1924) (Tintner 10). D'Annunzio did live in the Casetta Rossa adjacent to the Santa Maria di Giglio on the Grand Canal. The D'Annunzio association is crucial because Cantwell points out that D'Annunzio was brave, even though he was "a more miserable character than any that I know" (52:31–32), just as he will later say something similar about Dante (87:25–26, 201:12–14), distinctions he will also make about himself.

As Hemingway would have known through his readings, D'Annunzio's last name at birth was Rapagnetta, before he and his father appended the new surname. D'Annunzio was not Jewish. The comparison of "arms" (53:6, 53:7, 53:8) of women and of the military, of course, recalls the dual meaning of the title, *A Farewell to Arms*.

Hemingway uses parentheses seven times in the novel, twice to clarify a term, and five times to insert a phrase, the first of which is seen here, in his speculation about D'Annunzio's original surname.

52:33 the man I think of to compare him with never put the chips on the line and went to war: This intriguing example of Hemingway's iceberg theory invites the reader to speculate that Cantwell is linking D'Annunzio to Mussolini in their shared propagandist fervor for fascist Italy. However, in the manuscript, Hemingway wrote that D'Annunzio was more miserable than anyone "except Jed Harris" (JFK 1), the volatile Broadway producer with whom he briefly dealt in 1938 regarding Hemingway's play, *The Fifth Column*. Harris (1900–1979) thought the play needed more sweeping revisions than did Hemingway.

Mary referred to the cliché "when the chips are down" as one of Hemingway's catchphrases that eventually grated on her nerves (*How It Was* 248).

53:10 d'Annunzio had lost an eye: According to Virginia Jewiss's preface to a translation of D'Annunzio's *Notturno*, she claims that D'Annunzio suffered a detached retina in his right eye during a flying mission on 16 January 1916 over Trieste. She writes that he conceived *Notturno* and wrote it on scraps of paper during his convalescence in Venice (vii). This injury would be particularly resonant for Hemingway, who as he was beginning the writing of *Across the River and into the Trees* in March 1949 contracted a severe case of erysipelas, which caused an infection in his eye.

53:11 **Pola:** This southern Croatian town, also called Pula, served as a central naval base for the Austro-Hungarian Empire. Only the Adriatic Sea separates Pola from Venice.

53:14 **the Veliki . . . San Michele:** The Veliki, in present-day Slovenia, was the site of severe bombing at the start of the Battles of the Isonzo, 16 June 1915 (Cavallaro 172).[1]

San Michele al Tagliamento is a town in the province of Venice. Hemingway visited San Michele in 1948 and found the postwar modernization a disappointment (Zorzi and Moriani 51). Mount San Michele sits at the northern peak of the Carso, nine hundred feet in elevation, and changed hands many times during the first six battles of the Isonzo. The Italians captured San Michele in the sixth battle on 6 August 1916, at the cost of 100,000 dead since their first attempts to secure the summit (Macdonald with Cimprić 91). During the extended battles, the Austrians used phosgene gas to devastating effect against the poorly equipped Italian army (31).

53:27–28 **as white as the belly of a sole:** This insult recalls Huck Finn's description of his father's face: "a white to make a body's flesh crawl—a tree-toad white, a fish-belly white" (*AHF* 31). In *Islands in the Stream,* a hammerhead shark "rose white-bellied out of the sea" (88). The shark's belly is then described as "shining an obscene white" (89), before it turns black and red from bullet holes. In Hemingway's unpublished early short story, "The Woppian Way," the narrator refers to "the great amourist who had exhausted the love of women and now was wringing the last drops from love of country onto his white hot soul" (JFK #843), a clear reference to D'Annunzio.

Faulkner's *Sanctuary* (1931) contains a simile that also anticipates this image: the "ranked intent faces" of the courtroom are "white and pallid as the floating bellies of dead fish" (284).

53:30 **Morire non è basta:** Italian for "to die is not enough" is "morire non basta," without the "è." It is probable that Hemingway never heard D'Annunzio speak—Zorzi and Moriani suggest otherwise (50)—but here he places a young Cantwell in the audience of some of D'Annunzio's fiery rhetoric. For Cantwell to strike on the recollection of this cliché, a couple of days away from death, would be as galling for him now as it would have been when he was a young soldier. Hemingway quotes this phrase (correctly, without the "è") at the end of a 1923 article for the *Toronto Star,* translating it and then glossing it: "You must survive to win" (*DLT* 320). More than twenty-five years later, Hemingway views the same slogan with a considerable increase of satirical bite.

53:31 **What the muck more:** Hemingway can always be counted on to skewer wartime jingoism or empty sloganeering. His most famous passage is the evisceration of such tired wartime invocations in *A Farewell to Arms* (184–85).

As a euphemism for "fuck," "muck" is used six times in *Across the River and into the Trees* (also 61:4, 92:3, 92:4, 204:21, and 232:1), oddly puritanical given that "cunt" is used twice (204:6, 204:13). "Muck" is also used euphemistically thirty-two times in *For Whom the Bell Tolls*.

54:9 *Evviva d'Annunzio:* That is, "Long Live D'Annunzio."

54:21 **But now he was passing the house:** This long internal monologue (51:17–54:29), motivated by the vision of the house of Contessa Dandolo, the houses of other people he knows, Alvarito's mother's house, Byron's former house, and then D'Annunzio's house is now brought back into the present in a remark to Jackson, with a clear reminder of Cantwell's temporal and spatial position. As in "Snows of Kilimanjaro," Hemingway is usually meticulous about indicating temporal changes, even during relatively experimental narrative modes; Faulkner or Joyce would not necessarily be so conscientious to give readers a "But now" as a handrail.

Hemingway uses the same technique on 28:1.

54:22–23 **his great, sad, and never properly loved actress:** D'Annunzio lived with Eleonora Duse, the iconic Italian actress. He was consistently unfaithful and subjected her to much cruelty and derision. Cantwell does not know where either were buried, but D'Annunzio was buried in Il Vittoriale degli Italiani, Gardone Riviera, Lombardia, Italy, and Duse was buried in Asolo, in the province of Treviso, where she lived the last four years of her life. Duse is interred in the cemetery of Sant' Anna. Duse's "wonderful hands" (54:23)—a clear contrast to Cantwell's—were also praised by an admiring writer: "Her hands were always her true voice . . . and they could laugh, weep, run, silence, kill and die, as tenderly and as ruthlessly as so many saints and demons" (Del Riccio 7). D'Annunzio's friend and often more histrionic than historical biographer described this relationship: "The meeting of such creative and interpretative genius was therefore of interest to all thinking humanity" (Antongini 310).

55:2–3 **fair English translations:** Although Cantwell implies that he is an expert judge of the quality of the translations of D'Annunzio's work into English, according to the most reliable sources on the books Hemingway owned during his life, he owned only one of D'Annunzio's books, an early copy of *The Flame*.

55:9 **nor be difficult:** This motif of Cantwell constantly checking his own temper and behavior continues. At this point in the novel, actually, he has not been terribly difficult. He needles Jackson for being exceedingly concerned about side roads (31:12–13) and then rages at him because he has to repeat an order to him (42:3–5). The novel is not over, though (see 280:9–11).

55:15 Notturno: Adeline R. Tintner argues that this 1921 volume is actually more important to *Across the River and into the Trees* than is *The Flame of Life*. This book was not translated into English during Hemingway's lifetime but has since been published, in a 2011 translation by Stephen Sartarelli. Hemingway could conceivably have read the French translation available at that time. *Notturno* was written on strips of paper while a blind D'Annunzio convalesced from a plane crash. The effort, where D'Annunzio often reflects on his war experience as he describes his painful physical condition, is classified as a memoir. D'Annunzio's daughter in *Notturno*, as in his life, is named Renata.

55:17 Santa Maria del Giglio: This church, for which Giuseppe Sardi (1624–1699) began the facade in 1678, is, in the words of art historian Deborah Howard, "ostentatious" and "flamboyant" (229), which "could hardly be described as elegant" (230), with a facade that has—like Cantwell himself—"a swagger verging on vulgarity" (236). At the beginning of chapter 9, Cantwell compares this church to a war plane and wonders who built it (76:14–15), not knowing Sardi's name. As Hemingway wrote the manuscript, he did not recall this church's name and left it blank, to be filled in later.

55:29–30 Every move she makes: The old motor boat becomes a clear objective correlative for Cantwell himself, a "triumph of the gallantry of the aging machine" (55:30).

55:31 old Traveller: Cantwell refers to Robert E. Lee's (1807–1870) warhorse.

55:31 Marbot's Lysette [*sic*]: Cantwell's allusion is to Baron de Marbot (1782–1854) the French soldier and memoirist, whose mare Lisette is depicted in the "Lisette at Eylau" episode in Hemingway's *Men at War* (531–39). General Marbot describes his warhorse, after being stabbed with a bayonet: "Her ferocious instincts being restored by the pain, she sprang at the Russian, and at one mouthful tore off his nose, lips, eyebrows, and all the skin of his face, making of him a living death's-head, dripping with blood" (535). In Hemingway's introduction to the compilation, he notes: "There is quite a bit of Marbot in the book" (xxii). Eylau, in East Prussia, was the site of a February 1807 battle between Napoleon's army and the Russian army.

56:17–18 the members of the Order: The facetious and fictitious Order—*El Ordine Militar, Nobile y Espirituoso de los Caballeros de Brusadelli*—to which Cantwell belongs receives its first mention here. We know that the "second waiter" belongs (117:26–27), and that the night porter "may be member material" (170:17). The barman in Chapter 7 "was not a full paid-up member of the order" (57:9). Barone Alvarito (122:18) and Count Andrea (72:17) are also members. Renata becomes a member (super honorary secretary) at 248:10, by decree of the *Gran Maestro*. The Order is also discussed at 62:17–63:14 and 67:9–13.

Miriam Mandel speculates that the inspiration for the invention of this group might have been Hemingway's own designation as a cavaliere di gran croce al merito in the Knights of Malta, awarded during his 1948–49 trip to Venice ("Reading the Brusadelli Stories" 334). See entry at 59:23.

56:21 **Grand Master:** This character, the headwaiter at the Gritti, is only mentioned three times with his fictitious title in English (56:30, 57:21), is usually the *Gran Maestro*. In this novel, he serves as a kind of equivalent to Montoya in *The Sun Also Rises*, a dependable, judicious figure whom the protagonist respects and trusts completely. Cantwell and the *Gran Maestro* fought together during World War I. He is "two years older" than the Colonel (58:8), or fifty-two. *Gran Maestro*'s short speech about abstaining from alcohol while on duty, while working, is a classic statement of Hemingway's ethical "code," and it is not surprising that Cantwell replies with an offer of praise: "Not for nothing are you the *Gran Maestro*" (59:1). Of course, a couple of paragraphs later, the Gran Maestro does have a quick *Carpano punto e mezzo* (59:3). In a biographical corollary, it is said that Hemingway is the only customer with whom Giuseppe Cipriani (1900–1980), the owner of Harry's Bar, ever drank (Greene 129).

NOTE

1. At this point in the manuscript, it is impossible to determine from Hemingway's handwriting if he wrote "Veliki" or rather "Vilesse," which is a small commune in Gorizia, close to the Slovenian border. By the first typescript, however, Hemingway settled on "Veliki."

CHAPTER 7

57:2–3 **not the accurate term:** Cantwell reveres the bar to the extent that he believes "lobby" does not convey its majesty. Language falls short. The theme of accuracy, precision, propriety, correctness, and efficiency continues to emerge. Cantwell has a compulsive fixation on accuracy, precision in description, comportment, payment, and action, and this neurosis often takes on a linguistic inflection.

57:3, 4 **Giotto . . . circle . . . math:** For a discussion of Giotto and the theme of circles, see 22:8–9. For a discussion of math, see entries at 26:17 and 35:7. Here is the wonderful anecdote from Vasari's *Lives of the Painters:*

> Pope Benedict IX of Treviso sent one of his courtiers into Tuscany to see what sort of man was Giotto, and of what kind his works, having designed to have some pictures made in S. Pietro. This courtier, coming in order to see Giotto and to hear what other masters there were in Florence excellent in painting and in mosaic, talked to many masters in Siena. Then, having received drawings from them, he came to Florence, and having gone into the shop of Giotto, who was working, declared to him the mind of the Pope and in what way it was proposed to make use of his labour, and at last asked him for some little drawing, to the end that he might send it to His Holiness. Giotto, who was most courteous, took a paper, and on that, with a brush dipped in red, holding his arm fast against his side in order to make a compass, with a turn of the hand he made a circle, so true in proportion and circumference that to behold it was a marvel. This done, he smiled and said to the courtier: "Here is your drawing." He, thinking he was being derided, said: "Am I to have no other drawing but this?" "'Tis enough and to spare," answered Giotto. "Send it, together with the others, and you will see if it will be recognized." The envoy, seeing that he could get nothing else, left him, very ill-satisfied and doubting that he had been fooled. All the same, sending to the Pope the other drawings and the names of those who had made them, he also sent that of Giotto, relating the method that he had followed in making his circle without moving his arm and without compasses. Wherefore the Pope and

many courtiers that were versed in the arts recognized by this how much Giotto surpassed in excellence all the other painters of his time. (38–39)

Hemingway owned Vasari's six-volume edition (Reynolds, *Hemingway's Reading* 196).

57:8 Privy Counsellor: A privy counselor is a member of the private council of a leader, such as the group that advises the British Crown.

57:15–16 Across the Canal was the old Palace: Cantwell identifies a palace in front of the Gritti, his destination.
    The phrase "Across the Canal" nods to the title of the novel.

57:19–20 a very dry Martini. . . . A double: It is implied that Cantwell drinks at the first bar (gin and Campari is sent for, and Cantwell pays), but Cantwell here explicitly orders his first drink of what will be many in the novel. The sheer volume of alcohol seems antithetical to both how he would treat his failing health and also his quest to enjoy himself with Renata. It will be interesting to note how future behavior relates to his alcohol intake. As John Paul Russo writes, "His entire experience of Venice is suffused in a haze of alcohol. . . . The highly revealing 'stupidity' of the dialogue may be the result of intoxication" (404, 405). Ultimately, it is impossible to determine the effects of drinking with any kind of certainty.

How much does Cantwell drink in the novel?

1. The first bar [indeterminate number]
2. a Gordon's gin and Campari (44:14–15)
3. Before he meets Renata at the hotel (seven drinks)
4. a very dry martini . . . a double (57:19–20)
5. a small *Carpano punto e mezzo* (59:3)
6. another dry martini (63:5)
7. another dry martini . . . a double (65:19)
8. In the hotel room with the waiter
9. gin and Campari (71:28)
10. With Renata at the bar (four drinks)
11. two very dry martinis (80:15)
12. two super Montgomerys (96:31–32)
13. **With Renata at dinner**
14. (a bottle of?) Capri Bianco (111:8)—drinks it at 113:18–19
15. a bottle of Roederer Brut '42 (128:20)
16. another bottle of Roederer (131:30)
17. a bottle of Perrier-Jouët (135:33)

18. **In the hotel room alone before bed**
19. two glasses of Valpolicella (at least) (153:2–3, 155:2)
20. **In the hotel room / bathroom when he wakes up**
21. another glass of Valpolicella (156:10)
22. a second bottle of Valpolicella (160:8)
23. **At breakfast with Renata**
24. a flask of decanted (purified) Valpolicella (189:25)
25. **Back at the hotel with Renata**
26. a glass of Valpolicella (207:20)
27. a glass of Valpolicella (212:9–10)
28. "let me fill your glass" (219:1)
29. a glass of wine (236:6–7)
30. **At Harry's Bar before farewell**
31. two very dry martinis (243:23)
32. a glass of Valpolicella (248:6)
33. a bottle of wine from Vesuvius (249:24–25)
34. **On the duck hunt**
35. grappa passed around (257:2)
36. Gordon's gin, since there is no water (258:30–31)
37. swallow of gin (270:22)
38. sip of gin (272:17)
39. **After the duck hunt**
40. grappa on the table (277:33)

58:10–21 **He advanced smiling . . . in their youth:** This somewhat tortuous passage is 113 words with 22 commas, a semicolon and only two sentences. The back of the Scribner's paperback applauds Hemingway for writing in "short, declarative sentences," but moments like this one show that the stereotype is not always true. The phrase "triumphant in defeat" (58:20–21)—a theme in Hemingway, like "The Undefeated" or *The Old Man and the Sea* that goes along with *Winner Take Nothing*.

"Spatular," an adjective that compares the *Gran Maestro*'s fingers to a spatula, is an unusual, yet correct vocabulary choice. This paragraph also provides the most precise information about Cantwell's injured hand, that it has been "shot through twice" and has become "slightly misshapen" (58:15–16). We will learn that it is his right hand (243:28–29), which Renata calls his "real hand" (111:32). He despises the condition (227:3–4). After his street fight with the two sailors, Cantwell laments that he will have "bad hands in the morning" (261:28). For further discussion of Cantwell's hand, see entry at 66:13.

The motif of the hand will turn out to be one of the most prominent in the novel. Renata asks Cantwell if she may feel his wounded hand, saying she has dreamed about it and conflated it with "the hand of Our Lord" (82:17).[1] Cantwell responds by asking if she is "on the junk" (82:20). The narrative repeats that Cantwell was wounded twice in the same (right) hand (82:27). Cantwell does not like looking at it (83:3, 95:17) and generally finds it far less fascinating and erotic than does Renata.

58:29 Fornicate forbidden: Twice, Cantwell euphemizes "fornicate" for "fuck." Later, he and the *Gran Maestro* will both use this euphemism with respect to the Condottieri (65:25), Italian mercenary soldiers. In the manuscript, Hemingway wrote the actual obscenity on all occasions.

59:3 *Carpano punto e mezzo*: Carpano Punt e Mes is a brand of vermouth. This vermouth can be used when making either the Americano or Negroni cocktail.

59:6 to the *ordine*: "Ordine" is Italian for "Order."

59:23 particularly notorious multi-millionaire: For readers who are interested in the Brusadelli strain to this novel, Miriam B. Mandel's "Reading the Brusadelli Stories" article is an essential resource. The historical source of this figure is Giulio Brusadelli (1878–1962), who, according to Mandel, was "an Italian businessman whose scandalous doings" and "unsavory financial affairs" were "front-page headlines during Hemingway's visit to Italy in late 1948 and early 1949" (335).

60:1–2 new and more distinguished shameful acts: As Mandel explains, Brusadelli was complicit in "tax evasion, stock manipulation, and other illegal dealings" ("Reading the Brusdalli Stories" 336). As part of his defense, Brusadelli claimed that his wife made excessive sexual demands upon him, so he could not be held responsible for his actions (335–36). *Across the River and into the Trees* alludes to these acts from 59:24–28.

60:5–6 he can roast in hell: This vivid insult continues the Dantesque theme of Cantwell consigning his enemies to various circles of hell. The verb "roast" also prefigures the later mention of a German dog that is eating a "roasted German kraut" (235:3–4), a soldier who has been scalded by white phosphorus.

60:7 Giorgio: This barman, from Piemonte, with a pale face "as white as a leper" (66:27–28), does not care for Cantwell and appears in the novel only in this chapter.

60:14 eleven hundred tomorrow in the lobby: Contrary to this arrangement, Jackson will not appear in the text until chapter 39, when he is "in the boat with the luggage" (252:4). It is certainly not at 11:00 A.M., since Jackson meets up with Cantwell after lunch.

At this point in the manuscript, Jackson gets off his best one-liner, that they will meet the next day "at this gritty hotel" (JFK 1), a play on Gritti. One wonders how the novel might be different if Jackson were a more raucously funny character (or even consistently malapropistic) to offset Cantwell's sententiousness and pedantry.

60:16–17 **son of a bitch:** This epithet is used fourteen times in the novel. Jackson has previously called him "a mean son of a bitch" (42:8). Cantwell uses the term affectionately, to describe all of the wounded whom he loves, but he generally reserves it for himself, ultimately calling himself a "lucky son of a bitch" (281:30). He also uses it pejoratively to describe the surly boatman (267:30) and the pockmarked writer (84:20).

60:17 **as crazy as they say:** Jackson's aside is a fascinating one, since it provides insight into Cantwell's general reputation. In Hemingway's next book, *The Old Man and the Sea,* Santiago is also reputed to be insane. "If the others heard me talking out loud they would think that I am crazy," Santiago says. "But since I am not crazy, I do not care" (39).

60:28 **T5:** This term refers to the technician fifth class, the rank of corporal, as opposed to sergeant (T4) or staff sergeant (T3). Jackson is "T5 Jackson" (151:4, 252:4).

60:28 **100678:** This serial number is valid, assigned, incidentally, to Helen M. Davis of Maine, a member of the Women's Army Corps in World War II.

61:14–15 **Grappa, Pasubio and the Basso Piave:** These three sites are said to be "key points" where Cantwell and the *Gran Maestro* fought together, "where it all made sense" (62:11). Cantwell later refers to himself as a Grappa boy, a Pasubio boy, and a Basso Piave boy (151:9–10).

The Grappa, previously mentioned as the site of the death of the boatman's brother (50:26, 50:27), refers to the fighting around Monte Grappa, which is seen as emblematic that the Italians' mettle had not been eliminated after Caporetto (Thompson 322–23). The Battle of Vittorio Veneto, the final clash of the war on the Italian front, began on the Grappa on 24 October 1918.

61:20–21 **not thinking that he who dies on Thursday:** This quotation has tremendous resonance in the entirety of Hemingway's career, his life, and the evolution of his thought about war and death. This novel mangles the beautiful quotation from Shakespeare's *2 Henry IV*, in which Feeble says, "A man can die but once. We owe God a death. I'll ne'er bear a base mind. An't be my destiny, so; an't be not, so. No man's too good to serve's prince. And let it go which way it will, he that dies this year is quit for the next" (3.2.216–20). This line is celebrated in Hemingway's *Men at War*, in which Hemingway admits, "I was very ignorant at nineteen and had read little and I remember the sudden happiness and the feeling of having a permanent protecting talisman when a young British officer I met when in the hospital first wrote out for me, so that I could remember them, these lines: '*By my troth, I care not: a man can die but once; we owe God a death . . . and let it go which way it will, he that dies this year is quit for the next.*' That is probably the best thing that is written in this book and, with nothing else, a man can get along all right on that" (xii, emphasis in original). This same quotation has a central appearance in the short story "The Short Happy Life of Francis Macomber," in which the white hunter Wilson also refers to Feeble's words (*CSS* 25). The unnamed British soldier who taught it to Hemingway was Chink-Dorman Smith, who is a partial inspiration for Cantwell's experiences.

For an extended discussion of this quotation, see Cirino, *Thought in Action* (162n16).

61:31 gonorrheal pus: In his introduction to *Men at War*, Hemingway writes: "There was much trouble with self-inflicted wounds in Italy during the last war [World War I]. The men became very skillful at it and often a pair would team up to shoot each other, usually wrapping sandbags around the arm or leg, to avoid any evidence of a close discharge of the rifle" (xxv), a loose restatement of 61:21–23. Hemingway also writes of those who "deliberately contracted venereal disease in order to leave the lines" (*MAW* xxv), which restates 61:31–32. Cantwell goes on to tell Renata about "gonococci brought from Schio" (51:13), which the platoon would then share.

62:1–2 ten centime pieces to produce jaundice: From *Men at War*, Hemingway writes of soldiers who "would hold copper coins in their armpits to get a yellow cast of complexion and simulate jaundice" (xxv).

62:4 paraffin: In the introduction to *Men at War*, Hemingway writes: "There were doctors in Milan who did a thriving trade in injecting paraffin under the kneecaps of their clients to induce lameness" (xxv).

62:6–7 garlic could be used to produce certain effects: Although garlic was commonly applied to war wounds—mostly by Russian soldiers—to avoid gangrene, Cantwell is here describing its ill effects.

62:11 where it all made sense: Cantwell is distinguishing the battle sites of the Pasubio, Grappa, and the Piave from the "earlier stupid butchery" on the Isonzo and the Carso. In his introduction to *Men at War*, Hemingway refers to the years 1915–17 as "the most colossal, murderous, mismanaged butchery that has ever taken place on earth" (xiii). Later historical studies have corroborated Cantwell's claim, which is that the incessant Italian forays against Austria on the Carso were doomed to failure and promised to gain very little. *A Farewell to Arms* begins in 1915, with "the whole thing going well on the Carso" as a dry, devastatingly ironic remark (6).

62:18–19 **only five members:** The five members of the Order are

1. Cantwell, the supreme commander
2. The *maître d'hotel,* the grand master or *Gran Maestro*
3. The cook, the commendatore, which does not quite mean "Commander" in the military sense, but "knight commander" in the chivalric tradition
4. The manager of the hotel is the *cavaliere ufficiale* (knight officer).
5. Alvarito, the barone.

If by now the reader begins to accuse Cantwell and/or Hemingway of obsessing about a juvenile club, we should also note that Hemingway was inducted into the Knights of Malta, also a "noble, military, and religious" order. As Kim Moreland suggests, despite the abject silliness of this group, "these men gain a measure of dignity and self-confidence from their knightly identities not present in their own lives" (177).

Also central to Hemingway's tendency to form clubs or orders at this time is "The White Tower, Inc.," a name given to the organization he shared with Adriana Ivancich, who titled her memoir *La torre bianca* and explained the motivation behind the club in that work as well as in her 1965 article, "I Am Hemingway's Renata," in which the most important qualities were "to be nice and . . . creative and artistic" (263).

See entry at 56:17–18 for further discussion of the Order.

62:23 **comported himself as a man:** One of the cook's positive traits, then, is his sexual energy, even as a man—like Cantwell and the *Gran Maestro*—of at least fifty. The day after Hemingway's fiftieth birthday, he wrote to Scribner that he, too, "fucked three times, shot ten straight at pigeons (very fast ones) at the club, drank with five friends a case of Piper Heidsick [sic] Brut and looked the ocean for big fish all afternoon" (*SL* 658). Depending on your reading of the gondola scene later, Cantwell also comports himself thusly three times. As Mary coyly puts it in her memoirs, "Brown and healthy from the sea, soft and sure of movement, confident in his work on his new book [*Across the River and into the Trees*], Ernest on his fiftieth birthday seemed to me to show little of time's attrition" (242).

According to an unpublished letter to Colonel Lanham during the writing of *Across the River and into the Trees,* Hemingway wrote 573 words on 21 July 1949, his fiftieth birthday.

In the manuscript, he uses "fucked" instead of "comported himself as a man" (JFK 1). One wonders, then, if this passage was written after July 1949 and if so, by how much. Did art imitate life, or vice versa?

62:27 **chary:** The word is being used in the sense of "wary" or "cautious," and perhaps punning on "cherry" (see next entry).

62:31 **Anch'io:** Italian for "me, too"; that is, "I also remember when he was known as the cherry buster," the deflowerer of virgins. See also 263:27, where the same phrase is used, but in its uncontracted form: "Anche" (also) and "io" (I).

63:5 **another dry Martini:** This "another" follows up the double he ordered at 57:19–20.

63:7 **San Marco:** This defining landmark of Venice that honors its patron saint is mentioned twice, here and at 116:29.

63:10–11 **at this moment:** That is, because of the controversy currently embroiling Brusadelli, November 1948 or after (Mandel, "Reading the Brusadelli Stories" 336n9).

63:25–26 **the bravest of these are the Belgians:** Julius Caesar begins his *Commentarii de Bello Gallico*, his commentaries on the Gallic War, which Hemingway read in high school (Reynolds, *Hemingway's Reading* 106), by identifying three ethnic groups in Gaul and observing: "The Belgae are the bravest of the three peoples, being farthest removed from the highly developed civilization of the Roman Province, least often visited by merchants with enervating luxuries for sale" (29). This Caesar quotation is referenced again at 188:9.

63:31 **Flanders in the old days:** The *Gran Maestro*'s vague reference to the "the old days" in Flanders, a town in Northern Belgium where the Battle of Hastings took place in 1066, suggests the First Battle of Flanders in World War I, which occurred 19 October to 22 November 1914, when he and Cantwell were both fifteen. The Second Battle of Flanders, the so-called Battle of Passchendaele, was 11 July–10 November 1917. See also 228:11. The Third Battle of Flanders was 9–29 April 1918.

The characterization of Belgian tourists as "locusts" recalls the straight-talking prostitute Georgette in *The Sun Also Rises* who, pleased to learn that Jake Barnes is an American, confesses, "I detest Flamands" (24).

63:34 **fought with the Condottieri:** The Condottieri were Italian mercenary soldiers in medieval Italy through the Renaissance. See also 65:3.

64:7–8 **Vicenza, Bergamo and Verona:** Vicenza is a town in the Veneto (also mentioned on 243:6). After World War I, in 1922, Hemingway took his first wife to Vicenza (Sanderson 11). In *A Farewell to Arms*, Frederic Henry vomits on the train past Vicenza (77). Bergamo, later lauded by Cantwell as "a good town" (88:4), is north of Milan in Lombardy, at the base of the southern Alps. Verona (also mentioned on 243:6), is the second-largest city in the Veneto and the setting of Shakespeare's *Romeo and Juliet* and *Two Gentlemen of Verona*. Book 1 of *A Farewell to Arms* ends with Frederic eating an orange on a train "in the yards outside of Verona" (77).

64:10–11 **He was a general now again, and he was happy:** The central theme of Cantwell's character is this schizophrenic division between being a civilian (i.e., being civil) and being a general, a soldier, Faulkner's notion of "the human heart in conflict with itself" ("Address" 649). He constantly battles to suppress the instinct to be cold, brutal, deadly—qualities indispensable to the battlefield but inappropriate to everyday life. Although these references are frequent in the novel, it is surprising here that Cantwell is characterized as being "happy" about slipping into his formal mode of thought. Perhaps being with the *Gran Maestro* provides a safe opportunity to behave in this way. Although Cantwell is far from a happy-go-lucky character, it should be noted that this adjective is often attributed to his state of mind: he is happy when he knows he will be entering Venice (39:15) and seeing the fishing boats and gear along the canal (39:34–40:2) or that he contributed to Venice's defense in World War I (49:19). These references lead toward Renata's assertion that she wants Cantwell to die with "the grace of a happy death" (220:5–6). When planning to meet Renata for the first time, he asserts: "I'll damn well find happiness, too" (69:20).

Cantwell also asks both Jackson and the *Gran Maestro:* "are you happy?" (34:25, 63:20), which might allude to Robert Browning's classic poem of Venice, "A Toccata of Galuppi's," which asks, too: "'Were you happy?'—'Yes'—'And are you still as happy?'—'Yes—And you?'" (l. 22).

64:11 **Brescia:** Brescia is a city in Lombardy, at the base of the Alps.

64:14–15 **out of his depth:** As with Jackson (55:8) and later with Renata (136:11–14), Cantwell has a tendency to overestimate his audience's military acumen. Hemingway would later accuse the novel's critics of the same shortcoming, that they were not accustomed to the complexity of this novel. However, he also contradicted himself in a 24 August 1949 letter to Charles Scribner, claiming that this novel's main strength was its simplicity and universality: "It is a beauty novel; short and clear and even those saw-dust headed goons and ghouls that work for you in that deject edifice could probably understand it" (JFK, Outgoing Correspondence).

64:16 **He was at home:** This extraordinary paragraph leaves Cantwell's consciousness and explores the *Gran Maestro*'s mindset and attitudes, his nostalgia for Treviso and the natural splendors of the Sile River. It also allows the *Gran Maestro* a limited military expertise, as the command of a company but not a brigadier general like Cantwell, who would have commanded a division or four battalions.

64:25–27 **as far beyond him as calculus is distant from a man who has only the knowledge of arithmetic:** This simile has had great permanence in Hemingway's description of his own writing, particularly regarding *Across the River and into the Trees*. Just as Cantwell determines the site of his wounding "by triangulation"

(26:17), Hemingway viewed this figurative comparison as a key to understanding the novel. See entry at 35:7.

64:31 Mantova: Mantova, or Mantua, is a town in Lombardy, the site of Romeo's banishment in *Romeo and Juliet*. During one interview, Hemingway listed Mantova as one of his adopted hometowns (see entry at 41:18). Mantova is also mentioned at 243:6. In a 1949 letter to two of his sons before their trip to Italy, he advises them, "be sure to see Mantova, Virgil's home town. Plan to stay overnight and walk around in it in the dark if you want to see a real medieval town" (JFK, Outgoing Correspondence). Dante's presence in the novel is emphasized, then, by the reference to the town of Virgil, his mentor's birth. Dante refers to Mantua's origins in *Inferno* XX, and the pilgrim and Virgil encounter a fellow Mantovan in *Purgatorio* VI.

65:4 Padova: A town in the Veneto, Padova, or Padua, was a central location on the Italian front and the Austrian objective for the sixth Battle of the Isonzo in August 1916 (Macdonald with Cimprič 81). In 1949, Hemingway stayed in a Padua hospital for the treatment of an eye infection, erysipelas (Sanderson 24). Perhaps because of this reason, Hemingway once recalled, "I hated Padova" (qtd. in Beegel 55).

Padova is also the setting of Shakespeare's *The Taming of the Shrew*.

65:9–10 "There aren't any such times any more," . . . **and the spell was broken:** Cantwell, first, is being literal, that the age of the Condottieri is obsolete by three or so centuries. However, he again sounds like the grandfather in Steinbeck's *The Red Pony*, who nostalgizes a lost age of westering and adventuring. Cantwell later says, "maybe there never was any spell" (65:11) and then in a short paragraph analyzes whether he was mired in a spell, or whether it might have been something else. It seems like ultimately he's content to call it a spell, as it returns—even if incomplete—on 66:15–16.

65:12–13 Cut it out and be a human being: As seen on 64:10 and 64:24, this tension defines Cantwell's character. The novel asks: How can a soldier integrate himself into the civilian world when he is not at war? Must the soldier always be at war with something? Cantwell will ask explicitly: "why am I always a bastard and why can I not suspend this trade of arms, and be a kind and good man as I would have wished to be" (66:17–19), with the tense implying that this internal battle is a lost cause.[2]

65:19 Another dry Martini: The reader who may be growing concerned about Cantwell's health will note that between the beginning of chapter 6, which was "late afternoon" (57:14–15) and now, which is still before dinner, Cantwell has ordered his third martini, two of which are explicitly doubles and the third of which is an implied double, since he orders "another" (63:5). Cantwell has also had a small Carpano, along with the gin and Campari he seems to have had at the first stop.

66:3 **Bassano:** Hemingway demonstrates that he is aware that Bassano is known for its white asparagus. He also makes a repugnant reference to the malodorous quality that commonly appears in urine after consuming asparagus. See entry at 50:26.

66:6 **Maitre d'Hotel:** This is the third time the *Gran Maestro* is referred to by his job title (58:23–24, 58:27); the other two times, the phrase is incorrectly italicized. In all three instances, it is unncessarily capitalized.

66:13 **his crooked hand:** This farewell handshake frames the salutary handshake on 58:14–23, when the hand is described as "shot through twice . . . slightly misshapen" (58:15–16). Here, the hand is "crooked." His injured hand is one of the central motifs of the novel and is referred to on more than twenty separate occasions. See entry at 58:10–21 for a fuller discussion.

66:23–24 **in the small time which remains:** This phrase, following 15:25–26 and 16:20–21, represents one of the earliest references to Cantwell's knowledge of his own impending death. See also Renata's references: "How can we go to sleep now when we have so little time?" (201:6–7) and "Don't lie to me please, darling, when we have so little time" (219:32–33), both of which reveal their shared knowledge of time running out.

66:31 **Piemonte:** Mentioned only once in the novel, Piemonte is an alpine region of Italy of which Turin is the capital. Hemingway paid tribute to Piemontese cyclist Bartolomeo Aymo in *A Farewell to Arms* (see Cirino, "A Bicycle Is a Splendid Thing").

67:10 **prisoner of war in Kenya:** This refers to the East African campaign of World War II in 1940 and 1941. Hemingway visited Kenya on a 1933 safari with his second wife, Pauline, and would write about it in *Green Hills of Africa*. He would return in 1953 and 1954 with his fourth wife, Mary, a trip that led to his African novel, the posthumous *Under Kilimanjaro* (2005).

67:13 *cavaliere ufficiale*: This title, a degree of knighthood, refers to the manager, another member of the order.

67:26 **slight hydraulic inaccuracy:** Cantwell is insistent on competence and precision, from those who serve under him as well as from himself, to say nothing of his superiors. The boy's feeble excuse, that the "current is not stable" has greater resonance, specifically the Colonel's health. Indeed, the last sentence of chapter 7 anticipates Jackson's fecklessness in the last sentence of the novel (283:3–4).

NOTES

1. In *The Old Man and the Sea*, Santiago's wounded hands are a clear allusion to Christ's.
2. A passage in Stephen Crane's *The Red Badge of Courage* (1895) is an early description of the soldier's psyche after the battle: "His mind was undergoing a subtle change. It took moments for it to cast off its battleful ways and resume its accustomed course of thought" (102). "Battleful" is a wonderful, rare word to describe Cantwell's tendency toward confrontation. *The Red Badge of Courage* is printed in full in Hemingway's *Men at War*.

CHAPTER 8

68:4–5 Naturally, since it had been a palace: Cantwell's room is at the Gritti Palace. See entry at 46:30.

68:7–8 found the walk long, although it was a very short one: The omniscient narrator offers another indication of Cantwell's failing health. Let us recall, however, that Cantwell has just consumed more than seven drinks, which may or may not be contributing to his current lack of vigor.

69:4 Arnaldo: Also known as "the boy" (68:1), "the waiter" (68:8), or "the glass-eyed waiter" (71:9–10), Arnaldo is the keeper of Cantwell's room. He has obviously been wounded in battle. Later, when he tells Cantwell that he took a chance by buying alcohol for him and that "We have both taken many" (69:31), he is clearly alluding to this shared experience. Arnaldo's eye injury recalls D'Annunzio's similar injury (53:10–12) and may also conjure up the severe eye infection Hemingway experienced during his stay in Italy in 1949 (see entry at 65:4). Arnaldo reappears on 153:9 and 165:4. Arnaldo's name was "Enrico" in the manuscript.

69:16 The Contessa is not at home: The only previous mention of any contessa in the novel was the fictitious Contessa Dandolo (51:15). However, here Cantwell is referring for the second time to Renata, the young Italian woman he will soon meet.

69:21 Happiness, as you know, is a moveable feast: This phrase will automatically invoke the title of Hemingway's posthumous memoirs, *A Moveable Feast* (1964). During the drafting of *Across the River and into the Trees* in 1949, Hemingway experimented with various titles for memoirs. In fact, next to this line in the manuscript, Hemingway wrote:
Title for Memoirs
The Things That I Know
Hemingway must have been fond of the "moveable feast" phrase, since he reuses it later in this novel (250:16). The epigraph for *A Moveable Feast* reads: "If you are lucky enough to have lived in Paris as a young man, then wherever you go for the

rest of your life, it stays with you, for Paris is a moveable feast" (np). In *Under Kilimanjaro*, Hemingway writes, "Love is a terrible thing that you would not wish on your neighbor and, as in all countries, it is a moveable feast" (351–52). To William W. Seward Jr. on 6 July 1949 he explained—"I wrote it as well as I could but all journalism is a movable feast" (JFK, Outgoing Correspondence).

A moveable feast is a "religious feast day which, though always on the same day of the week, does not occur on the same calendar date each year" (*OED*).

69:29 **"I agree," the Colonel agreed:** This sentence, so appallingly amateurish, might cause us to wonder what was the editorial process for *Across the River and into the Trees*. Did anyone at Scribner's challenge Hemingway on any aspect of this material or dare to point out the clumsiness of a sentence such as this? Following the death of Hemingway's longtime editor, Maxwell Perkins, in June 1947, his publisher had no one to caution Hemingway about his writing and offer editorial suggestions. Hemingway used Italian friends and also A. E. Hotchner as informal readers, but no one with the authority, as F. Scott Fitzgerald did with *The Sun Also Rises*, to urge sweeping changes.

69:32 **3200 lire . . . 800:** The Gordon's Gin, then, was about $5.91, and the Campari was $1.48 in 1948 dollars (see entry at 26:30). Arnaldo, then, has laid out slightly less than $7.50 in anticipation of Cantwell's program of drinking.

70:9 **those fat iron-curtain ducks:** Cantwell had obviously in the past given Arnaldo a gift of ducks he had hunted, which were greatly pleasing to the waiter and his wife. These ducks, according to Cantwell, originated in eastern Europe and flew along the Danube, a massively long river from Germany to the Black Sea. Hemingway told Lillian Ross, similarly, that the ducks he hunted in the Veneto came from "the Pripet Marshes" (43), a vast expanse that occupies southern Belarus and northern Ukraine. On 9 September 1949, Hemingway wrote Taylor Williams that the ducks "come down from the Pripet Marshes and the Misurian Lakes and are fine and in wonderful shape as they feed on grain all the way down" (JFK, Outgoing Correspondence).

Alvarito will later report to Cantwell that the ducks for the hunt "are coming in heavily from the north" (123:4–5).

70:10–11 **splinter flight:** According to Hemingway, the ducks came in a main flight from the Danube and then in a "branch flight" come from as far as the Pripet marshes. This is one of the latter sort.

70:27, 29 **Russians . . . our potential enemy:** In addition to anticipating the Cold War, Cantwell furthers a common theme in Hemingway: the identification with and respect of the enemy. In discussions of war, Cantwell's own government and superiors are typically criticized more than the ostensible enemy from another country. A similar point recurs when discussing "Krauts," or Nazis (164:10–12). Cantwell will eventually tell Renata, "I love my enemies, sometimes, more than my friends" (263:18).

71:10–11 He did not want it, and he knew that it was bad for him: This remark echoes "The Snows of Kilimanjaro," when Helen tells her dying husband not to drink whisky. "I know it's bad for you," Helen says. Harry replies, "No . . . It's good for me" (*CSS* 40).

71:12–14 wild-boar truculence . . . cat-like when he moved: Cantwell is compared to a boar and a cat in this single sentence, and he will also be compared to Richard the Lionhearted. He also asserts that during the breaking of the ice in the duck hunt, he "worked like a horse" (14:1). See when his "*gueule*" is referenced (107:12). He has also tried to restrain his "wild boar blood" (66:23). When Cantwell nearly fights the two fascists in the street, he wonders if the youths did not know "what sort of animal they were dealing with" (175:15). After Cantwell's heart attack, he is compared to a hawk (183:13), and in the army, he is forced to "obey like a dog" (222:22).

71:16–17 as though Degas had painted it: The narrative refers to Edgar Degas (1834–1917), the great French impressionist. According to Margaret O'Shaughnessey, Degas was "hardly associated with gray" (204), although she does endeavor to discover Degas paintings where gray would have been prominent. As O'Shaugnessey also notes, Hemingway told journalist Lillian Ross that Degas was, along with Cézanne, "another wonder painter. I've never seen a bad Degas. You know what he did with the bad Degas? He burned them" (87).

71:22–23 He only loved people . . . who had fought or been mutilated: This line is absolutely crucial to understanding Cantwell's attitude, a "sucker for crips" (71:28), those who had "received the castigation" (71:26). Although this limitation would seem to exclude Renata, she has actually in her own right had a horrific experience from the war, through the loss of family members, including her father. In this respect, she joins the war-scarred love interests from *The Sun Also Rises, A Farewell to Arms,* and *For Whom the Bell Tolls.*

The first sentence of this short paragraph directly quotes Cantwell's thoughts: "I wish . . ." (71:21–22). The second is from the third-person perspective: "He only . . . he thought . . . " (71:22–23).

71:31 his other, good, side: In a novel where Cantwell the soldier will be vying for supremacy with Cantwell the civilian, this exchange is revealing.

In this exchange, Cantwell's "good side" believes in love, and Cantwell finally admits that he does too. As he wakes up from his nap to begin chapter 32, he has "turned bad" (224:4), showing the two-hearted division of his personality; just as he has one good hand and one bad and a good leg and a bad leg, he has one good side and one bad side.

See the end of *For Whom the Bell Tolls* for a similar phenomenon, of the rigidly disciplined soldier debating with the "human being" over what to think and how to act. See also "The Strange Country," where the protagonist has an argument with his alter ego, named "Conscience" (*CSS* 635). In Mark Twain's *Adventures of Huckleberry Finn*, Huck's conscience becomes a character, haunting him: "What had poor Miss Watson ever done to you" (110). See Cirino, *Thought in Action* (154n4).

72:7 **Cipriani has not come in:** Giuseppe Cipriani founded Harry's Bar in Venice in 1931. Cipriani is mentioned in Hemingway's fable "The Good Lion" and also, naturally, in the audio recording of "In Harry's Bar in Venice" (See Appendix 2 on pp. 210–11 of this volume), in which the narrator describes the sacred place of Harry's felt by those who enjoyed "the credit and the hospitality of Cipriani." See also 87:3, when Ettore offers to ask Cipriani for information about the pockmarked writer's elderly dining companion.

72:16 **Ettore:** Ettore appears in chapters 8 and 9. He shares not just the name but also the characteristics of Ettore in *A Farewell to Arms,* in their mutual "love of joking" (85:18) or "hectoring" those around them (see Cirino, "You Don't Know" 56).

Ettore is also the name of Ettore Sottsass, the husband of Fernanda Pivano, Hemingway's principal Italian translator, both of whom he spent time with during the period of writing *Across the River and into the Trees*.

72:17 **Andrea:** A tall, friendly, heavy drinker for whom Cantwell has genuine affection. Like Cantwell, he is in poor health. He is also the person who introduced Cantwell to Renata (266:1). Andrea will be at Harry's Bar when Cantwell arrives (77:29). Later, Renata will say jokingly that Andrea is the only person she would want to hit (218:9). Andrea—a loose anagram for "Adriana"—is named Carlo in the manuscript, for Hemingway's hunting friend Count Carlo Di Robilant. As Adriana Ivancich writes in her memoirs of this description: "This is Carlo Robilant, dear Carlo" (*La torre bianca* 139).

72:20 **a Greek Princess:** A reference to the Princess Aspasia, with whom the Hemingways spent time in Venice in the late 1940s and early 1950s. Aspasia Manos (1896–1972), the widow of King Alexander of Greece, died in Venice. Princess Aspasia was also part of one of Hemingway's dinner parties at the Gritti in January

1950. According to Carlos Baker, she "once declared herself mad for Ernest, and offered to build him a special house in her garden if he would come and live there" (*Life Story* 481). Adriana Ivancich recalled:

> One evening, I remember, he wanted to explain to us how to perform a corrida. He had invited Princess Aspasia of Greece and some of our friends to Ciro's. After dinner he cleared the table, took the tablecloth, and said to his wife Mary, "You are the bull." Right in the middle of the room he began to fight the bull; "Aha, aha, toro," we shouted, clapping our hands. He seemed like a real torero. His face was also transformed, serious, intense. Around us the waiters watched us a little bit bewildered while, seated in the corner, Aspasia observed the scene with a kind and understanding smile. ("I Am Hemingway's Renata" 260)

Adriana recounts a version of the same story in *La torre bianca* (31–32).

According to Mary's diary entry of 18 March 1949, while she was away, Hemingway "had an afternoon of good, solid drink and talk" with Princess Aspasia ("Harry's Bar" 62).

In Hemingway's absurd monologue, "In Harry's Bar in Venice," is a mangled, satirical retelling of *Across the River and into the Trees*, an eighteen-year-old colonel "is mad about" Princess Aspasia. See Appendix 2 on pp. 210–11 of this volume.

In *Under Kilimanjaro*, Hemingway attempts to instruct Debba, a young African woman, in the manners of European royalty: "I had tried to teach her," he writes, "the lift of the wrist and undulation of the fingers with which the Princess Aspasia of Greece would greet me across the smoke-filled clamor of Harry's Bar in Venice" (377–78).

72:26–27 **Dome of the Dogana:** The Dogana is Venice's customs house, located off the Grand Canal. In Ezra Pound's third canto, the speaker sits on the Dome of the Dogana: "I sat on the Dogana's steps / For the gondolas cost too much, that year" (11).

72:33 **fall of its own weight:** The drunks, who do not need to be dealt with actively, will fall away, with the same phrase that was used to describe Brescia (64:11–12). In fact, soon after, Ettore will call from Harry's to report: "The position has fallen, my Colonel" (75:12)

73:7 **Keokuk:** A town in southeastern Iowa, close to the border of Illinois and Missouri. In an October 1940 letter to Charles Scribner from Sun Valley, Idaho, Hemingway describes his future travel plans with Martha Gellhorn, who would become his third wife: "Her idea of fun . . . is to go to the Burma Road. . . . But I like everything once it starts so I guess I will like the Burma Road and then will probably want to stay out on the Burma Road and Martha will want to go to Keokuk Iowa. Well I guess I will like Keokuk Iowa too. They have a nice damn [sic] there" (*SL* 519), meaning Lock and Dam #19.

73:18 **1918:** The fourth and final explicit mention of Hemingway's crucible year (also 26:2, 39:17, 51:2), the year of his Red Cross service to the Italian army and his wounding.

73:23 **Carroll:** Cantwell is referring to B. Harvey Carroll, the Italian consul in Venice in 1918. Per the entry in the *Handbook of Texas Online*, Benajah Harvey Carroll Jr. (1874–1922), author, educator, minister, chaplain, journalist, editor, and U.S. consulate; was ordained a minister in Waco in 1894 and served churches in both Kentucky and Texas; and headed the department of history and political economy at Baylor for a short time (J. A. Reynolds). He volunteered for service in the Spanish-American War. He first served as captain and field chaplain of the 1st U.S. Volunteers, Texas Cavalry, before being appointed lieutenant colonel and aide-de-camp in the Texas National Guard. In 1914 he served as U. S. consul to Venice during World War I. He also later served as consul to Naples, Italy, and Cádiz, Spain. Carroll also published a translation of D'Annunzio's poetry in an Italian newspaper during Hemingway's stay in Italy in 1918 (Gerogiannis 80).

74:22 **what's the news from the Rialto now?** Cantwell, in inquiring about the financial center of Venice, is alluding to Shakespeare's *The Merchant of Venice*, in which Shylock asks Antonio: "What news on the Rialto?" (1.3.33). Later, Solanio asks Salerio, "Now, what news on the Rialto?" (3.1.1). See also 173:28 for the novel's other mention of the Rialto.

Hemingway also appropriated this line in "God Rest You Merry, Gentlemen," a story from *Winner Take Nothing*, in which Doc Fischer, a Jewish doctor, asks, "What news along the rialto?" (*CSS* 299).

74:28 **the Torcello part:** It is unclear what this elliptical reference means, the apparent suggestion that Cantwell has had a notorious history in Torcello. Although the specific incident is unknowable, the omission figures as a typical component of the Colonel and Arnaldo's badinage.

74:33 **Questura:** This word refers to the "offices responsible for police work, public order and relative administrative services" (*Concise Oxford Paravia Italian Dictionary*).

75:20 **day after tomorrow:** This conversation is on Friday and the duck hunt is on Sunday morning.

75:21 **botte**: The Italian word for "barrel," this method of hunting was the one Hemingway employed in the Veneto in 1948 and 1949. See the entry at 12:21.

75:26 **An ugly face:** Cantwell's self-criticism recalls the garrulous Bill Gorton in *The Sun Also Rises,* who, when shaving, asks, "My God! . . . isn't it an awful face?" (108). See a similar instance of a self-critical Cantwell at 107:6–7. He later tells Renata he "would not sign" for his face (120:25).

CHAPTER 9

76:1 **Colonel Cantwell:** The protagonist is only referred to as "Colonel Cantwell" three times in the novel: here, in identifying himself on the phone to Ettore (75:11), and on the phone again to Renata (182:9).

76:2 **the last sunlight of that day:** Chapter 9, then, opens at dusk on Friday.

76:9–10 **the paved street which turned off on the right:** The street that turns off on the right from the square outside the Hotel Gritti is Calle Ostreghe.

76:11 **the church of Santa Maria del Giglio:** The seventeenth-century Venetian architect Giuseppe Sardi designed the baroque facade of this church, which was erected in 1678–1681. "To a great extent," explains scholar Deborah Howard, "its flamboyant character is due to the wishes of the patron, Antonio Barbaro" (229), who envisioned a monument to himself and his family. This church's ostentatious facade is an objective correlative for its blustering observer. See entry at 55:17.

The P47 to which Cantwell likens the church (76:14) is Republic Aviation's P-47 Thunderbolt, a heavy, heavily armed fighter aircraft used commonly in World War II.[1] In the manuscript, Cantwell compares the church to a P51.

Whether or not it is an exact match, it is nevertheless telling as with a Rorschach test that Cantwell can only process this religious architecture in terms of weaponry.

76:16 **All my life:** Cantwell realizes the irony of this phrase, given what he knows to be the brevity of the rest of his life. Hemingway uses this same mode of irony when Francis Macomber, in "The Short Happy Life of Francis Macomber," realizes that he deserves his wife's derision "for the rest of my life now" (*CSS* 7), only a matter of hours.

76:18 **No horse named Morbid ever won a race:** This line anticipates *Islands in the Stream,* in which Thomas Hudson "had traded in remorse for another horse that he was riding now" (369). In *Under Kilimanjaro,* Hemingway muses, "Remorse is a splendid name for a racehorse but it is a poor lifetime companion for a man" (367–68).

This phrasing also recalls a 1950 letter to Chink Dorman-Smith: "We ought to own and run a horse called Remorse out of Other People's Orders and Sorrow's Brother" (qtd. in Greacen, "Irish Soldier" 9). "Other people's orders," of course, becomes one of the key phrases of *Across the River and into the Trees* (194:12, 222:18–19). Cantwell asserts that he has never felt remorse over the people he has killed (117:4).

Cantwell decides not to give his medals to Renata because it would be morbid (267:21). Earlier, he stated that he would not want to ask Alberto if he could be buried on his property because it would be morbid (40:13). Cantwell learns of the boatman's family's casualties during World War I before it becomes "morbid" (51:11). See also when Renata entrusting the stones to Cantwell is not "crazy or morbid" (157:5).

76:20 **charcuterie:** A store that sells cooked meats.

77:1 **hams from San Daniele:** As Hemingway would know, San Daniele del Friuli is a region renowned for its ham or prosciutto; it hosts a prosciutto festival every June.

77:8 **only the buzzing:** Ringing or buzzing in the ears is common to the high blood pressure that plagues Cantwell. The buzzing, compared to locusts (77:9), is in the manuscript compared to cicadas.

77:10 **young Lowry:** Although it is conceivable that this reference is to novelist Malcolm Lowry (1909–1957), whose *Under the Volcano* was published in 1947, Cantwell is more likely referring to Robert James Collas Lowry (1919–1994), author of *The Big Cage* (1949), who, unlike Malcolm, actually served in North Africa and Italy during World War II. In a 1949 letter to Malcolm Cowley, Hemingway refers to Robert Lowry as a Texas Leaguer (*SL* 681), a common Hemingway putdown for fellow writers, particularly during this vituperative period of his life. Hemingway owned copies of both of Malcolm Lowry's novels and five Robert Lowry books (Brasch and Sigman 231).

77:14, 23 **twinges . . . twinging:** In addition to the two mentions of twinges on this page, twinges are also mentioned when Cantwell and Renata are walking onto a bridge against the wind (101:1).

78:8–9 **Us healthy bastards shall inherit the earth:** Cantwell puts his own earthy spin onto the familiar verse in Matthew 5:5, "Blessed are the meek, for they shall inherit the earth." See also Psalms 37:11: "But the meek shall possess the land, and delight themselves in abundant prosperity."

78:15 ***la vie militaire:*** French for "the military life," this phrase also is the title of a segment of Honoré de Balzac's *Human Comedy*, "Scenes from a Military Life"

(*Scènes de la vie militaire*) consisting of *The Chouans* (1829) and *A Passion in the Desert* (1830). Hemingway owned Balzac's complete works in English and many other volumes in French (Brasch and Sigman 61).

78:17 San Relajo: Since "relajo" is the Spanish word for "relaxation," Cantwell is humorously emphasizing to Andrea that his days of arduous military service are over. In a novel of compulsive allusions to actual cities, one should not fall into the trap of believing that San Relajo is an actual Italian city. In Fernanda Pivano's translation of *Across the River and into the Trees,* she fails to convey Cantwell's humor. Rather than Hemingway's "don't make jokes in Spanish," she writes, "*non parlar spagnolo*" (*Di là dal fiume* 63), or "don't speak Spanish," which entirely misses the point.

78:24 one of your girls: Andrea may just be joking, but his is an odd comment nevertheless. Cantwell's devotion to Renata is never in question, and although he does notice beautiful Venetian women as he walks down the street (77:15–19), this comment is the only indication that Cantwell has a coterie of Italian mistresses.

78:30 she came into the room: Although her presence has been lightly foreshadowed (e.g., 50:6, 50:9, 69:16, 71:7), Renata enters the novel slightly more than a quarter into the action. Given Hemingway's framing device, Renata is physically absent in chapters 1–8, and then again from chapters 40–45.

78:32–33 a profile that could break your, or any one else's heart: Hemingway loved to look at Adriana Ivancich in profile and always posed her that way in photographs. Without disparaging Hemingway's taste or Adriana's appearance, the effect is always a bit comically overwrought, because Adriana appears to be looking off majestically in the distance. Later in this chapter, Cantwell will tell Renata, "Turn your head and raise your chin once for me" (81:13) and "Turn your head sideways, beauty" (91:15–16). He says to her, "You *could* stand sidewise" (108:8). Renata reports that she is aware that her profile resembles that of Marie Antoinette (131:21–22), to which Cantwell responds, "Please turn your head" (131:26). Cantwell will also instruct the portrait of Renata to "keep your God-damn chin up so you can break my heart easier" (160:29–30). As Cantwell and Renata take their final walk to breakfast, he "saw the profile" (187:8).

79:6–7 Her voice was low and delicate and she spoke English with caution: Hemingway is paraphrasing King Lear's words over the dying Cordelia: "Her voice was ever soft, / Gentle, and low, an excellent thing in women" (5.3.267-68). As a sleepy Renata will ask Cantwell to continue his lengthy anecdote, "Tell me very low and soft" (224:14).

79:8 **How is Emily:** Renata's mention of Emily, Andrea's wife, is interesting for at least two reasons. First, of the fifteen characters that are given names in the novel, Emily, Renata, and Contessa Dandolo are the only females mentioned by name, of whom Renata is the only named character we see.[2] Emily, however, may also refer to one of the novel's literary and symbolic touchstones, *Othello*, in which Emilia is Iago's wife. Following the joke about the "wicked Andrea" (77:33), a wife named Emily would be appropriate.

79:31 **Caro:** Italian for "dear." Since Andrea's name was Carlo in the manuscript, Hemingway makes a deft, economical revision, merely removing the "l" and leaving an incorrectly capitalized replacement.

79:33–80:3 **He turned his fine, long . . . :** In a rare, albeit brief, sequence, compressed into a single sentence, Andrea leaves Renata and Cantwell and looks at himself in the mirror. We read the objective description of him leaving the table and looking in the mirror, but we are also privileged to his subjective judgment, which is that, like Arnaldo and Cantwell, he does not like how he looks in the mirror. We are also told the reason establishments put mirrors behind bars. This moment echoes Cantwell's reaction to his reflection at the end of chapter 8 (75:26–27).

According to Catherine Bourne's aphorism in *The Garden of Eden*, "You can't fool a bar mirror" (103).

80:15 **Two very dry Martinis:** Cantwell, who has already had three doubles and a Carpano, has ordered his first drink since 65:19, his fourth martini of the evening. We know that the waiter in Cantwell's hotel room has secured Campari and gin for him, but we are never told whether he has had any drinks from it.

80:15–16 **Montgomerys . . . Fifteen to one:** The Montgomery martini is fifteen parts gin to one part vermouth. The drink is so named due to British field marshal Bernard Montgomery's alleged preference to have a fifteen-to-one ratio of his troops to enemy troops on the battlefield. As Cantwell will later say during the epic chapter 12, "Monty was a character who needed fifteen to one to move, and then moved tardily" (119:13–14). Montgomery is further disparaged on 127:8–10. Legend has it that Hemingway ordered the first Montgomery in the history of Harry's Bar. Hemingway owned Montgomery's *Normandy to the Baltic.* (Brasch and Sigman 258). Cantwell's description of Monty as "a British General" (119:21) is, in the manuscript, simply "a jerk."

In an interview published the same week as *Across the River and into the Trees*, Hemingway asserted that he would rather be executed than pay homage to Montgomery, the man, he claims, "who took our gasoline to do what he could not do" ("Hemingway Is Bitter about Nobody" 110). In the early 1980s, a Hemingway favorite, "Lightning" Joe Collins recalled, "Monty was always waiting, waiting until he got everything in line. He wanted a great deal of artillery, American artillery mostly—American tanks, also. Then, when he got everything all set, he would pounce. . . . Too cautious, entirely" (Wade 11).

80:17 who had been in the desert: The "desert" alludes to the western desert campaign from 1940 to 1943, which invites further consideration of Montgomery's presence in the conversation. Montgomery served as one of the Allied leaders against Italy and Germany, including the "Desert Fox," Erwin Rommel, who will also be mentioned several times in the novel. See entry at 116:14.

80:19–20 nice . . . beautiful . . . lovely . . . I love you: Cantwell constantly praises Renata and usually gushes about her beauty. However, the phrase "I love you" and its derivatives, the meaning of which Renata initially questions, serves as a refrain for the entire novel, almost a compulsive tic to which Cantwell returns. Lest the reader believe Cantwell is a hateful cynic, or even ready to say farewell to an impractical, impossible love as does Jake Barnes at the end of *The Sun Also Rises*, Cantwell explicitly says that he loves Venice (49:19) just as he loves any man who has been wounded in action (71:30); in fact, he asserts that a man as grand as he loves more than the ordinary man, too (72:3). As he will tell Renata, succumbing to this compulsion, "I love you and I love you and I love you" (89:4). Often, Renata and Cantwell will challenge each other about their love of the other, including demands for affirmation, that the other make the declaration out loud.

It is important to appreciate the way Hemingway wished to depict this relationship, as two people absolutely adoring each other, despite the external complications.

The "I love you" chart
(80:19–20) Cantwell → Renata: "You're also very beautiful and lovely and I love you."
(80:28) Renata → Cantwell: "I love you very much, too, whatever that is."
(82:9–10) Cantwell → Renata: "I love you and my trade can gently leave."
(84:17–18) Renata → Cantwell: "I love you when you are gentle."
(86:8–9) Cantwell → Renata: "When will you learn that I might joke against you because I love you?"
(88:18) Cantwell → Renata: "And you are most beautiful and I love you."
(89:4) Cantwell → Renata: "I love you and I love you and I love you."
(89:29) Renata → Cantwell: "I just love you."
(92:8–9) Renata → Cantwell: "I love you and I only wish we could be cheerful tonight."
(92:32) Cantwell → Renata: "I love you very truly . . ."
(92:33) Renata → Cantwell: "I love you very truly, too."
(93:1–2) Renata → Cantwell: "I also love you in Italian, against all my judgment . . ."

(93:25) Cantwell → Renata: "I love you and your mother both very much."
(94:20–21) Renata → Cantwell: "Do you see now why I love you when I know better than to do it?"
(96:23–24) Renata → Cantwell: "And that's one more reason why I love you."
(106:10, 106:14) Cantwell → Renata: "I love you . . . I love you only . . ."
(108:31) Cantwell → Renata: "I love you very much the way you are . . ."
(109:14–15) Renata → Cantwell: "I love you to be in your trade and I love you."
(109:19) Cantwell → Renata: "I love you, devil."
(126:9) Renata → Cantwell: "I love you, you know . . ."
(133:9) Renata → Cantwell: "I love you."
(133:14) Cantwell → Renata: "I love you Period."
(137:30–31) Cantwell → Renata: "I love you very much."
(142:3–4) Renata → Cantwell: "We are in our home and I love you."
(142:8) Cantwell → Renata: "I love you."
(142:10) Cantwell → Renata: "I love you and I know whatever that means."
(144:18) Cantwell → Renata: "I love you true . . ."
(147:14) Renata → Cantwell: "I say it because I love you."
(148:15–16) Cantwell → Renata: "I will tell you, now, a military secret. . . . I love you"
(154:12) Cantwell → Renata: "Please know I love you . . ."
(186:17) Cantwell → Renata: "I love you and it is cold and hard."
(186:32–33) Cantwell → Renata: "I love you . . . Take it frontally and formally please."
(195:8) Renata → Cantwell: "I love you my last true and only love . . ."
(195:24) Cantwell → Renata: "I love you truly, finally and for good."
(206:27–28) Cantwell → Renata: "I love you."
(207:18) Renata → Cantwell: "and I love you."
(239:11) Cantwell → Renata: "I love you."
(249:9–10) Cantwell → Renata: "Did I tell you, Daughter, that I love you?"
(249:11–12) Renata → Cantwell: "But I love you."
(250:13) Cantwell → Renata: "I love you . . ."
(262:17) Cantwell → Renata: "I love you much more than before . . ."
(262:18–19) Renata → Cantwell: "I love you more since I saw that thing."
(264:5–6) Cantwell → Renata: "I love you with two moderately swollen hands and all my heart."

80:24 **Nearly nineteen:** Hemingway met Adriana Ivancich in December 1948, when she was one month shy of her nineteenth birthday. Renata's age is also mentioned on 88:28 and 92:26. Hemingway (and presumably Cantwell) was nearly nineteen when he was wounded in World War I. During their last couple of hours together, Renata tells Cantwell he does not know "how long a week can be when you are nineteen" (215:29–30).

80:29–30 **Let's not think about anything at all:** Rather than view this line as an indication of Hemingway's anti-intellectualism—or Cantwell's—let's recall that Renata and Cantwell spend their time trying to avoid the obvious, the elephant in the room, which is that this meeting and the next day will be the last they will ever spend together. This kind of metacognitive impulse, where the hero and heroine must shield themselves from the real world in order to savor the senses and secure even the slightest enjoyment, is perhaps Hemingway's trademark in his treatment of consciousness.

80:34 **chin-chin:** Actually "cincin" or "cin cin," this onomatopoeic sound is an Italian toast, mimicking the sound of clinking glasses. Cantwell's warning against toasting recalls Count Mippipopolous's similar admonition to Brett Ashley in *The Sun Also Rises* (66).

81:22 **Queen of Heaven:** Peter Ackroyd's study of Venice is subtitled *Pure City,* continuing the connection between Venice and the Virgin Mary, whom Catholics designate as Queen of Heaven. Ackroyd writes of various artistic depictions of the city: "The coronation of the Virgin in heaven by Christ was then employed, in painting and poetry, as the victorious image of Venice. The Queen of Heaven is also the Queen of the Sea" (270). The Venetian painter Paolo Veronese (1528–1588), for instance, painted *The Apotheosis of Venice,* or *The Triumph of Venice.*

In a 1952 letter to his friend Bernard Berenson, Hemingway wrote of his failed marriage with Martha Gellhorn, "Anyone confusing a handsome and ambitious girl with the Queen of Heaven should be punished as a fool" (*SL* 789).

81:30 **Please never look at me like that:** Renata refers to Cantwell's glare. See 197:9 and entry on 42:7.

81:31–32 **slipped into my trade:** Whether this is a self-glorifying, self-justifying excuse or a candid, self-aware explanation, it begins Cantwell's explicit struggle between treating Renata as would a kind, doting lover and treating her as would his other incarnation, Colonel Cantwell, whose trade was to kill armed men (65:20–21). Stating his case, Cantwell ascribes the lapse to unconscious or instinctive behavior: he is telling Renata that he did not do it on purpose, but after more than thirty years in the business, it is no longer something he can easily turn off.

82:17 **the hand of Our Lord:** In addition to furthering our understanding of Cantwell's injured hand, Renata is here revealing that she finds religious significance in it, as she will later derive sexual excitement from it. She fetishizes the hand as an object that chronically appears in her dreams. In chapter 14, following Renata and Cantwell's sexual dalliance in the gondola, Cantwell asks, "Why do you like the hand?" (148:7) which had been the source of Renata's sexual gratification. Later, Renata will refer to it as the "one I love and must think about all week" (208:4–5).

In *To Have and Have Not* (1937), Marie Morgan gains sexual excitement from Harry's severed arm. As she tells him, "Go ahead. Go ahead now. Put the stump there. Hold it there. Hold it. Hold it now. Hold it" (114).

82:27–28 the two times that had made it that way: Carlos Baker points out that Stonewall Jackson was similarly wounded twice, in the hand and in the arm (*Writer as Artist* 268).

83:3 I don't like to look at it much This moment in the novel begs a comparison with a similar topic in *The Sun Also Rises,* during which Jake Barnes has an anguished private moment as he undresses in front of a mirror in his Paris apartment. Unlike Cantwell, Jake seems compelled to look at his far more recent wound, but he is fairly close-lipped about it. Of course, Jake's wound is to the genitals, not the hand. See a similar moment featuring a naked Cantwell on 168:2–11.

As Renata will ask Cantwell if she might take his hand, he repeats, "It's so damned ugly and I dislike looking at it" (95:17).

83:14–15 *ancora due Martini*: That is, "another two Martinis."

83:26 what am I doing here anyway? It is wicked: What aspect of Cantwell's relationship is he criticizing? He seems to be voicing the complaints of the skeptical, perhaps of unknowing onlookers. Indeed, one sentence later, he reassures himself that he is acting on true love.

83:33 Lady Diana Manners: Lady Diana Cooper, born Lady Diana Olivia Winifred Maud Manners (1892–1986) was an English socialite and actress. Her obituary describes her as a "legendary beauty" and, as per Cantwell's reference, explains that the "vehicle that launched her to fame was a spectacular, although lightweight, pageant called 'The Miracle,' by Max Reinhardt. Off and on for 12 years, she toured with it from London to the shires, from the cities of the Continent to New York and across the United States." The obituary goes on to say, "She encountered such diverse figures as Ernest Hemingway, whom she dismissed as the biggest bore of Paris" (Saxon).

Reinhardt, an Austrian theater and film director and actor (1873–1943), put on *The Miracle* in Germany in 1911, London in 1912, and then on Broadway from January through June 1924 at the Century Theatre; in all three, Cooper starred as the Madonna. This play dramatizes a nun from the Middle Ages who runs away from her convent with a knight.

In 1961 Hemingway requested, in one of the final letters he would write, that a volume of Lady Diana Cooper's memoirs be sent to him, her *Trumpets from the*

Steep (*SL* 911). In 1958, he ordered a copy of her first memoir, *The Rainbow Comes and Goes*. According to *Hemingway's Library,* Hemingway also owned a copy of the second volume of the three memoirs, *The Light of Common Day* (Brasch and Sigman 112). Cooper also became a close friend of Hemingway's third wife, Martha, in the mid-1930s.

84:13 **You are nice when you are gentle:** In other words, Cantwell is *gentile* when he is gentle.

84:14 **Do you suppose the word:** At this point, we might review the topics of conversation between Renata and Cantwell: They address their teasing of Andrea. They order drinks. They exchange "I love yous." They agree not to think and not to toast with their drinks. Renata updates Cantwell about her plans to go to school. Cantwell asks her to sit in profile, which excites him and then he asks if she would be Queen of Heaven, then withdraws the question. Cantwell then looks too aggressively at Renata, which he then explains as a byproduct of his trade and for which he apologizes. They then discuss his wounded hand, before agreeing to discuss their fellow patrons, focusing primarily on a group of potential lesbians.

With respect to Cantwell's etymological query, the word "gentleman" comes from the Middle English translation of Old French *gentilz hom,* a good man, of good breeding and status.

84:20 **that son of a bitch:** Cantwell and Renata's game of talking about the other people in the bar, which Renata agreed to with the understanding that it would be done without "malice" (83:12–13), has taken a darker turn. In fact, the character at the third table to whom Cantwell refers is a barely veiled screed against novelist and 1930 Nobel laureate Sinclair Lewis (1885–1951), whose novels include *Babbitt* (1922); *Main Street* (1925); and *Dodsworth* (1929), which is partially set in Venice and refers to it as "the friendliest city in the world" (415).

This uncomfortable thread will become an obsession with Cantwell, whose preoccupation with the avatar for Lewis remains Cantwell's least appealing rant, rivaled only by his venomous remarks, which are unmistakably about Martha Gellhorn. For a man in the last day or two of his life, just minutes into seeing the love of his life for the last time, to descend into brutal attacks on the physical appearance of someone else in a bar minding his own business is hateful, unfunny, and pathetic. As Renata implores Cantwell, "Let us skip him. . . . Please skip the man. He didn't come here to do anyone any harm" (87:4, 87:10–11). She articulates what frustrated readers might be thinking: "When we have so little time, Richard. He is rather a waste of time" (87:6–7). Likewise, he is a waste of words, a waste of pages and paragraphs. Philip Young calls this sequence in the novel, "savage and quite irrelevant" (*Reconsideration* 117). To Jeffrey Meyers, it is "Hemingway's cruelest passage" (*Hemingway* 468).

Hemingway targeted Lewis for perceived slights the older writer made when they were both in Venice at the same time. In March 1949, Hemingway and Mary dined at the Gritti in Venice with Sinclair Lewis and Katherine Powers, the mother of Lewis's former mistress. Mary's autobiography contains a similarly negative recollection: "I found it just barely possible to look at Mr. Lewis. His face was a piece of old liver, shot squarely with #7 shot at twenty yards. His hands trembled when he ate, blobs of everything oozing out between his lips" (234). In *Across the River and into the Trees,* the writer is described as "chawing at his food" (117:33–118:1). In a lengthy postscript to a 22 July 1949 letter to Charles Scribner, Hemingway recounts the source of this tension: "When I was in the hospital in Padova he nailed Mary on a three hour diatribe, 'I love Ernest BUT.'" Hemingway catalogues Lewis's criticisms of Hemingway, after which Lewis ultimately expressed sympathy that Mary was married to Hemingway. (For the full statement, see *SL* 660–61.)

Although Hemingway derided Lewis and *Main Street* in a 1925 letter to F. Scott Fitzgerald, his first wife, Hadley, recalled "how deeply and carefully Ernest had once studied *Main Street*" (Baker, *Life Story* 161). Kenneth Lynn confirms that in addition to reading Havelock Ellis and histories of World War I, *Main Street* was one of Hemingway's most important postwar texts (132). One of Hemingway's most irate letters to Maxwell Perkins was his complaint about Scribner's neglecting to transcribe Lewis's speech honoring *For Whom the Bell Tolls* in 1941. "Scribners not haveing [*sic*] it taken down as I requested as a favour," wrote Hemingway only four days after Pearl Harbor was attacked, "was the most careless, shiftless and callous action I have ever met in civil life" (*Only Thing* 315). Lewis praised Hemingway at the conclusion of his own Nobel Prize speech in 1930, showing prescience by also praising William Faulkner.

Although Hemingway's anger toward Lewis may very well have been justified, this novel suffers for the inclusion of this vengeful attack. For instance, during a conversation with Renata later in this chapter, an entirely incongruous mention of the writer mars an expression of love:

> "I love you and your mother both very much."
> "I must tell her," the girl said.
> "Do you think that pock-marked jerk is really a writer?" (93:25–27)

And then later:

> ". . . forgive me for talking about my trade."
> "I hate it but I love it."
> "I believe we share the same emotions," the Colonel said. "But what is my pitted compatriot thinking three tables down?" (120:7–11)

Furthermore, the repetitiveness of the insults is wearying: his hair did not go with his face (84:33–85:1–2, 85:22–25). In the manuscript, Cantwell speculates that no Indian would ever scalp this man, because it would "spook" him (JFK 3).

In an unpublished Hemingway story of World War II, "Indian Country and the White Army," a marching soldier reads *Arrowsmith* (1925), another Lewis novel, and judges, "it stands up pretty good" (JFK 496B). Hemingway also invokes Lewis in *The Torrents of Spring*, asserting that he is available for artistic advice at the Café du Dôme "any afternoon, talking about Art with Harold Stearns and Sinclair Lewis" (47). In *Green Hills of Africa*, Hemingway's hunting companion Kandisky declares, "Sinclair Lewis is nothing" (8). Later, when asking Hemingway to name the greatest writer in America (the same conversation that provoked Hemingway's declaration that all modern American literature comes from *Adventures of Huckleberry Finn*), Kandisky interposes: "Certainly not Sinclair Lewis" (19).

On 17 November 1940, Lewis wrote Hemingway a laudatory letter about *For Whom the Bell Tolls*: "Jesus, that's a great book, 'Bell Tolls.'" (JFK, Incoming Correspondence). According to Lewis's biographer, one of his complaints to Mary was that Hemingway never wrote anything kind about him, while he consistently praised Hemingway (Lingeman 531). In a brutal letter to John Dos Passos on 29 May 1949, Hemingway wrote: "The only trouble with Venice was that Sinclair Lewis showed up there" (JFK, Outgoing Correspondence, box 49).

In addition to this character, whom we may call "the pock-marked writer" or "the pitted compatriot" entering here, he is also referred to nine more times (113:32–33, 117:32–118:20, 122:11–12, 123:22–26, 130:30–33, 188:7–8, 188:15, 192:5–6, 248:18–20).

For a fuller discussion of the Hemingway-Lewis connection, see McLaughlin.

84:28 **Goebbels' face:** Joseph Goebbels (1897–1945) was the Reich minister of public enlightenment and propaganda (see also 85:27).

85:6–7 **elderly, wholesome looking woman:** As Cantwell reports, Sinclair Lewis travelled with the mother of his ex-mistress, Marcella Powers. This figure is also mentioned on 118:1. The novel sets up a clear distinction in which the pitted compatriot is associating with someone old enough to be his mother, while Cantwell is associating with someone young enough to be his daughter. This dynamic is also lampooned in "In Harry's Bar in Venice," in which Hemingway's young colonel "meets an Italian or rather, should we say, a Venetian countess aged 86."

85:9 **The Ladies' Home Journal:** *Ladies' Home Journal* is a magazine that began in 1883 and continues to the present day. According to Emily Yellin, it was a venue for government communication to housewives during World War II (23). *Ladies' Home Journal* contacted Hemingway for the serial rights for *Across the River and into the Trees* when it was a work in progress, and in a 17 July 1949 letter, he informed them that he was engaging in no negotiations on the serial rights until the writing was done. His claim was not true; the rights had already been promised to his friend A. E. Hotchner at *Cosmopolitan,* where it was published in five issues from February to June 1950 for an $85,000 fee.

85:26–27 **Verdun:** The comparison of the pockmarked writer's face to this hilly region of northeastern France refers to the major World War I battle between Germany and France, from 21 February to 18 December 1916, one of the longest and most brutal battles in history, resulting in more than three hundred thousand deaths and a half a million wounded.

85:28–29 **playing at Götterdämmerung:** In other words, courting the apocalypse. This phrase is taken from the last of Richard Wagner's four operas in the Ring of the Nibelung, *Twilight of the Gods.* Götterdämmerung refers to "the complete downfall of a regime, institution, etc" (*OED*).

85:29 ***Komm' Süsser Tod:*** Meaning "Come, sweet death," the phrase is taken from Johann Sebastian Bach's (1685–1750) church cantata "Komm du Süße Todesstunde" (1736). This desire for a heavenly afterlife is a thematically crucial reference to the "sweet death" upon which Cantwell must inevitably be meditating.

86:1 **Bach:** Hemingway frequently claimed that Bach had a primary influence on his writing, particularly the fugues and contrapunto that he claimed were influential in his drafting of *A Farewell to Arms.* Bach is included in the list of thirty influences that Hemingway catalogued in his interview with George Plimpton ("Art of Fiction" 118). In 1949, Hemingway told Lillian Ross that he learned from Bach, particularly in the first paragraph of *A Farewell to Arms* by using the word "and" as Bach "used a note in music when he was emitting counterpoint" (88). Hemingway continued to say, "I can almost write like Mr. Johann sometimes—or, anyway, so he would like it" (88). Cantwell's characterization of Bach as a "cobelligerent" references Germany's partnership with Austria during World War I.

87:8 **Goya:** The painter Francisco José de Goya y Lucientes (1746–1828) receives his only mention in the novel. Unlike the Baroque or Renaissance painters who have been invoked, Goya is synonymous with the grotesque and with being an unflinching depicter of violence (see Cirino, *Thought in Action* 106). In *Death in the Afternoon,* Hemingway recalls that he began attending bullfights in order to learn how to represent violence as authentically as in Goya's harrowing series, *The Disasters of War.*

87:23–24 **the method of Dante:** The first of several mentions of Dante Alighieri (1265–1321). Although most scholarly treatments of *Across the River and into the Trees* note Hemingway's references to Dante, this novel's use of Dante's *Inferno* is largely superficial. As some commentators suggest, Cantwell does join Dante in consigning his foes to hell, and does speak of circles, just as the poler reminds us of Charon, the surly boatman in *Inferno* III. Hemingway was interested in Dante at the time of writing *Across the River and into the Trees*. He apparently favored the Longfellow translation but later also owned John Ciardi's translation. He owned Eliot's study of the poet, *Dante* (Brasch and Sigman 135) as well as Paget Toynbee's biography (370).

Dante is mentioned as part of Hemingway's litany of influences in Plimpton's "Art of Fiction" (118). Renata would prefer that Dante immortalized her and Cantwell's relationship, rather than the pockmarked writer (118:21–22). After Renata particularly approves of Cantwell's imagery (122:7–11), she suggests that he share the phrase with the pockmarked writer, but Cantwell prefers to tell it to Dante (122:13). Renata vows to read Dante during the week while she and Cantwell are apart (201:1, 201:11), Cantwell embodies Dante, consigning various military figures to hell (225:28–31), and then Renata somewhat inanely affirms Cantwell's praise of the Italian language by asserting that Dante also approved of it (247:11).

Rather than these superficial references to Dante, which would not require a particularly profound understanding of the *Commedia,* Dante's importance to Cantwell and to Hemingway is instead his vexed role as both a person and a writer. Is it possible to be a soldier and also to be a good person? Is it possible, furthermore, to be a writer who is militantly devoted to his craft and still to be kind and humane? And human? One of the central explorations of this novel is to test one's ability to maintain the purity of professionalism and still to exist and to love in the real world. Cantwell is clear to distinguish his dislike for Dante as a man from his feelings for him as a writer. In a 1949 letter to John Dos Passos, Hemingway wrote: "Since trip to Italy have been studying the life of Dante. Seems to be one of the worst jerks that ever lived, but how well he could write! This may be a lesson to us all" (*SL* 677). In a conversation with Renata, Cantwell calls Dante "an execrable character" (201:12), and Renata responds, "But he did not write execrably" (201:14)—this distinction is a crucial one for Cantwell and Hemingway. When Cantwell later says, "I am Mister Dante . . . For the moment" (225:29), his identification becomes explicit.

A passage in *Islands in the Stream* views Dante with more ambivalence, with Thomas Hudson learning that "hell was not necessarily as it was described by Dante" and that, in fact, hell "had many circles and they were not as fixed as in those of the great Florentine egotist" (195).

87:25 **vieux con:** French for "old jerk," or a similar pejorative.

87:28, 30 **Firenze . . . Florence:** Although Dante is Italy's national poet, he is particularly associated with Florence, where there is a museum of his former house, the Casa di Dante. Just as Cantwell's love of Italy is clearly provincial in favor of the north, in a passage from the manuscript of *Death in the Afternoon,* Hemingway writes: "It was the north of Italy that I cared about. I never gave a damn about any part of the peninsula south of Milan" (qtd. in Beegel 54). Cantwell says, "Eff Florence" (87:30).

88:2 ***deposito:*** As Cantwell asserts, this word is Italian for "depot." It is significant that Hemingway is clear to note that this conversation, or at least this word, takes place in Italian. (See Cirino, "You Don't Know" 55).

88:5–6 **Milan . . . Bologna . . . Bergamo:** Cantwell designates as "good" these three cities in northern Italy, although he praises only a fraction of Milano. In this novel, Milan and the Milanese are associated with industry, commerce, and those who profited from the wars in which Cantwell fought. Bologna has already been labeled a tough town where one eats well (41:24–25). Cantwell had previously taken Bergamo when he was play-acting as a general with the *Gran Maestro* (64:8).

88:13 **Bank of Odessa:** Cantwell's joke references the Bank of Odessa, founded in 1889 in Missouri, while simultaneously punning on Odessa, the city in the Ukraine.

88:30 **a little bluntly:** Not only does Renata summarize the situation "bluntly," but Hemingway also succumbs to his occasional habit of reviewing the novel's plot in an encapsulating paragraph (88:28–30). Indeed, Renata's line could serve as a spoken summation if a trailer of the movie were ever made. Would Renata ever speak such a raw, artless line, or was Hemingway merely regaining his footing after a long stretch of discursive dialogue?

88:32 **I never cry:** Renata will break this rule three times during the action of the novel: when Cantwell glares and snaps at her and reduces her to tears (135:5), when he proposes that they will live "happily ever after" (150:5), and upon her farewell to him (254:3).

89:10 **"No," he lied:** According to the exchange in chapter 2, the doctor never explicitly tells Cantwell any bad news. Either the conversation was off-stage, or it was simply understood without being spoken aloud. Cantwell could have recounted Wes's glowing report about Cantwell's heart without telling an overt lie.

89:24–25 **as your grandfather's Purdey shot-gun:** A reference to James Purdey & Sons, the British gun manufacturer. As Hemingway recalls in *Under Kilimanjaro:* "The Purdey was not a Purdey but a straight-stocked long-barreled Scott live-pigeon full choke in both barrels that I had bought from a lot of shotguns a dealer had brought down from Udine to the Kechlers' villa in Codroipo" (392). In a September

1949 letter to Taylor Williams, Hemingway reveals that the two duck guns he used were "a Scott British-made pigeon gun with very long barrels tightly choked" and a "Beretta over and under" (JFK, Outgoing Correspondence).

Toward the end of the novel, Cantwell imagines giving Renata one or two Purdeys (266:27, 266:29).

89:30 *oficio:* As with "*deposito*" (88:2), our narrator intrudes here to tell us that a word is spoken in a different language, in this case Spanish. See also 93:31 for a translation of this word. Phrases are translated into Spanish on three occasions (198:6, 244:9, and 246:11). When Adriana wrote letters to Hemingway, she would write in Italian or passable English, with the occasional Spanish phrase thrown in.

90:3 **Es un oficio bastante malo:** Spanish for "It's a pretty bad job," which is intended to restate, "It isn't much of a trade, is it?"

90:5 **Don't you write any more poetry?** This question may be unexpected, given the context of Cantwell and Renata's conversation, but Adriana Ivancich was interested in poetry and the arts, and Hemingway was effusively supportive of her aspirations. Mondadori published a book of Ivancich's poems, *Ho guardato il cielo e la terra* (1953), which has been alternately described as "delicate" (Hotchner, *Papa* 90), "wretched" (Lynn 535), or "poor" (Meyers, *Hemingway* 451). In a 1 October 1952 letter to Adriana, Hemingway wrote, "Because I am not a critic, I cannot tell you why they are good. But I believe that they are, all of them" (Ivancich, "I Am Hemingway's Renata" 263).[3] He also referred to Adriana as "a great poet" and wrote that he knew "of no better young writer" (Doyle and Houston 31).

Renata's own self-criticism of her work as "young girl poetry" (90:6) may reflect Adriana's own belief; she did not publish any more poetry after her first effort, at twenty-three. During their correspondence, Adriana would often include the poetry she had been writing.

90:14 **because of her sorrow:** One of the unstated tensions of the book is that Renata's mother, like Adriana's mother, is a recent war widow. If the Renata-Cantwell conversation and relationship parallels Hemingway and Adriana's, we should note that Adriana's father died when she was fifteen, only three years earlier, although he was apparently murdered by Italians and not by Germans.

90:15 **if we had a baby:** This non sequitur is surprising, given that Cantwell would only have one night left in which to impregnate Renata, and he would never meet his child. One wonders how this reference relates to the menstruation that is later implied. Renata's physical state is at issue, with some critics even arguing that Renata is pregnant (Wylder 188).[4]

90:21 It is just a decision: "Decision" is another critical word in the novel. Renata admires Cantwell's facility for making "lovely quick decisions" (99:20). She, in turn, makes a decision not to marry Cantwell (113:10). The Colonel also makes a "quick decision" about where he would like to be buried (209:11). As Cantwell prepares to say goodbye to Renata, Hemingway offers a one-sentence paragraph: "He had made another decision" (244:22), an ambiguous declaration that may mean more than Cantwell's intention to repay Cipriani for the small statue with a check. Cantwell also orders Renata, "Make a decision, Daughter" (247:23), referring to ordering dinner. Finally, Renata reneges on her "decision" not to cry (254:4).

90:27–28 Three is plenty in my trade, and I made all three: In a novel where the number three takes on symbolic importance, Cantwell may be referring to three strategic errors in battle just as he may be referring to his three wives, of whom he later says he has "lost them thrice" (91:21). The connection is soon made explicit when, through interior monologue, Cantwell remarks that one loses a woman the same way one loses a battalion (91:22). See also "I have loved three and lost them thrice" (160:12). "I made all three" seems to be Cantwell taking responsibility for the death of others and not blaming it on the unwise orders of his superiors.

90:30–31 They beat the hell out of me to remember them: In the manuscript, Cantwell says, "They bore the shit out of me to remember them" (JFK 1), a significant difference. As it stands, Cantwell is implying that it is difficult to remember his three errors; in the manuscript, it is merely wearying, tiresome to recall them.

91:1 true love: Cantwell repeats this phrase so compulsively—a variation of it is used eleven times—that it becomes a conspicuous refrain. Hemingway invokes a courtly, chivalric, baldly anachronistic parlance, recalling, for example, Shakespeare's Sonnet 61, which refers to "Mine own true love that doth my rest defeat" (*Sonnets* 55). E. B. White skewered this language in his *New Yorker* satire, "Across the Street and into the Grill," which begins, "This is my last and best and true and only meal" (28).

Cantwell's Homeric Epithets:

91:1–2	"My last and only and true love"
92:6	*"Ma très chère et bien aimée"*
106:14	"my best and last and only and one true love"
134:32–33	"his last and true and only love"
161:5–6	"my one true love or whatever it is"
162:7–8	"his own true love"
184:28	"his true love"
185:1	"His true love"
206:22	"You're my last and true and only love"

| 229:32 | "His true love" |
| 231:1 | "my true love" |

Renata returns this phrase, if only to suggest that "I love you my last true and only love" is more euphonious in English than in Italian (195:8). In *The Sun Also Rises*, Brett Ashley mocks this kind of overtly chivalric sentiment, explaining to Jake, "I couldn't live quietly in the country. Not with my own true love" (62). In a 1944 poem, Hemingway refers to Mary Welsh, soon to be his fourth wife, as "My own true love" (*Poems* 108).

91:20–21 I have loved but three women and have lost them thrice: Cantwell is quoting Edmond Rostand's (1868–1918) *Cyrano de Bergerac* (1897), where Roxane says, "I never loved but one man in my life, / And I have lost him—twice" (193). This formulation will later express for countries what Cantwell currently laments about women (160:12). In the manuscript, Hemingway writes, "Thank you Mr. Rostand and do not mind the transposition" (JFK 1). this line would have invited a consideration of Hemingway's biography, too, as he was in his fourth marriage. As this comparison continues (91:26–27), Hemingway's biography continues to intrude; his fourth wife was his dedicatee, but Renata is a stand-in for Adriana Ivancich, which makes for something of an awkward reference.

91:22 You lose them the same way: Hidden in this meditation is one of the keys to Cantwell's backstory, which is that he was demoted for "orders that are impossible to fulfill," the same "other people's orders" that he later bemoans (194:12, 222:18–19).

91:30 Council of War: A meeting held to determine a plan or a strategy for action. Cantwell has lapsed into a vivid reverie about the women and military incidents he has mismanaged.

91:31–32 GENERAL WHERE IS YOUR CAVALRY? Hemingway takes this Civil War quotation from Lieutenant General J. A. Early's missive to General John C. Breckenridge on 16 June 1864 from Charlottesville: "Where is your cavalry?" (*War of the Rebellion* 763). *Under Kilimanjaro* repeats this reference (98). This quotation appears almost as part of Cantwell's stream of consciousness, the same spell as during Cantwell's earlier discussion with the *Gran Maestro* (see 64:10–65:10).

Cantwell's vivid, haunted consciousness recalls Gail Hightower in Faulkner's *Light in August* (1932), a man trapped in memory—"dissociated from mechanical time"—who cannot escape the sound of galloping hooves from the cavalry in his own Civil War memories (366).

Hemingway told friends that the correct answer to this question is, "up shit's creek and about to take off."

92:5 **Cavalry:** This iteration of "cavalry" is unnecessarily capitalized; while it may be an error, Hemingway's punctuation ultimately conflates "cavalry" with "Calvary," the hill where Jesus was crucified.

92:6 *Ma très chère et bien aimée:* French for "My very dear and good love."

92:28 **Gondoliere:** This word for the boatman on a gondola should not be capitalized and should be italicized, the error occurs on 141:13, 145:23, 150:15–16, and 181:2. On 181:2, "gondoliere" is given an English plural form: "gondolieres," rather than the Italian word, "gondolieri."

92:33 **Whatever that means:** In what is apparently an inside joke between Renata and Cantwell, the sense is that the speaker will question a term or a phrase that has a loaded emotional charge or would tend to be taken too seriously, such as "I love you" or "British General" or "happiness" or "woman, or a girl."

Renata also proposes that they have a good time on the gondola ride, despite the circumstances, "whatever they are." She remarks that she learned the phrase from him, and then he relearned it back from her.

The "Whatever That Means" Inside Joke:

PAGE	SPEAKER(S)	LINE
80:21–22	Renata	"I don't know what it [I love you] means but I like to hear it."
119:21–22	Cantwell	"I simply think he is a British General. Whatever that means."
121:29–30	Renata	"But I will love you, whatever that means, and you and I know what it means very well."
138:23–27	Cantwell	"he did not want the man to have even a journalist's look into happiness." "Whatever that is." "I learned that phrase from you and now you have relearned it back from me."
139:8–9	Renata	"Even under the circumstances, whatever they are."
142:8–10	Renata, Cantwell	"I love you." "Whatever that means." "I love you and I know whatever that means . . ."
145:4–5	Renata	"I am just a woman, or a girl, or whatever that is."
167:20	Cantwell	"the five corners of the world; wherever that is . . ."
189:18	Renata	"Wherever that [Canada] is."
189:20–21	Cantwell	"Wherever that [Canada] is . . . And I know damn well where it is."

195:34	Renata	"Whatever that [the average high school valedictorian] is."
207:24–25	Renata	"I am not an inquisitor; or whatever the female of inquisitor is."

93:8 **That boy:** Renata continues the discussion of the twenty-five-year-old painter, who hides his homosexuality. She also reveals that he painted her portrait two years ago, which she offers as a gift to Cantwell and he accepts. Thus, the narrative of the portrait spans 93:9 through 279:3 and is one of the prominent threads of the novel. The portrait that will become such an important object was done when Renata was not even seventeen, two years prior (164:14–16, 167:16–17).

93:13 **rising from the sea:** Renata is evoking Titian's *Venus Rising from the Sea* (see entry at 49:23). Sandro Botticelli's (1445–1510) *The Birth of Venus* (1486), a painting that hangs in the Uffizi, also depicts such a scene.

93:16–17 **Daddy paid him adequately:** This reference is curious and potentially inconsistent, particularly if we are to believe that Renata's father died during or at the end of World War II. If the painting were done two years prior to the action of the novel, then it would have been unlikely that he was alive.

Adriana dedicated her book of poetry to her father, Carlo.

93:22 **lovely mother:** Hemingway knew Adriana's mother, Dora, and she and Adriana were guests of the Hemingways in Cuba from October 1950 to January 1951, until they received word of a scandalous article in a French periodical that suggested Hemingway's improper relationship with her daughter and her friend, Afdera Franchetti, was the inspiration behind *Across the River and into the Trees*. See Ivancich, "I Am Hemingway's Renata" (265n38).

94:10 **Did you ever have a daughter?** It is unclear whether Cantwell ever had a child at all. Furthermore, it is stunning that this major aspect of Cantwell's life would never have arisen in past conversation. Hemingway had three sons—Jack (1923–2000), Patrick (b. 1928), and Gregory (1931–2001)—and no daughters.

Particularly when anticipating a discussion of incest, Renata's question also recalls Quentin Compson's question to Dalton Ames in William Faulkner's *The Sound and the Fury* (1929): "Did you ever have a sister?" (92), which becomes a haunting refrain that Quentin poses to the other men in his and his sister's life.

94:11 **I always wanted one:** It is part of the Hemingway mythology that his entire life he desperately wanted a daughter. Although he cites no evidence, biographer Jeffrey Meyers asserts that Hemingway "always desired a daughter" (*Hemingway* 244).

Bernice Kert refers to an incident in which Hemingway cradled the young daughter of an Argentinian pilot and expressed his "longing for a daughter" (362). Martha's unwillingness to bear his child and Mary's inability following her ectopic pregnancy made this dream an impossibility.

Soon after this reference and elsewhere, however, Cantwell's wish is to marry Renata and "have five sons" (see entry at 95:4), a curious contradiction.

Aaron Latham writes, "He had hoped to have a daughter but never did and so began calling younger women, including his wife, 'Daughter'" (8). In a rather defensive letter to Malcolm Cowley on 25 April 1949, he defended his use of the word, in reaction to Cowley's recent depiction in *Life* magazine:

> I don't go around trying to be everybody's father even if Life knows I do. I've called girls daughter since I can remember. You say it in Spanish or in Ojibwa (Chippewa) or in Cheyenne to anybody females from kids, to whores, to Countesses or Duchesses or, with me, to any woman but that does not mean you want to be their father except that usually, or 90 percent of the time, they are in love with their father and it is as good approach as any. (JFK, Outgoing Correspondence)

Cowley, whose profile had referred to Hemingway as "grizzled and paternal" ("Portrait" 35), writes, "Sometimes his friends describe him as having a papa complex, which they explain, is exactly the opposite of a father complex. Instead of seeking for a substitute father to support and protect him, he keeps trying to protect and lay plans for others . . . he talks to them as if he were ninety years wise instead of only forty-nine" (41). Reviewers would level a virtually identical charge against Cantwell.

Meyers also points out that had Gregory been a daughter, "as both he and Pauline desired" (*Hemingway* 441), she would have been virtually the same age as Adriana Ivancich.

94:18 voice was thickened: This discussion of sexuality and daughterhood and incest inspires the same signifier—the thickening of the throat—that is so prominent in *For Whom the Bell Tolls*. On this topic, Carl P. Eby presents a thorough case about Hemingway's use of throat swelling as an indicator of sexual excitement, in which he is often "choked with desire" (*Fetishism* 41).

95:4 five sons: Cantwell introduces a strange motif, to recur five times (105:21, 108:9, 113:7, 167:19, 210:2). Rather than understand this comment as a literal wish, it seems Cantwell is longing for a legacy, for permanence to his relationship with Renata, as he intuits time is expiring. As inscrutable as the recurrence of "five sons" may be, the notion does operate within a religious, mythical, and classical tradition of patriarchy. In the biblical tradition, Shem is the father of five sons, who were credited with forming five nations, which is consistent with Cantwell sending his progeny off to the five corners of the world (95:6–7). Gawain is also one of five sons. In Walt Whitman's (1819–1892) "I Sing the Body Electric," he writes, "I knew a man, a common farmer, the father of five sons, / And in them the fathers of sons, and in them the fathers of sons" (ll. 33–34). See also Abraham Lincoln's famous 1864 letter to Lydia Bixby regarding the loss of her five sons in war, a historical antecedent to *Saving Private Ryan*.

This suggestion also picks up on the five brothers whom the boatman lost on the Isonzo (51:7–9).

95:26 **I want to be the moon, too:** Renata's association with the moon prefigures her inconveniently timed menstruation. She will later say, "I'll be the moon" (95:31). As chapter 11 closes, Cantwell tells Renata, "I don't care about our losses because the moon is our mother and our father" (109:19–21). He explains to her that lobsters become full as the moon does, so the lobster they order at the Gritti is large like the moon (112:10). When talking about the waves at Mont-Saint-Michel, he thinks "the hours of the tides change each day with the moon" (240:7–8).

95:30 **Only that's an airplane:** Cantwell cannot restrain himself from pointing out that the Lockheed-049 Constellation was a World War II aircraft, followed by subsequent updates to the Constellation series.

96:7–8 **get killed sometime:** Cantwell upbraids himself for losing his soldier's vigilance and is quite optimistic to believe that he will die from carelessness, rather than imminent heart failure. The theme of concentration and distraction is a central one in Hemingway's work, one that forms the central tension to perhaps his greatest short story, "Big Two-Hearted River." Cantwell's gloss that distraction "is a form of concentration" (96:9) is deft, a beautiful and accurate assertion; to be distracted is just to concentrate on the wrong thing, the inconvenient or inefficient or untimely thing. Cantwell tells Renata, "I'm not lonely when I'm working. I have to think too hard to ever be lonely" (99:29–30), an apt statement about his powers of concentration.

He also remarks when his "attention has been faulty again" (108:12–13), distracted by Renata's face and not focusing on her body. After his thoughts distract him from witnessing the street scenes on the way to the market on Saturday morning, he laments, "Hardly noticing is bad" (176:19).

96:32 **super Montgomerys:** A super Montgomery is garnished with a garlic olive. (See Boreth 95, 189–90).

NOTES

1. The Thunderbolt P-47 was made in Evansville, Indiana, just like this book.
2. The full list of named characters is Cantwell, Renata, Arnaldo, Andrea, Jackson, Burnham, Enrico, Ettore, Contessa Dandolo, Alvarito, Wes, Cipriani, Giorgio, Domenico, Emily, and the *Gran Maestro*.
3. The words are not exactly Hemingway's; I have translated Adriana's translation of Hemingway's original letter of 1 October 1952. All quotes from *La torre bianca* are my translations.
4. Wylder alludes to Robert W. Lewis agreeing with him, although he never cites a source. Lewis later recanted (Russo 793n32).

CHAPTER 10

98:1–2 **the right side of the street that led to the Gritti:** Renata and the Colonel are walking on Calle Larga XXII Marzo, which becomes Calle delle Ostreghe. The walk from Harry's Bar to the Gritti should take less than ten minutes, even for a man with a bad heart who is laying more than a dozen drinks. The street XXII Marzo, or March 22 is so named because of a historic victory in Italy's independence in 1848, culminating the so-called Five Days of Milan, in which Milan was liberated from the Austrian empire. It is thus fitting that although Cantwell does not name the street, which carries historical and thematic resonance, he does refer to it.

98:2–4 **The wind . . . about her face:** This two-sentence prose sequence is a flash of classic Hemingway, with a pitch-perfect repetition; the wind "blew the girl's hair forward" (98:3) and then, parting her hair, "blew it forward about her face" (98:4). This kind of care in the variation of language in its precision—long Hemingway's style—is not a trademark of this novel.

98:6 **jewelry shop:** Although Cantwell does not name the shop, he is referring to Codognato's jewelry store, a favorite of the Hemingways, which is not far from Harry's Bar at 1295 San Marco. Mary refers to a day in March 1949 during which she "paused on the way home as usual to inspect the jewelry in Codognato's window" ("Harry's Bar" 62). According to Zorzi and Moriani, Codognato is renowned for its "moretti" (31), the Venetian brooches of the kind that Cantwell gives to Renata. Adriana Ivancich mentions Codognato in *La torre bianca*, recalling that she never revealed to Hemingway her longing for the beautiful jewels (27).

Cantwell will think that he and Renata must go to the "jewelry place" (235:27), which they will at the beginning of chapter 36 (237:1–2).

98:15 **PX:** The abbreviation for "post exchange," the store available on army posts.

98:18 **presents of hard stones:** This phrase is a clear allusion to the classic study of Venice, John Ruskin's *The Stones of Venice* (1851–53), his three-volume treatise on Venetian art and architecture. No evidence exists that Hemingway ever owned or read Ruskin's magnum opus, although Hemingway does allude to him in "In Harry's Bar in Venice," his humorous spoken-word piece.

Beyond the allusion to Ruskin, the present of the stones for Renata serves as a counterpoint to the portrait Renata will give Cantwell. The stones continue as a theme, reified by Renata's "square emeralds" (99:2–3), family heirlooms she gives to Cantwell (100:12–13) so he will have a piece of her with him at all times. They immediately become a fetish object, as in the close of this chapter, when Renata derives pleasure from telling Cantwell to touch the emeralds in his pocket, and he, too, finds that "They feel wonderful" (101:6). She twice tells Cantwell to feel inside his right pocket (103:23, 103:30). Her instruction changes when she requests of him, "tell me how *you* feel" (111:33, emphasis added). And instead of describing the emeralds as feeling wonderful, he responds by saying that he feels "Wonderful" (112:2) and then that the emeralds "feel wonderful" (112:32). She asks him to feel the stones again (125:5–6), and he does (125:8–11).

Cantwell believes that the stones are "not worth more than a quarter of a million" (154:24–25), but it is unclear whether he is exaggerating or has no idea about the actual value. He acknowledges having the "damned stones" (157:1); he buttons the stones in the "inside left pocket of his tunic" (169:10–11) and then tells Renata (182:25–26). He says the stones are put in a safe in "your name" (208:7), which he later repeats to her (238:19–20). As he catalogues his debts at the end of the novel, he will assert that she gave him the hard stones "which I returned" (267:14–15).

Although it is not necessary, these stones also reinforce the referent in the title, Stonewall Jackson, so that the stones of Venice and a modern evocation of Stonewall coincide. According to Michael Reynolds, D'Annunzio was given three stones by his muse, Eleonora Duse (*Final Years* 212).[1]

99:2 on Army pay: In October 1949, Cantwell would receive an 0–5 pay scale as a colonel and with his lengthy service receive $584.26 a month, just over $7,000 a year.[2] In chapter 11, the lobster Renata wants would cost the *Gran Maestro* a week's pay (103:26) but Cantwell only a day's pay (103:29). As the novel ends, Cantwell wishes that he could bequeath Renata his "retired Colonel's pay" (267:12), as he seems to be leaning toward retirement.

100:10–11 for better or for worse: Cantwell here invokes the marriage ceremony in the *Book of Common Prayer*: "to have and to hold from this day forward, for better for worse, for richer for poorer, in sickness and in health" (279). Cantwell will also say, "For better or for much worse" (157:8–9), as well as "for better or worse, or something, or something awful" (168:10–11). When Cantwell wonders why he cannot "have her and love her and cherish her" (167:18), he is also conjuring up the phrase from the marriage vows from the *Book of Common Prayer*: "to love and to cherish" (279). As Cantwell concludes his catalogue of debts in the second-to-last chapter, he thinks,

"With all my worldly goods I thee endow" (267:13), also citing the same chapter, the "Solemnization of Matrimony." In *For Whom the Bell Tolls,* Hemingway puts forth a wry Freudian slip: "For better and for worse. In sickness and in death" (168).

100:17 **surly**: Renata accuses Cantwell of the same attribute—surliness—of which Cantwell accused the poler (12:31).

100:22 **that small Negro with the ebony face**: The *moretto* is a Venetian tradition, of the kind that Codognato sells (see entry for 98:6). This gift would also bring to mind Othello the Moor and deepen this novel's association with the literary and cultural traditions of Venice, just as do the earlier allusions to Ruskin and to XXII Marzo. The thread of this narrative continues (244:1–4, 244:13–15, 244:19–21, 246:2, 267:4–6). She gives him the portrait; he gives her the Moor. It is described as "carved in ebony with his fine features, and his jeweled turban" (231:4–5). They examine two heads and torsos "carved in ebony and adorned with studded jewels" (237:3–4).

100:29 **No. Give it to me**: Although Renata is generally accused of being reverential and obsequious, she is often assertive in conversation with Cantwell, as she is during their sexual encounter in chapter 13. In this short chapter, she insists that he take the emeralds (100:5) and then thank her (100:12), and then she asks for the small ebony Moor as a pin (100:22) and instructs Cantwell about when to give it to her (100:29). Later, she will correct him about how to bargain with the store owner (237:14–15) and then where they will get the money (238:13).

In chapter 11, too, during some of Cantwell's rough joking, she refutes him repeatedly (104:8, 104:12, 104:16), showing a forcefulness that readers of the novel rarely remark upon. By all accounts, Adriana was not shy about speaking her mind, even telling Hemingway that she disliked both *Across the River and into the Trees* and the character of Renata.

101:1 **twinge**: The third stated instance of twinges in the novel. See 77:14 and 77:23.

NOTES

1. See also Tintner (11), who reports that D'Annunzio tended to pawn Duse's gifts.
2. I have used "Historical Military Pay Rates," www.military.com, as a source.

CHAPTER 11

102:1–3 **They came in . . . :** Note the Hemingwayesque accumulation of prepositions: "came in" (l. 1); "out of the wind and cold" (l. 1); "through the main entrance" (ll. 1–2); "into the light and warmth" (ll. 2–3). Just as the novel's title will depend on the power of prepositional phrases, the reader must appreciate that Renata and Cantwell are "out of the wind and cold" that "lashed at them" (100:33) and have entered some kind of beatific "light and warmth" (102:2–3). The Gritti Palace is such a holy place for Cantwell that the mere unlocking of his hotel room door "was not a simple process, but a rite" (105:4–5).

102:17 **my Countess:** This is the only time the word "Countess" appears in the novel, strange, since an Italian maître d' hotel is speaking to an Italian woman. All other times, it is "contessa." One of Adriana's principal objections to this novel was the representation of someone of her refinement and breeding who drinks a lot—"to swallow one Martini after another like they were cherries" ("I Am Hemingway's Renata" 263)—and is promiscuous. As Renata says when visiting Cantwell in his hotel, "it is also known who my family are and that I am a good girl" (104:24–25). Renata does come from a wealthy, established family; later she will describe her family hosting the British ambassador (191:33).

103:4 **commence:** This slightly anachronistic verb may give Hemingway's prose biblical grandeur, but it also gives it linguistic authenticity. The Italian verb for "begin" is "cominciare," which would lend itself to a graceful transliteration of "commence."

103:11 **conscious of using the word:** As mentioned (see entry for 94:11), the appellation "Daughter" carries massive importance for Renata as well as Cantwell. Beyond the romantic and sexual excitement it has already been established that the word inspires, we also know Cantwell has never had the biological daughter he so desired, and we also know that Renata's own father was killed during or after the war, which would make a man calling her daughter fraught with emotion. Renata is a stand-in for the daughter Cantwell has always wanted; Cantwell is a stand-in for the father Renata has just lost. This line prefigures the tension when *Gran Maestro* refers to Renata as Daughter, to which Cantwell says, "I'm the one who calls her Daughter" (189:12). For her part, Adriana Ivancich rejected the notion that in Hemingway she was seeking a replacement for her late father. In her memoirs, she writes: "Perhaps one imagines that I wanted Hemingway to be as a father. Not so. My father was rigidly honest, absolute moral rectitude.... Hemingway belonged to another culture" (*La torre bianca* 141).

At another moment, when Cantwell pities Renata's inability to have sex with him, he calls her "poor Daughter" (106:3) and the narrator reports that "there was nothing dark about the word" (106:4), a curious remark: when does the word ever contain anything dark or ominous or negative? "Dark" seems to be a synonym for "sexual" in this instance, as the possibility for conventional intercourse is removed. Renata is incapable of having sex with Cantwell just as his ex-wife was biologically incapable of bearing a child, just as Jake was physically incapable in *The Sun Also Rises* and Catherine Barkley was ultimately incapable in *A Farewell to Arms*. In *For Whom the Bell Tolls*, Maria cannot have sex with Jordan due to pain resulting from being raped by Fascists.

At this moment, the narrator reports on the consciousness of three different characters at the same time, a subtle reminder that Cantwell's voice is the loudest and most frequent one, but it is not the only controlling perspective of the novel. This brief paragraph demonstrates that the narrator is actually omniscient, and the protagonist only swaggers that way.

103:18–19 **She said this in Italian:** In Fernanda Pivano's 1965 Italian translation of the novel—the only one ever published—she renders Renata's statement, "La maionese piuttosto dura" (Hemingway, *Di là dal fiume* 83).

103:22 *Ay hija mia:* "Oh my daughter." Cantwell dismisses Renata's concerns about the money as he again refers to her as Daughter, but this time in Spanish. He will also use the Spanish word on 244:9.

103:27 **TRUST:** As the narrator goes on to explain, TRUST was the Trieste United States Troops, a body of troops stationed in Trieste from 1947 to 1953, to maintain order in the free territory.

104:18 **comb my hair:** As is the case with many of the love interests of Hemingway's protagonists, Renata's hair becomes a continuing fixation in the novel. Cantwell asks Renata to grow her hair as long as it is in her portrait (137:30). He has a fantasy of her sleeping with her hair spread out on her pillow (167:2–3). When Renata enters the novel, "the carelessness the wind had made of her hair" is mentioned in the first sentence (78:31–32).

Renata is well aware of the excitement that her combing her hair inspires in Cantwell (107:31–108:27). She also bemoans combing her "too heavy hair" (113:4). Cantwell also fantasizes about Renata's hair on 167:1–9. During one of their final kisses in a Venice side alley, Renata and Cantwell kiss with her hair "beating silkily against both his cheeks" (239:15–16).

After the duck hunt that followed Hemingway's first meeting with Adriana, her hair was snarled from being in the rain, and Hemingway broke his comb in half and gave it to her as a present ("I Am Hemingway's Renata" 259, *La torre bianca* 13–14).

On Hemingway's thematic focus on hair in his work and life, see Eby's book-length study, *Hemingway's Fetishism*, which shows how this interest is present in virtually all of Hemingway's work.

105:19 **"Oh," . . . Then, "Oh."** The "Then" in between the "Oh"s in this line, in Hemingway's work, typically implies the omission of something, an action or behavior that is being elided from the description. See two instances in *The Sun Also Rises* where something sexual is effaced by such a phrase (61, 62).

105:20 **We owe nothing:** This fairly wretched pun on the homophones "oh" and "owe" is particularly clumsy and distracting given that Renata and Cantwell have begun a sexual encounter.

105:25–26 **the buttons of your uniform:** That Renata is pained by Cantwell's aspect of being an officer, yet simultaneously aroused, is captured by this request (see also 106:8–9, 201:19).

105:27–28 **I have a disappointment:** In the classic Hemingway style of omission, Renata is implicit in her disappointment, which suggests that she is menstruating and will be unable or unwilling to have sexual intercourse. In Othello's phrase, it is "the very error of the moon" (5.2.118). In *For Whom the Bell Tolls,* Maria uses a similar phrase to tell Robert Jordan that she is unable to have intercourse: "I do not wish to disappoint thee but there is great soreness and much pain. . . . I am not good to receive thee as I wish to" (341). As Maria indicates, of course, her reason is different from Renata's.

Since Renata is not as explicit, Hemingway is inviting us to speculate on the other possibilities. Could she be pregnant? Cantwell's response is telling: "You are positive" (106:1), a phrasing one would associate with a pregnancy rather than a period (Wylder 188, Lewis).[1] Could she also be expressing disappointment that she is menstruating and thus is not pregnant with the child for which Cantwell might have hoped?

Comley and Scholes conclude think similarly, believing, "we must assume . . . that she has her period" (68). In the manuscript, this oblique moment reads: "'And the famous hay,' she said. 'You remember the famous hay that was in the Noel Coward play? I cannot go to the famous hay now.'" Renata here refers to *Hay Fever*, Coward's 1925 play. In Henry Reed's contemporary review of *Across the River and into the Trees* in the *Listener*, he refers to Renata's "transitory physical condition" (515), a vague description of a vague Hemingway indirection. The general critical consensus is that Renata is on her period, but nobody is confident about it, and critics seem anxious to change the subject as quickly as possible.

Fittingly, Cantwell compares this instance to receiving bad news on the battlefield (105:31–33). Cantwell's inability to have sexual intercourse with Renata—at least conventionally—on their last encounter forces Renata to conclude, "we don't have too much luck do we?" (106:23–24). Robert Jordan also laments the bad luck: "it was not good luck for the last night" (*FWBT* 341).

107:12 **guele or a façade** A "*gueule*" is the snout of an animal or the mug of a face; "*façade*" literally means frontage or face. Cantwell tends to associate himself with both animals and monuments or buildings.

107:15 **what an ugly man:** Cantwell's self-assessment echoes a similar moment of looking in the mirror, but his criticism has escalated from "An ugly face" (75:26) to "what an ugly man," a harsh thing to say or think about oneself. The narrator continues in the subsequent paragraph with flattering remarks about Cantwell's face (107:16–20). After seeing himself in the mirror on Saturday morning, he calls himself "a beat-up, old looking bastard" (157:33), bemoaning that he must look at his face while he shaves.

107:22 **miserable:** The correct but unusual use of "miserable" as a noun may be a nod to Victor Hugo's epic novel, *Les Misérables* (1862). Hugo also wrote of the Veneto in his short play, *Angelo, Tyrant of Padua* (1835).

107:22 **Should we rejoin the ladies?** This non sequitur alludes to J. M. Barrie's one-act play, *Shall We Join the Ladies?* (1929), a drawing-room mystery, of which "And now, shall we join the ladies?" is the last line of dialogue (34). Sir James Matthew Barrie (1860–1937), Scottish writer, is more renowned as the author of *Peter Pan*.

107:27–28 **Où sont les neiges d'antan? Où sont les neiges d'autre fois? Dans le pissoir toute la chose comme ça.** The text—it seems like this is Cantwell's stream of consciousness—is invoking the refrain from the French writer François Villon's (1431–1463) poem, "Ballade des Dames du Temps Jadis" (Ballad of the ladies of times past), that asks, "Where are the snows of yesteryear?" This is a common touchstone in literature, praised in Hugo's *Les Misérables* as "so exquisite and so famous" (986) and serving as part of the conclusion of Umberto Eco's *The Name of*

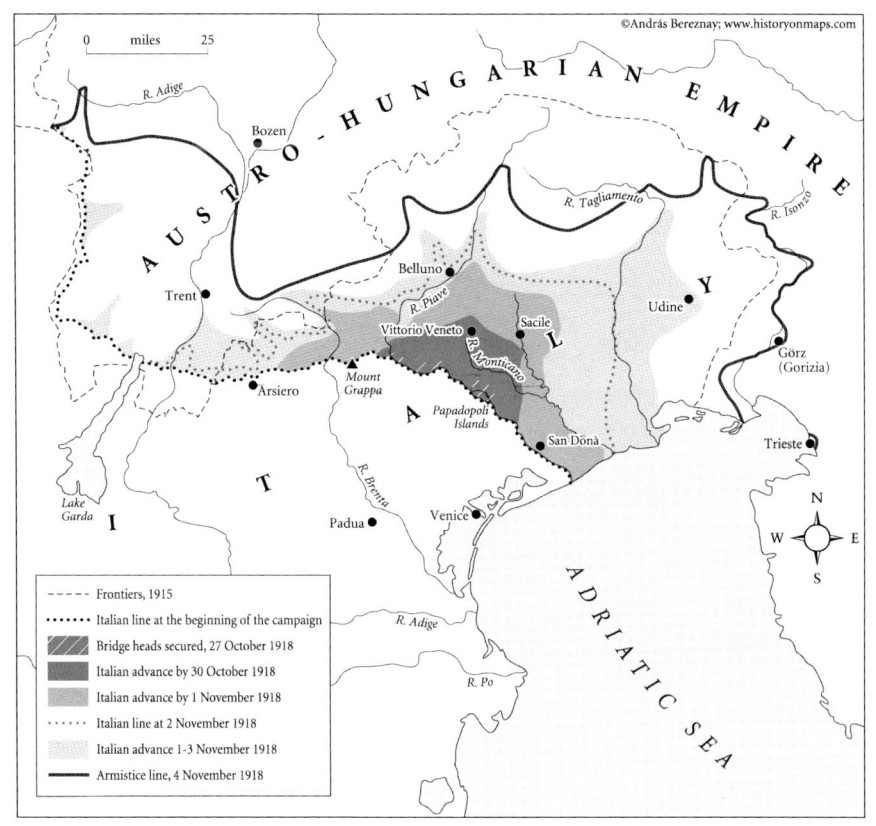

Colonel Cantwell served in the Battle of Vittorio Veneto, 24 October to 3 November 1918. This battle, a response to the devastating losses at Caporetto, was the great triumph for the Italians in World War I.

VENEZIA

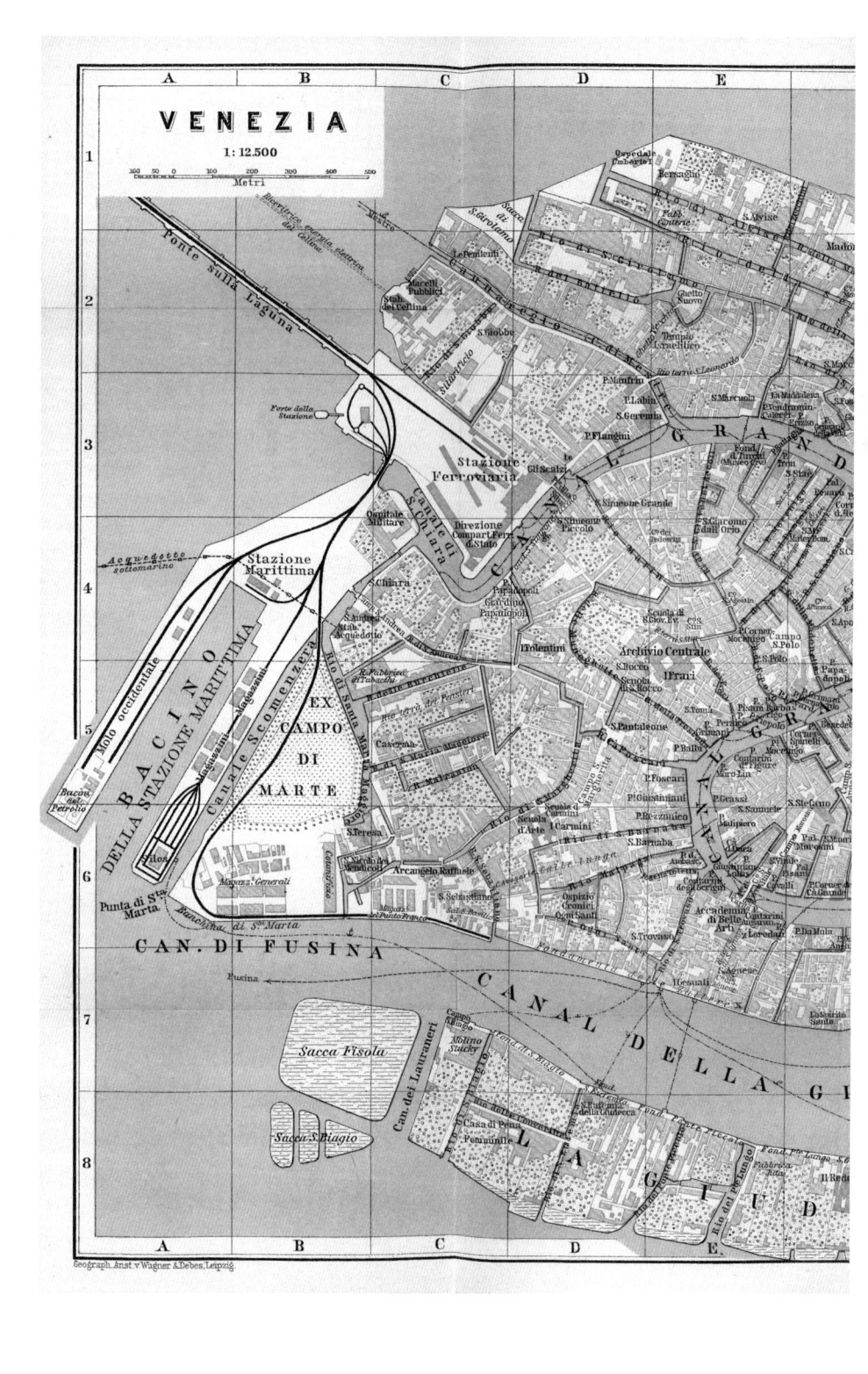

1 : 12.500

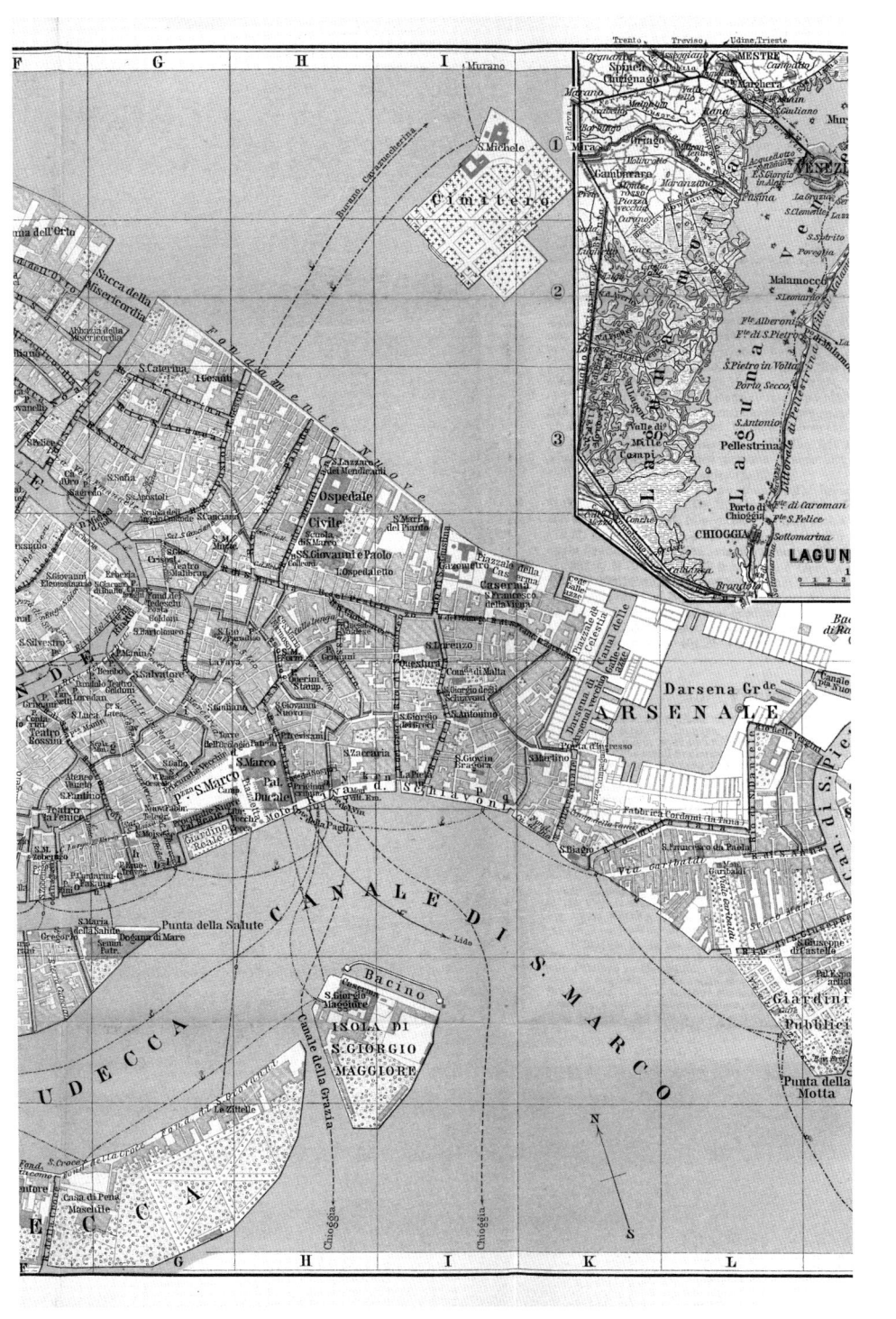

This map of Venice appeared in the 1909 edition of Baedeker's *Italy,* which Hemingway owned. In chapter 12, Colonel Cantwell criticizes a fellow American, the "pitted compatriot," for relying on Baedeker. As with most Hemingway heroes, Cantwell distinguishes between traveling like a tourist and enjoying the authentic experience.

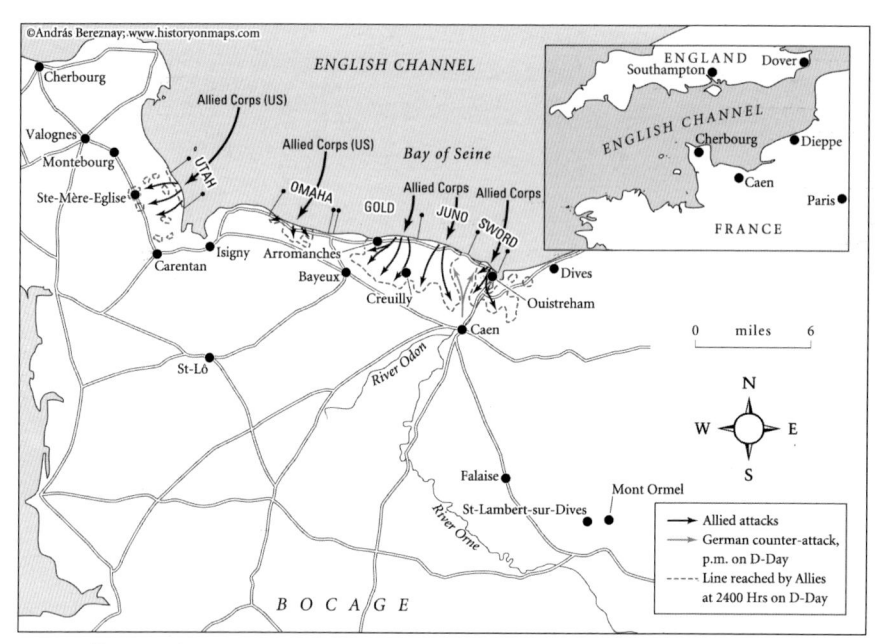

Cantwell's 4th Infantry Division served at the invasion of Normandy on 6 June 1944 and the breakthrough that followed.

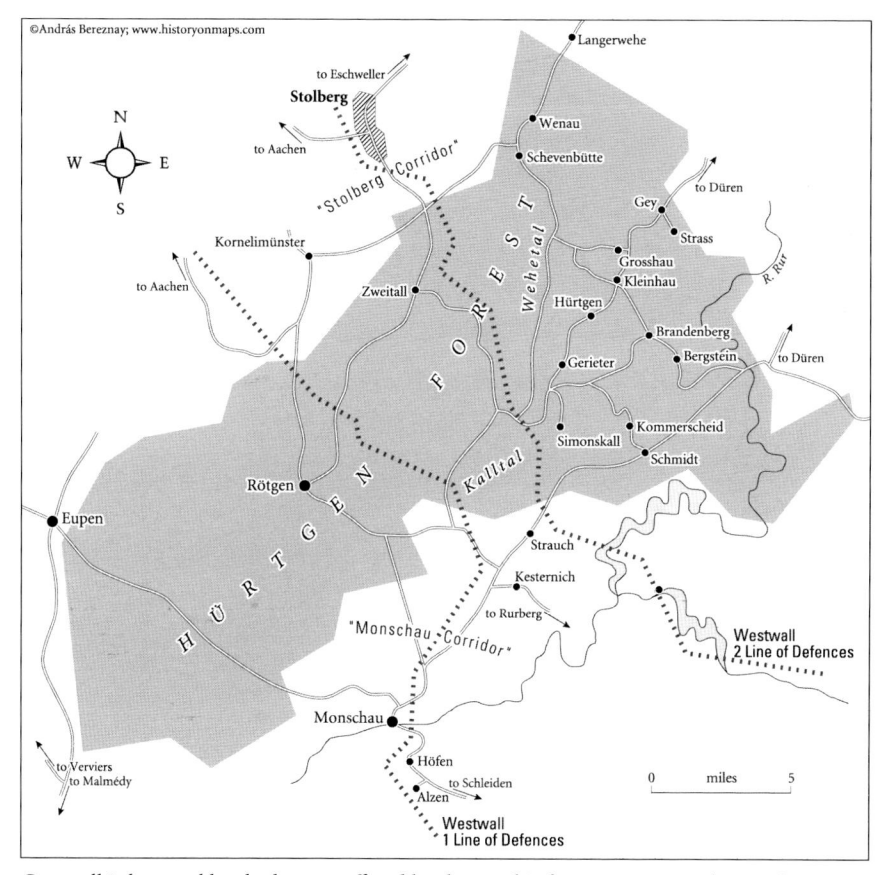

Cantwell is haunted by the losses suffered by the 22nd Infantry Regiment during the Battle of Hürtgen Forest, September to December 1944.

Adriana Ivancich, self-portrait in a bathroom mirror, 1954. Ivancich was the main inspiration behind Renata in *Across the River and into the Trees,* and designed the original book cover for Scribner's. (Ernest Hemingway Photograph Collection in the John F. Kennedy Presidential Library and Museum, Boston)

Adriana Ivancich poses in Venice, Italy, 1954. Hemingway admired Ivancich in profile; in the novel, Cantwell declares that Renata has a profile that "could break your, or any one else's heart." (Ernest Hemingway Photograph Collection in the John F. Kennedy Presidential Library and Museum, Boston)

Ernest Hemingway, Giuseppe Cipriani (owner of Harry's Bar), and server Ruggero Caumo at Harry's Bar, Venice in 1948. Cipriani appears in *Across the River and into the Trees* as the *Gran Maestro*. (Ernest Hemingway Photograph Collection in the John F. Kennedy Presidential Library and Museum, Boston)

the Rose (501). D. H. Lawrence impishly restates Villon's question when remarking on the elimination of the Native Americans in a chapter considering James Fenimore Cooper (40). Early in Tennessee Williams's *The Glass Menagerie,* the stage directions instruct "Ou sont les neiges" to be included as a legend on a screen (30), which later becomes "Ou sont les neiges d'antan?" (34).

After Villon's first sentence, Cantwell's response in French can be translated as "Where are the snows of other times? In the pisser like all other such things." In a 1919 letter to his father, Hemingway wrote that he had read Villon's *The Larger Testament* (*Letters 1,* 209).

107:29 **whose first name was Renata:** This articulation is a strange designation for the novel's sixth mention of the name Renata. Hemingway also uses awkward punctuation; a comma would be called for after "girl," or should be removed after "Renata."

Commentators have remarked on the thematic significance of the name Renata, as providing a "rebirth" for Cantwell. It is also notable that Renaissance painters and architects have occupied a fair presence in the setting of the novel. Hemingway also used the surname Bourne for the protagonist of his posthumously published *The Garden of Eden.*

In addition to the thematic resonance, Hemingway might have chosen Renata as a tribute to Renata Borgatti, with whom he and his first wife, Hadley, vacationed in Cortina d'Ampezzo in 1923. D'Annunzio's daughter, born in 1893, was named Eva Renata Adriana, the latter two names combining the fictional character along with her biographical namesake. D'Annunzio's daughter Renata also appears in his *Notturno.*

In the manuscript, Hemingway first names her Nicola, but then adds a question mark.

108:9 **All contours:** The manuscript has Renata saying, "Those two things" (JFK 1).

108:28 **Pablo Casals:** Casals (1876–1973), Catalan cellist and conductor, is one of the most celebrated cellists in history. He is particularly renowned for his recordings of Bach suites. Hemingway received at least one letter from Casals in the 1950s.

109:7 *sale métier*: French for "rotten job" or "dirty trade," as the manuscript originally put it and Renata eventually translates it (109:9). As ever, "he was a General again without thinking of it" explains the vulgar expression that Renata calls "rough" (109:5, 109:6). By "skinning a dead horse" (109:4), Cantwell is intending to praise Renata, since she is alive and a portrait will be no replacement.

Hemingway uses the same phrase in his short story of World War II, "Black Ass at the Cross Roads": "We were specialists in a dirty trade. In French we said, '*un métier très sale*'" (*CSS* 581).

109:17 **heart broken:** The romantic implications aside, this phrase is also a comment on the condition of Cantwell's actual heart. He later picks up on Renata's adjective "disheartening" (127:24), repeating it and then telling her, "you are not supposed to have a heart in this trade" (127:24–25). He will close chapter 41 by referring to his "lousy chicken heart. . . . bastard heart" (270:19–20), and he also asks Renata, "what if you haven't a heart, or your heart is worthless?" (112:26–27).

109:19 **devil:** Although this is the only time Cantwell will call Renata "devil," this epithet is used incessantly in Hemingway's posthumous novel *The Garden of Eden*. As Comley and Scholes point out, women in Hemingway narratives "become devils when they seduce their fall guys into sexual transgressions" (52).

NOTE

1. On Lewis, see chapter 9, note 4.

CHAPTER 12

110:2 **both his flanks covered:** Just as the bathroom in the Gritti is evaluated for its military soundness (107:2–3), Cantwell's instinct is to feel vulnerable if not protected, even in civilian life. See entry at 96:7–8.

110:16 **Georgie Patton:** Cantwell's mocking name for George Smith Patton Jr. (1885–1945), the notorious World War II general.

Cantwell fought in Normandy, where he and his army "made the break for Georgie Patton's armour to go through and held it open on both sides" (125:28–29). The Colonel uses Patton as an example of a fundamentally deceitful person (111:18–19), one of the Deceivers in his circles of hell.

Cantwell is implying that Patton cries insincerely. In Hemingway's unpublished "Indian Country and the White Army," tears shine in the protagonist's eyes "just like Georgie Patton could make them" (JFK 496B).

George C. Scott won the Academy Award for his portrayal of Patton in the 1970 film *Patton*. Scott would go on to play the protagonist of Hemingway's posthumous novel *Islands in the Stream* in the 1977 film version. His son, Campbell Scott, is virtuosic in a spoken-word performance of the 2006 Audioworks production of Hemingway's *For Whom the Bell Tolls*.

111:8 **Capri Bianco:** Cantwell bucks tradition by ordering a white wine from southern Italy, the isle of Capri. He compares its paleness and coldness to the wines of Greece, perhaps because of Capri Bianco's similar lineage to Greco Bianco wine. He then compares its body's fullness and loveliness to that of Renata. In *A Farewell to Arms*, this wine is a favorite of Frederic and Catherine. Hemingway and his first wife, Hadley, also share it during a vignette in *A Moveable Feast*.

111:21 **four times:** Is Cantwell referring to his four wives, or is Hemingway doing the same? Perhaps Cantwell is referring to untruths uttered to army officials? It is unclear. In fact, Cantwell asserts that his honesty while in the army impeded his promotions (111:28–29).

112:16 **Dalmatian coast:** The Dalmatian Coast, in current-day Croatia, is on the east of the Adriatic, just as Italy is on the west. The Ivanciches hailed from Dalmatia.

114:22, 23 **Quite rare . . . "** *Al sangue.* When Renata indicates that she wants her steak "quite rare," it echoes Cantwell's earlier opinion that a man who does not lie is "quite rare" (111:17). *Al sangue* is Italian for "rare"; *sangue* is Italian for "blood." The manuscript has the French word: *saignante.*

114:23 **as John said:** Although it is uncertain, if Cantwell is making a wildly allusive joke about John the Baptist, it is a crude reference, indeed.

114:24–25 ***Crudo, bleu,* or just make it very rare:** *Crudo* is Italian for "raw"; *bleu* is French for "raw" or "barely cooked."

115:2 **Valpolicella:** This oft-mentioned wine that originates in the province of Verona is first written of here. In his return to Italy in 1948, Valpolicella is a constant accompaniment to all of Hemingway's activities. Gianni Moriani's book of photographs depicts Hemingway touring the casks of Valpolicella (120).
 Cantwell also drinks Valpolicella before going to bed on Friday night (153:2–3, 155:1–2).

115:6 **thirty centesimi:** One centesimo is 1/100 of a lira; thirty centesimi would be less than six cents. See the entry at 172:2.

115:14 *fiamme nere:* Meaning "black flame," this insignia was worn on each lapel of the Arditi uniform, the special operations shock troops that were introduced in Italy in 1917. This emblem was also the designation of the 9th Battalion, which fought in the Grappa during World War I.

115:28 **who was a sub-lieutenant again now:** Rather than lapsing into the identity of a general or a colonel, Cantwell becomes the young soldier that he was during the Battle of the Piave in World War I, when he served alongside the *Gran Maestro.* As Hemingway tends to write, Cantwell "sat thinking" (115:30) but unlike Hemingway's traditional technique of omission, in this instance he soon tells us the content of the memory.

115:31–32 **massif of Grappa with Assalone and Pertica and the hill I do not remember the name of on the right:** Cantwell refers to Monte Asolone and Monte Pertica and has failed to recall Monte Tomba; these are the three peaks of the Grappa, where the Italian army was forced to hold its line during the Battle of Vittorio Veneto in October 1918. The battle on Asolone occurred from December 1917 through January 1918

(Russo 421). This location is also mentioned in "The Snows of Kilimanjaro," where Harry remembers speaking with an Austrian about "*the fighting on Pasubio and of the attack on Perticara and Asalone*" (*CSS* 42, emphasis in original).

See the similar phrasing in *A Farewell to Arms,* in which Frederic Henry mentions three villages: "Chernex, Fontanivent, and the other I forget" (291).

Cantwell refers to himself as "a Basso Piave boy and a Grappa boy straight here from Pertica" (151:9–10). In a 1925 letter, Hemingway tells a friend that he "Would like to be in Venice and get a little romantic fucking and Compari's [sic] and get a meal and a real bed to sleep in at the best hotel I know in Vicenza . . . and go up to Grappa and Monte Pertica and Asalone and climb—how swell it is that there isn't a war on" (*SL* 169–70).[1]

116:14 **Erwin Rommel:** Erwin Johannes Eugen Rommel (1891–1944), known as the "Desert Fox," fought on the Italian front during World War I and served as the German field marshal during World War II. Hemingway's close friend from World War I, Eric "Chink" Dorman-Smith, served as Auchinleck's chief of staff and played a major role in engineering Rommel's defeat in North Africa. For a discussion of parallels between Smith's career and demotion and Cantwell's, see Meyers, "Chink Dorman-Smith."

Rommel has won Cantwell's respect, even as an adversary when he fought in the Battle of Caporetto, which he considered a high point of his military career (Macdonald with Cimprić 169). Rommel committed suicide to avoid a military court hearing regarding his involvement in a plot to kill Hitler. When Cantwell recalls that he and Rommel "used to ski together" (116:20–21), it echoes the italicized reverie in "The Snows of Kilimanjaro," in which the dying writer Harry has a memory of "*the same Austrians they killed then that he skied with later*" (*CSS* 42, emphasis in original).

Adriana's brother Gianfranco fought with Rommel in the tank corps in North Africa, before being wounded in the autumn of 1942 (Kert 437). Hemingway mentions this connection in *The Dangerous Summer* (45).

By saying "halfway from Cortina to Grappa" (116:14–15), Cantwell is referencing the Battle of Vittorio Veneto. Later, he declares that Rommel would understand one of his military riffs (212:4). See also 229:2–3. Rommel is quoted as saying that besides victory, "All the rest is cabbage" (263:13).

116:23 **Ernst Udet:** Colonel General Ernst Udet (1896–1941) was a German flying ace in World War I, ranking second to the Red Baron. He is mentioned favorably, along with Rommel (also on 212:8, 229:3). Like Hemingway, he died from a self-inflicted gunshot.

116:27–28 **killed my father and burned our villa on the Brenta:** The Brenta is a river that runs from Trentino into the Adriatic, south of the Venetian lagoon (see

40:6–7). Renata's reference invites a link to Adriana's biography; Carlo Ivancich was murdered on 12 June 1945, most likely by political enemies. In Adriana's memoirs, she refers to "extremist elements" who killed him (*La torre bianca* 140), those who feared that Carlo knew of corruption during the war. Therefore, Adriana suggests not that Germans killed her father, but rather Italians seeking to protect themselves and to ascend in the postwar power vacuum.

117:1 **One hundred and twenty-two sures:** Cantwell's claim that he killed 122 men is precisely identical to Hemingway's assertions of this time, which are almost certainly exaggerated. Michael Reynolds, Hemingway's principal biographer, concludes that the number of Hemingway's alleged victims "increased in direct ratio to his drinking" (*Final Years* 154). In an 11 August 1949 letter to William Seward, a college professor, Hemingway cited 122 victims (qtd. in Reynolds, *Final Years* 205). In a 2 May 1950 letter to Chink Dorman-Smith, he wrote: "I have it completely and accurate and straight now that have killed 122 (armeds not counting possible or necessary shootings)" (qtd. in Reynolds, *Final Years* 222). In a 2 June 1950 letter to Fitzgerald biographer Arthur Mizener, Hemingway wrote, "I . . . have killed 122 sures beside the possibles" (*SL* 697). He repeats the claim to Charles Scribner a month later (*SL* 702), as he does elsewhere in letters during spring 1950, claiming the same number of 122 when writing to journalist Lillian Ross and to actress Marlene Dietrich. Hemingway's brother Leicester stated, "Any number in excess of a hundred is really putting a little gloss on it" (qtd. in Brian 161). Hemingway's son John declared noncommittally, "I suspect he killed some" (qtd. in Brian 161). Whatever the facts may be, it is certainly telling that Hemingway and Cantwell share the exact number: 122; Cantwell, a soldier in two world wars, and Hemingway, a writer, journalist, and volunteer for the Red Cross.

In the manuscript, the one-word sentence "Armeds." follows this phrase.

Islands in the Stream mentions the Florida island of Bahia Honda, "where they had shot one hundred and twenty-two American volunteers" (241).

118:7 **everywhere in Baedeker:** Sinclair Lewis actually did travel with the Baedeker guidebook, even, as his biographer puts it, using it "as his docent" (Lingeman 530). See T. S. Eliot's 1920 poem, "Burbank with a Baedeker: Bleistein with a Cigar," which mentions the Rialto. Eliot's poem also quotes from an inscription on Mantegna's "St. Sebastian" (circa 1490), Henry James's *The Aspern Papers* (1888), *Othello* (1603), Robert Browning's "A Toccata of Galuppi's" (1855), and Théophile Gautier's "Sur les Lagunes," all literature or art set in Venice.

It should be observed that these rather superficial putdowns of the pitted compatriot—his Italian is poor; he is condescending; he uses a Baedeker guide; and he eats and drinks ignorantly—are the opposites of qualities Cantwell prizes in himself: he can enjoy Venice as does a native, he is an expert at the dinner table and a polyglot, and he is less condescending to others, certainly to the wait staff at the bar and hotel, whom he has befriended.

Furthermore, Cantwell accuses his pitted compatriot of being undiscerning and unselective when writing, the exact charge that would redound onto Hemingway so ferociously following *Across the River and into the Trees*.

Renata continues the association with Baedeker on 120:13. The *Gran Maestro* refers to the pitted compatriot's lady as "Miss Baedeker" on 248:20.

Hemingway had Baedeker volumes for the Austria region, Italy, and Spain (Brasch and Sigman 59).

118:24 **Can you tell me anything about the war?** If the novel's dialogue suffers from one weakness, it is the tendency of the secondary characters to interview Cantwell, rather than to engage more equally with him, to challenge him, surprise him, or possibly even to be questioned by him. When Renata says, for instance, "if I may ask" (195:26), it reinforces the notion of an entirely Socratic dialogue structure. She asks Cantwell if he will tell him about the war for her "education" (199:17). So, Cantwell is the teacher and Renata is the eager pupil.

Even the staunchest supporter of Hemingway's craft in this novel would concede that the action was sputtering and Renata's questions invited many pages of Cantwell's memories.

One reasonable explanation for this mode of questioning is that Renata senses that Cantwell is in need of purgation—both a psychic and spiritual catharsis—before he dies, and she constantly seeks to take his confessional with her benign, often vapid prompts. For Renata, "tell me" is an insistent refrain. In addition to this instance, she asks Cantwell to tell her about his erroneous decisions (91:5, 91:10), what a jerk is (93:29), how the emeralds in his pocket make him feel (111:33), if he fought a lot (116:13), the previous war (125:17), when he was a general (128:18), his heart condition (130:19), any anecdote about the war (131:11), true things about fighting (133:7), "more true episodes" about fighting (134:26), Paris (146:25, 147:11, 200:13), and so on.

The complaint that Cantwell is engaged in an extended "interview" with Renata is true, but the real problem rests in the skill of the questioner. For instance:

"Did you fight much? I know you did. But tell me."	(116:10)
"Can you tell me anything about the war?"	(118:24)
"Tell me about the last war . . ."	(125:17)
"Tell me about when you were a General . . ."	(128:18)
"Could you tell me any anecdotes . . . ?"	(131:8)
"Tell me some true things about fighting . . ."	(133:7)
"tell me more true episodes later . . ."	(134:26–27)
"tell me some true things about Paris . . ."	(146:25)

| "Will you tell me some happy things I can have for during the week and some more of war for my education?" | (199:16–17) |
| "Please tell me some picturesque..." | (201:4) |

Renata asks, "Please tell me" eight different times. However, this supplication does have an interesting trajectory: her reason for asking questions changes dramatically as the novel progresses. She asks him to tell her about his decisions so that she might "share in your sad trade" (91:6). In the same way, she asks him to tell her about Paris and the loss of his regiment, so she might experience it vicariously (146:26–27, 211:19–20). She then asks for "happy things" she can savor during their week apart and also war anecdotes "for my education" (199:17). Renata's motivation then emerges less as adoring idolatry than benevolent friendship: she tells Cantwell that he should tell her "as true as you can, without hurting yourself in any way" (207:1–2), which implies that she thinks he needs to say these things for his own good. Soon after, she tells Cantwell, "tell me true until you are purged of it" (207:8), suggesting that through this facade of obsequiousness, she is actually coaxing a spiritual catharsis from him. She tells him that he needn't talk about the day of the Valhalla Express because "I know now it is not good for you" (207:22–23). As she states unequivocally: "I am not an inquisitor" (207:24). "Don't you see," she assures him, "you need to tell me things to purge your bitterness" (220:2–3). During the story of the breakthrough, Cantwell "was not lecturing; he was confessing" (204:22–23). As an argument for Renata's savvy in drawing out Cantwell's anecdotes as part psychoanalyst, part priestess, part drinking buddy, Cantwell expels his bitterness and remorse to a willing listener and an understanding ear.

See entry at 22:31 for further discussion.

118:27 What was General Eisenhower like? Dwight David Eisenhower (1890–1969) was a five-star general in the United States Army and the supreme commander of the Allied Forces in Europe. As Cantwell predicts (215:6), he became the thirty-fourth U.S. president, serving from 1953–1961.

In his 11 September 1950 *Time* magazine interview, Hemingway, responding in the third person, declared, "Hemingway has no opinion in regard to General Eisenhower except that he is an extremely able administrator and an excellent politician" ("Hemingway Is Bitter about Nobody" 110). Cantwell also damns Eisenhower with the identically faint praise: "excellent politician.... Very able at it" (118:30). Earlier, Hemingway was more complimentary. In July 1945, he wrote to Maxwell Perkins that Ike "has a hell of a good head and is a fine man.... a good man and a fairly good general" (*SL* 595).

In the manuscript, Cantwell elaborates on his criticism, claiming that Eisenhower was "complicated by someone named Kay Summersby," a reference to the secretary with whom he allegedly had an affair. Further, he is called an "excelent [sic] politician" and a "mediocre general" who "Never fought in his life" (JFK 1). In a 1950 letter to Chink Dorman-Smith, Hemingway asserted, "You can't be a good fighter and a good politician" (qtd. in Greacen, "Letters from Cuba" 10)

118:28 **Strictly the Epworth League:** Epworth League refers to a church youth group, associated with the Methodist Church.

118:32 **Let us not name them:** Just as Cantwell later says he will "not name names" (216:30), what is left out in the published novel is revealed in the manuscript, in which he has written, "I will name names." In this case, Cantwell criticizes General Walter Bedell Smith (1895–1961), Eisenhower's chief of staff at SHAEF, for being dishonest and for never having fought in his life. In fact, Smith was wounded near Chouy, France, during World War I on 18 July 1918, just ten days after Hemingway was wounded. Smith's "combat career," his biographer writes, lasted "less than thirty-six hours" (Crosswell 132).

119:1 **Rotary Club:** The Rotary International, or the Rotary Club, is a humanitarian organization that was founded in 1905. The Rotarians encourage service as a fundamental to their charge. In Gertrude Stein's *The Autobiography of Alice B. Toklas* (1933), Hemingway is characterized as being "ninety percent Rotarian" (207).

119:6 **Bradley:** Praised as a "good one," General Omar Nelson Bradley (1893–1981) was a United States Army field commander in North Africa and Europe during World War II. According to Hemingway's son Patrick, Hemingway received a Christmas card from Omar Bradley every year after the war. "After the war, I had to listen to endless discussions with members of the 4th Infantry Division and my father. He was revered by these people" (Kendall). Bradley's designation as a "schoolmaster" refers to his position as a teacher at West Point; Bradley was an exemplary student and was also the son of a schoolteacher.

119:7 **Lightning Joe:** This moniker refers to Joseph Lawton Collins (1896–1987), another general in the United States Army. In World War II, he served in both the Pacific and European Theaters of Operation. He earned the name "Lightning" for his aggressive, efficient style and also because it was his division's codename (Weigley 100). Collins was in command of the VII Corps during the D-Day invasion of Utah Beach on 6 June 1944. His corps "then spearheaded the breakthrough east of Saint-Lô, participated in closing the Falaise Gap, drove north into Belgium, broke through the Siegfried Line defenses, and captured Aachen" (Wade 2), precisely Cantwell's experiences.

Hemingway wrote Collins on 19 August 1949 to congratulate him on his appointment to chief of staff of the United States Army three days earlier, asserting that he would "be happy to serve under you in any capacity (preferably not one which involves writing) at any time, anywhere, and against any enemies of our country" (JFK, Outgoing Correspondence, 1949). Collins served until 1953.

Cantwell will again refer to Collins when discussing the taking of Cherbourg (203:10).

119:23 But he beat General Rommel: Renata's assertion that Montgomery beat Rommel is a controversial one, disputed even in Omar Bradley's autobiography. Cantwell concurs with his American colleague. In the manuscript, Cantwell asks Renata rhetorically, "And you don't think Auchinleck softened him up?" (JFK 1), referring to the British commander Claude Auchinleck (1884–1981). Auchinleck's chief of operations was Hemingway's lifelong friend and one of the models for Cantwell, Chink Dorman-Smith.

119:27 three to four against one: According to Mark Thompson's definitive study, "the Austrians were outnumbered almost three to one on the Carso" (221). Thompson then puts it at ten to four beginning in 1915 (279).

119:29–30 something over one hundred and forty thousand dead that year: In the Battle of the Piave, the Italians suffered about 80,000 dead or wounded. About 300,000 Italian casualties were suffered in the Battles of Isonzo. In 1915, about 150,000 Italians died. Roughly 650,000 Italians were killed in World War I.

119:32 It is such a sad science: Hemingway gives Renata a phrase that would much consume him after World War II. Hemingway told Lillian Ross that he was interested in the "godamn sad science of war" (51). Cantwell repeats this phrase (126:8) and then translates it loosely as the *"triste métier* of war" (231:3). In a 1949 letter to his son John, Hemingway writes in something of an awkward formulation, "I want you to make good very badly in this sad science that you are in" (*SL* 682).

The British writer Walter de la Mare (1873–1956) also uses this phrase in a long poem from 1933, "Dreams": "Let no sad Science thee suborn" (241), although there is no evidence that Hemingway ever read de la Mare.

120:22 she chewed well and solidly: A weird detail to notice and a weird way to describe it, but it contrasts Renata with the "chawing" of the pitted compatriot (117:33–118:1), who is three tables away from them at this point. E. B. White lampooned sentences like this one in his *New Yorker* piece: "She stepped into a public booth and dialed true and well, using her finger" (28).

120:26 "You," she said. "You." This line may not resonate according to Hemingway's intention, but it seems to be Renata's mock scolding of Cantwell's self deprecation.

121:3 **I've suggested it.** Cantwell is slyly referring to his marriage proposal (90:19, 95:4).

121:6–7 **chuck the army . . . retirement pay:** Cantwell decides to retire in Venice, committing to the city and to Renata rather than to future wars. As a marriage would be, Cantwell's retirement would be a symbolic gesture rather than a serious change of lifestyle, given the short time remaining in his life.

See also when Renata suggests that they could buy good Murano glass when he retires (133:20); also, Cantwell vows "I'm getting out of the business" (150:1–2). Cantwell's retirement pay would have been $619.88 a month (see entry at 49:3).

121:17 **Viterbo:** Viterbo is a town in central Italy, about fifty miles outside Rome, known for its medieval walls and gates, built in the eleventh and twelfth centuries.

At this point in the manuscript, Hemingway decides on the title. He writes: *Across the River and Into the Trees* and underlines it with a flourish. He capitalizes the "I" in "Into."

121:24 **the Pope:** The Pope (known in Italian as "Papa") at the time of composition of *Across the River and into the Trees* was Pope Pius XII (1876–1958), in office from 1939 until his death. The legacy of Pius XII's papacy is still debated, due to his perceived failure to condemn Nazi atrocities.

122:7 **some bare-assed hill where it was too rocky to dig:** Cantwell brings to mind the plight of the Italian soldiers on the Carso, forced to dig trenches into the mountain rock. The simile Cantwell is constructing compares the feeling of being loved to being protected at war, as opposed to being vulnerable. Cantwell's main rhetorical quirk is to compare aspects of civilian and romantic and sexual life to his war experiences to process it and vivify the emotion.

The bare-assed hill is where Cantwell received the wound to his hand (127:30). Cantwell will also recall a "bare-assed piece of hill" when describing the Battle of Hürtgen Forest (234:12).

122:10 **eighty-eights:** In World War II, The 88 mm gun was a German antiaircraft and antitank artillery gun (see 234:15).

122:18 **Barone Alvarito:** After previously having been mentioned as looking for Cantwell (56:27, 78:19) this pivotal secondary character first enters the novel at this point. Another member of the Order, designated as barone, he is modeled on the Baron Nanuk Franchetti, Hemingway's hunting friend. He is described as having a mysterious, shy smile and is "beautifully built" (122:22). Renata discloses their lifelong friendship; Alvarito, then, is about twenty-one years old (123:17). Nanuk Franchetti was born in 1929 (Meyers, *Hemingway* 628), which would have made him nineteen during the duck hunt of December 1948 and one year older than Adriana. In a bizarre comparison, Cantwell likens him to a "Bongo" (122:26), an antelope found in the dense forests of Central Africa. This odd compliment may also be invoking Byron, whose "favorite image of female desirability" was the antelope (Eisler 548).

Alvarito has many similarities to another young character admired by a Hemingway protagonist, Pedro Romero in *The Sun Also Rises*. The parallel becomes more convincing because just as Jake facilitates Pedro's dalliance with his love interest, Cantwell seems to do the same thing, albeit less explicitly.

Alvarito is the only one Cantwell believes is a better shot than him in Venice: "he's a kid and shoots faster" (268:26–27).

123:8–9 **meet at the Garage at two-thirty:** That is, Cantwell and Alvarito will meet the next afternoon—Saturday—at 2:30 P.M. in preparation to go hunting the morning after, Sunday. Cantwell will tell the concierge that the portrait of Renata should be packaged "for transport at noon tomorrow" (135:23–24).

123:28 *grand vin:* French for "grand wine." Although it has no official definition, it is a way to distinguish better wine from lesser offerings.

123:33 **Pinard:** Cheap, coarse, ordinary wine. One of Hemingway's fellow ambulance drivers in the American Red Cross, Richard T. Baum, was nicknamed "Pinard" (*SL* 89). When Hemingway was living in Paris, he wrote in a 4 August 1922 letter, "Dick Baum was in town. Very drunk!" (*Letters 1*, 348).

123:33 **Ritz:** The *Gran Maestro* is referring to the Hôtel Ritz Paris, considered one of the finest hotels in the world, where Hemingway stayed frequently. In fact, one of the bars in the hotel is named the *Bar Hemingway* in his honor. In *The Sun Also Rises,* Robert Cohn stands up his girlfriend, Frances Clyne, who then doesn't have the money to dine at the Ritz (53). Hemingway finished the draft of *Across the River and into the Trees* in the Ritz, where he stayed beginning late November 1949, often using hotel stationery for his writing.

124:11 *Chambertin:* A Burgundy wine, from the Grand Cru vineyard.

124:12 **use to drink:** As the first edition verifies, this line should be "used to drink."

124:14–15 **perfection for my money:** This attitude, so crucial to a reading of *The Sun Also Rises* and Jake's conversation with Count Mippipopolous, returns our focus to

Cantwell's demand for precision, accuracy, efficiency, and value. The Colonel does not mind spending money, time, or energy, but he refuses to waste it.

124:22 Something was going on in her mind: This paragraph suggests a connection between Renata and Alvarito that must be traced through the whole novel. It is stated through exposition rather than action or dialogue, so Hemingway is emphasizing the importance of this thread to the narrative. The iceberg principle of omission does much in *Across the River and into the Trees* to efface the history of Cantwell's demotion, but it does even more in maintaining the implicitness of the connection between Renata and Alvarito.

Renata reveals that she and Alvarito are roughly the same age and have been lifelong friends (123:16), that she can convince him to invite her to the hunting trip (133:27), that she was not asked on the hunting trip precisely because he did want her to come (185:15); this vague association becomes still more suggestive yet more prominent during Cantwell's circuitous exchange with Alvarito at the end of the novel (see entry at 275:15).

125:2 take it like a corn cob: Cantwell's indecorous comparison is that he would eat the cheese with the ferocity of eating corn on the cob.

125:27 only really difficult in Normandy: On 6 June 1944, Hemingway was present at the Allied invasion of Normandy as a noncombatant observer, covering the war for *Collier's*. See entry at 29:18.

125:33 St. Lo: Saint-Lô is the capital of the Manche department in Normandy. On 8 June, Allied forces bombed Saint-Lô in an effort to weaken the garrisoned German forces. After almost two weeks of attempting to capture Saint-Lô, General Bradley opted instead to put the Allied resources toward their Cherbourg objective (McManus 135).

126:4 Does this bore you? This rhetorical pattern continues, with Cantwell protesting that the war is not interesting, that it must be boring Renata, who, in response, always eggs him on. Each reader must judge whether she is genuinely fascinated by his lectures or is listening to his orations for his own psychic benefit, as a psychotherapist or priestess. Or we might also note that Renata is subtly gaining some benefit for herself, perhaps an increased knowledge of and intimacy with the man she loves, a vicarious thrill, and even erotic excitement.

See full discussion at 29:27.

126:23 people of Leclerc: "Leclerc" refers to Jacques-Philippe Leclerc (1902–1947), a French general during World War II. He was named marshal of France posthumously, in 1952, and in France is known as le maréchal Leclerc. Cantwell, always sensitive to people who gain undue credit or praise for other people's work, would be aware that Leclerc led his 2nd Armored Division into Paris following the U.S. 5th to receive Germany's surrender. Cantwell soon will describe delaying his entry into Paris so that Leclerc might lead the way (132:18–21). Cantwell later calls Leclerc "a high-born jerk" and "Very brave, very arrogant, and extremely ambitious" (200:22, 200:23–24). When Cantwell tells Renata, "He is dead," it will have been relatively recent news: Leclerc died 28 November 1947. In a June 1948 letter to a World War II general, Hemingway writes, "am glad that prick is dead" (*SL* 640). Hemingway met Leclerc, who dismissed him vulgarly—"*Buzz off, you unspeakables*" (qtd. in Baker, *Life Story* 413). Hemingway later commented that "a rude general is a nervous general" (*BL* 374), a withering, understated criticism.

Cantwell also tells Renata that Dante was "More conceited" than Leclerc and that Leclerc "could fight . . . Excellently" (201:12, 201:15).

126:23–24 **of the third or fourth water:** Cantwell uses a jeweler's term; "first water" refers to a pearl or jewel of the finest quality.

126:25 **Perrier-Jouët Brut 1942:** Perrier-Jouët is a champagne producer based in the Épernay region of Champagne. The house, founded in 1811 by Pierre-Nicolas-Marie Perrier-Jouët, produces both vintage and nonvintage champagne. Cantwell's recollection of the exact type of champagne is not surprising; as mentioned in entry 126:23, Leclerc died on 28 November 1947, within a year or two of the action of *Across the River and into the Trees*.

When the cold Roederer runs out after the second bottle, Cantwell orders Perrier-Jouët (135:33), which they then take into the gondola.

Catherine Bourne orders Perrier-Jouët in *The Garden of Eden* (48, 187). Hemingway also orders "a couple bottles" of Perrier-Jouët along with caviar when he and his wife were staying in the Sherry-Netherland in 1950 (Ross 45).

126:33 **SHAEF:** The Supreme Headquarters Allied Expeditionary Force was the headquarters of the commander of Allied forces in northwest Europe from late 1943 until the end of World War II. General Eisenhower commanded SHAEF throughout its existence, even though Cantwell's many references to it leave Eisenhower unnamed (see 208:24, 212:21, 214:6, 219:8, 228:25, 228:27). Likewise, the disparaging reference to "high brass, even from Kansas" (221:2–3) is clearly directed at Eisenhower, who was raised in Abilene, Kansas.

127:3–4 **a badge of shame in the form of a flaming something:** The SHAEF badge depicted a flaming sword against a black field pointed upward at a rainbow.

127:4 **we wore a four-leafed clover:** This clover appears on the badge of the 4th Infantry Division, which is also known as the "ivy" division, that is, the "IV" division. Hemingway was embedded with the 4th Infantry Division during World War II. The four-leaf clover is also referred to later (227:17, 228:22).

127:9 **the gap at Falaise:** The Falaise Pocket, fought from 12 to 21 August 1944, was the decisive engagement of the Battle of Normandy. The gap to which Cantwell refers was the German objective of a corridor that would allow for their escape.

127:14–15 **Bas Meudon:** A town in the southwestern suburbs of Paris. See 132:2.

127:15 **Porte de Saint Cloud:** Cantwell recalls that the bridge was secured at Porte de Saint-Cloud, a neighborhood of Paris (132:2–3).

127:17 **Etoile:** The Place Charles de Gaulle, historically known as the Place de l'Étoile, is a large road junction in Paris, the meeting point of twelve straight avenues, including the Champs-Élysées, which continues to the east.

127:17–18 **Elsa Maxwell:** Maxwell (1883–1963) was an American gossip columnist and hostess renowned for hobnobbing with the elite. Mary Hemingway mentions her as frequenting Harry's Bar ("Harry's Bar" 63). Hemingway also namedrops Maxwell in his article about bullfighting, from which *The Dangerous Summer* was published. Although the reference to Maxwell is excised from the subsequent book, the journalism describes the attack of "ptomaine poisoning" that Luis Miguel Dominguin suffered (*DS* 62). In the article, it is explained that this poisoning occurred "at a calf-teasing festival he had given at his ranch for Elsa Maxwell. None of this sounded too good and the pictures and reports of the Elsa Maxwell festivities looked and sounded worse" ("The Dangerous Summer" 91).

This anecdote about the kidnapping of Elsa Maxwell's butler can be presumed a preposterous stab at humor.

127:26–27 **in the time of the Grand Captains:** Renata is referring to an order of medieval knights, the Grand Captains of the Guard. See Shakespeare's *Antony and Cleopatra,* where Silius tells Ventidius, "thy grand captain, Antony, / Shall set thee on triumphant chariots and / Put garlands on thy head" (3.1.9–11).

128:1 **You ought to write:** In a novel where Hemingway's presence is so easily conflated with Cantwell's, this type of too-cute intrusion borders on the obnoxious, particularly when—falsely modest—he responds, "I have not the talent for it" (128:3). On the next page, Cantwell assures Renata, "I don't write, Daughter" (129:29–30). He then wryly tells her that he is not a writer "by the grace of God" (131:2). In Hemingway's previous novel, *For Whom the Bell Tolls,* Robert Jordan openly plans to write about his experiences in Spain; somehow that is a more authentic, less self-aggrandizing stance than Cantwell's, which drips with irony and only puts more focus on Hemingway than had he stated otherwise.

128:7 **Maurice de Saxe:** Marshal de Saxe (1696–1750) was a German in the French service who became marshal general of France. Saxe's writings explored the art of war, including *Mes Rêveries* (1757) and *Lettres et mémoires* (1794). General Montgomery was said to be a devotee of Saxe's writings. Hemingway told a *Newsweek* interviewer that for their "writings and understatement" he admired Saxe, along with Clausewitz, Frederick the Great, Grant, and De Picq [*sic*] ("New Hemingway" 95). In a letter to Chink Dorman-Smith, Hemingway imagines that one of the benefits of going to hell would be the opportunity to hear de Saxe speak while sitting on "a cooling pile of cinders" (*SL* 844).

128:7 **Frederick the Great:** Frederick II (1712–1786) was the King of Prussia, who wrote *Instructions for His Generals,* with a compendium: *Frederick the Great on the Art of War.* Hemingway owned George Peabody Gooch's 1947 study *Frederick the Great, the Ruler, the Writer, the Man* (Brasch and Sigman 165). In a 1938 piece for *Ken* regarding the Spanish Civil War, Hemingway praises Frederick the Great's ability for fighting a defensive battle during the Seven Years' War against the vastly superior Austrian army (*BL* 291).

128:7–8 **T'sun Su:** Sun Tzu, the more common spelling, was an ancient Chinese military general, strategist, and philosopher who is believed to have authored *The Art of War,* a massively influential book on military strategy. Sun Tzu is estimated to have lived in the fifth or sixth century B.C.

128:20 **Roederer Brut '42:** Roederer is a champagne company based in Reims, France. Louise Roederer inherited the company and renamed it in 1833. The firm also produces the luxury champagne Cristal. See entry at 126:25.

128:26 **G1, G2 . . . :** Cantwell's explanation of the hierarchy is sound: the commander is a general or a brigadier general; his chief of staff is the second in command and manages the headquarters; G1 is the branch responsible for personnel matters, including manning, discipline, and personal services; G2 is the branch responsible for intelligence and security; G3 is responsible for operations, including operational requirements, training, and combat development; G4 covers logistics and quartering; G5 is responsible for civil and military cooperation.

128:27 **Kraut-6:** Cantwell here refers to the German planning and communication. Hemingway possessed German maps on which he and army officials were able to predict German movement and strategy.[2]

129:6 **he translated:** As the motif of language continues, this phrase suggests that most of this extended dialogue about military matters is conducted in Italian. If Cantwell were translating correctly into Italian, he would have rendered it "*corpo d'armata*"; in Spanish, "corps" would be "cuerpo diplomatico." A staunch defender of Cantwell and/or Hemingway's linguistic skills would defend this as proof of his polyglotism, but more reasonably, it is evidence of his confusion. Hemingway put a question mark over the phrase in the manuscript, but he never corrected it.

129:19–20 **write to profit quickly from the war they never fought in:** Cantwell's screed mimics Hemingway complaints against his contemporaries and competitors, writers like Andre Malraux or Willa Cather, who would presume to write about war while either never going or not staying for what Hemingway deemed a significant period of time. In this way, Hemingway is equating some of his fellow writers with the *pescecani* who exploit the war for financial gain. When Cantwell declares that he does not know which category of sin such a transgression would belong to, one possibility is the Fraudulent, doomed to eternity in Dante's eighth circle.

Cantwell's focus on D'Annunzio, for instance, depicts a man who fought and was wounded in war and earned the right to write on that theme. Later, when Cantwell declares that Shakespeare "writes like a soldier himself" (159:16–17), it is his highest possible compliment, given to someone who fuses artistic excellence with the bravery and experience of a soldier. Just as Cantwell is battling his own dueling impulses between being a soldier and being a kind human, Hemingway believed the mentalities of a writer and soldier were antithetical. In his introduction to *Men at War,* he writes, "Learning to suspend your imagination and live completely in the very second of the present minute with no before and no after is the greatest gift a soldier can acquire. It, naturally, is the opposite of all those gifts a writer should have" (xxiv).

In the manuscript, this vituperation is directed at two people in particular: Irwin Shaw and Harry Butcher (1901–1985). Shaw (1913–1984), whom Hemingway would mercilessly lampoon in letters as a "Brooklyn Tolstoi," largely for having the temerity to write a book about World War II, the popular novel, *The Young Lions* (1948), later a film starring Marlon Brando, Montomery Clift, and Dean Martin. Shaw was also Mary's former lover, which no doubt contributed to the resentment.

129:26 **nylon-smooth Captain of the Navy**: Although previous commentators have argued that this remark alludes to Eisenhower (e.g., Cowley, "Old Soldier" 1), the manuscript reveals that with this epithet Cantwell intends to disparage Harry C. Butcher, who, as Cantwell says in the deleted passage, "had the rank of captain in the Navy and could not command a cat boat" (JFK 1). Cantwell also refers to Butcher's book, *My Three Years with Eisenhower* (1946), two copies of which Hemingway owned (Brasch and Sigman 91), as "My Six Years Brown-Noseing [*sic*] Eisenhower" (JFK 1). Cantwell will eventually banish this nylon-smooth man to hell, in response to Renata's relief that she will never meet him (225:23–25).

Butcher, as a commander of SHAEF, ordered Hemingway to report to the inspector general of the 3rd Army on 3 October 1944 as part of an investigation regarding Hemingway's activities at Rambouillet (Reynolds, *Final Years* 115, 384n11).

130:6–7 his heart rose and he felt it choke him: Cantwell's own heart condition is referenced as he sympathizes with the *Gran Maestro*, who has had two heart attacks to Cantwell's three.

130:18 there were more: "More" refers to Cantwell's heart episodes, not the wine.

130:24–25 Rolex Oyster Perpetual: The first waterproof wristwatch, the Oyster was introduced in 1923. When Hemingway critic Philip Young was writing his groundbreaking study of his work, Hemingway compared it to being "as though some curious person, not a watch-maker, should take apart his Rolex Oyster Perpetual. It is fine to say it does no harm and anybody has a right to take anyone else's watch apart. But I don't think they have a right while it is still ticking" (qtd. in Young, "Assumptions of Literature" 353).

131:19–20 Marie Antoinette in the tumbril: Maria Antonia Josepha Johanna (1755–1793) was an Archduchess of Austria, the Queen of France and of Navarre. She was the wife of Louis XVI (1754–1793), who is also mentioned (238:1). She rode in a tumbril, or an open cart, on the way to her execution for treason; the tumbril is mentioned at 238:3, 238:5, 254:24, and 265:16–18.

131:33 Clamart: Clamart is a commune in the southwest suburbs of Paris, about five and a half miles from the city center. Leclerc arrived on 24 August 1944. Hemingway would later write that the troops heading into Paris "proceeded past the wrecked airdrome of Villacoublay to the crossroads of Porte Clamart" (*BL* 380).

132:1 Montrouge . . . Porte d'Orleans: Two neighborhoods in the southern outskirts of Paris. Leclerc's 2nd Armored Division entered the city of Paris through the Porte d'Orleans on 24 August 1944, and he has been honored with a Metro stop and an avenue at this location. The *Famous Fourth* claims that they traveled North on d'Orleans on 25 August 1944 (17).

132:16–17 **Mount Valérien:** Fort Mont-Valérien is west of the Seine, overlooking the Bois de Boulogne.

133:2 **Rambouillet:** This commune in the southwestern suburbs of Paris represented one of the two passages into Paris. Hemingway entered Rambouillet on 19 August 1944, settling into the Hôtel du Grand Veneur the next day (Beistle 5). In October 1944, the inspector general of the Third Army interrogated Hemingway for conducting himself as an armed combatant from 22 to 25 August while a war correspondent at Rambouillet. In an unpublished letter, he claims to have been deceptive during the interrogation, having "swore away everything I felt any pride in" (qtd. in Reynolds, *Final Years* 116). According to Reynolds, Hemingway participated in the killing of two German soldiers at Rambouillet (205).

133:4 **Toussus le Noble and at LeBuc:** Like Rambouillet, Toussus-le-Noble and Buc are communes in the Yvelines region of north France. Hemingway's *Collier*'s piece "How We Came to Paris" begins with his meeting of Leclerc in Rambouillet and wondering about the resistance they would face the next day in Toussus-le-Noble; indeed, there is "a short but sharp fight" (*BL* 376). Hemingway goes on to describe the German opposition: "Past the airdrome toward Buc they had 88s that commanded all that stretch of road" (376).

133:9–10 **the Gazzettino:** *Il Gazzettino* is the daily local paper of Venice. See the photo in Moriani (96–97), in which Hemingway is reading this newspaper.

133:23 **I go duck shooting tomorrow:** That is, he will head off to the location of the duck hunt the next afternoon, which is Saturday, to be ready for the actual shoot the following morning, Sunday before dawn. As Cantwell clarifies: "the shoot is on Sunday" (134:6).

133:27 **I can make him ask me:** In the background since the short paragraph on 124:21–23, the thread of the understated relationship between Alvarito and Renata becomes more forceful with this comment. Renata is aware of her influence with Alvarito and is not too shy to remind Cantwell of the connection the two younger people share. The invitation is brought up again, when Cantwell discourages her from attending (253:17).

In the biographical basis for this strain, Adriana actually did attend a duck hunt with Hemingway and his hunting party, which included Alvarito's model, Nanuk Franchetti.

134:1 **visit my poors:** If this phrasing seems stilted, Hemingway intends to convey the actual Italian word for poors, "poveri"; Renata will take care of the poor people to whom she ministers.

134:1–2 I am an only child: Adriana Ivancich, incidentally, was not an only child. Hemingway was close friends with one of her two brothers, Gianfranco, who spent time with him in Cuba and Idaho, and who wrote a book about their time together, *Da una felice Cuba a Ketchum: i miei giorni con Ernest Hemingway* (2008). Adriana also had another brother, Giacomo.

134:9 pictures of Miss Bergman: Ingrid Bergman (1915–1982) was the iconic, Academy Award–winning actress whom Hemingway hand selected to play Maria in the 1943 film adaptation of *For Whom the Bell Tolls*. In a letter to Maxwell Perkins, Hemingway remarked that it was "marvelous" that Bergman was going to play the role and that "she should be marvelous" (*SL* 540). Hemingway tells a mordant story of drinking champagne with Bergman at a 1947 New Year's Eve party in Sun Valley, Idaho. While watching the wealthy guests embarrass themselves playing limbo, he remarked, "Daughter, this is going to be the worst year that we have ever seen" (*FTA*, Hemingway Library ix). In a 1954 letter to Adriana Ivancich, he writes that Bergman is "Sweet and good and honest and married to the 22 pound rat [the director Roberto Rossellini]" (*SL* 830–31).

134:13–14 I want to be like you. Can I be like you a little while tonight? On this note, Carl P. Eby argues that Hemingway is preparing us for the "transvestic hallucination" that occurs during the gondola scene in chapter 13. Eby identifies this moment as evocative of a larger pattern in Hemingway's postwar writings, in which "the experience produces a merger between lovers that threatens to become a reversal of roles" ("He Felt the Change" 81), what Eby elsewhere calls "a dream of erotic fusion" (*Fetishism* 27). Renata, then, introduces this theme, which will take on a more specifically sexual cast in the next chapter. Eby's reading is extreme and has been met with incredulity and even hostility, but the pattern of this language in Hemingway's work is overwhelming and ultimately impossible to ignore.

134:15–16 In what town are we anyway? In what seems a non sequitur, Cantwell is alluding to the historical licentiousness of Venice; prostitution, the tradition of the courtesan, the Carnevale were identified with Venice, particularly during the decadent sixteenth and seventeenth centuries and later, the lifestyle that led to the fame of Venice's own Giacomo Casanova (1725–1798). In the fourth canto of *Childe Harold's Pilgrimage,* Byron refers to Venice as "The pleasant place of all festivity, / The revel of the earth, the masque of Italy!" (221).

135:5–6 I wish to serve you: This tearful supplication is a restatement of one of the most beautiful passages in all of Hemingway, the Italian priest's explanation in *A Farewell to Arms* to Frederic Henry of what love is: "When you love you wish to do things for. You wish to sacrifice for. You wish to serve" (72).

135:14–15 **quite a large package:** At this point—slightly short of halfway through the novel—the portrait arrives that will essentially become its own character or an avatar of Renata.

136:2 **And besides he's dead:** Patton died on 21 December 1945 from complications following a car crash in Germany.

136:12 **beyond her depth:** For a man who has criticized the pockmarked writer for condescension (118:6), this instance is the novel's third example of his regret for being so lofty, so esoteric that those around him simply cannot follow. See entry at 64:14–15.

137:15 **Velasquez:** Diego Rodríguez de Silva y Velázquez (1599–1660) was a Spanish artist who created many historical paintings and portraits, including *Las Meninas* (1656), in the Prado. Velázquez is a staple of Hemingway's fiction, particularly his Spanish work, including an early mention in *For Whom the Bell Tolls,* in which a beautiful horse "looked as though he had come out of a painting by Velásquez" (13). Margaret O'Shaughnessy argues that Velásquez did not typically paint women and that when he did it was not always flattering, making this reference curious indeed (205).

137:17 **in our time:** Hemingway includes a slyly self-referential phrase that nods to his first collection of short stories, *In Our Time* (1925). The Colonel repeats the phrase (184:17–18, 213:14), just as one of the volume's titles, "Out of Season" is referenced at 240:18.

138:13 **without a pause:** Renata points out the difference between Cantwell's fluid courtesy—as opposed to, in recent instances, remembering to call her "Daughter" (135:10)—and remembering belatedly to say "please" to the *Gran Maestro* (135:33).

138:28–29 **What you win in Boston you lose in Chicago:** Cantwell's trite phrase about consequences and balance speaks to the larger Hemingwayesque theme of payment. This line concludes Lillian Ross's infamous 13 May 1950 *New Yorker* profile of Hemingway (94). See also the obnoxious essay "The Art of the Short Story," written about a decade later, in which Hemingway repeats this same line (5).

139:1 *calcio:* Italian for "soccer."

139:20 **Nothing . . . probably nothing:** This two-sentence rejoinder initially seems like a whimpering end to such a sprawling, allusive chapter; the 8,096-word chapter—the longest by far—spans about 12 percent of the entire novel, but the word "nothing" has always been more profound to a Hemingway text than to those of most other writers.

In an essay about the concept of nothing in "Big Two-Hearted River," Frank Scafella refers helpfully to this concept as "at once an absence and a presence . . . meaning that 'nothing' is 'something'" (77). The French philosopher Henri Bergson is more expansive about this idea. As one of the great commentators on this topic, Bergson states, "'Disorder' and 'nothingness' in reality designate therefore a presence—the presence of a thing or an order which does not interest us, which blunts our effort or attention; it is our disappointment being expressed when we call this presence absence" (*Creative Mind* 49). "'Nothing,'" Bergson goes on, "designates the absence of what we are seeking, we desire, expect. Let us suppose that absolute emptiness was known to our experience: it would be limited, have contours, and would therefore be something. But in reality there is no vacuum" (78). Bergson, arguing against the possibility of complete annihilation of thought, points out that to "represent 'Nothing,' we must either imagine it or conceive it" (*Creative Evolution* 278). Bergson's description is beautiful and quite anticipates Hemingway in "A Clean Well-Lighted Place": "It was a nothing that he knew too well. It was all a nothing and a man was nothing too" (*CSS* 291). Carlos Baker terms it—in a definition that has resonated—a "Something called Nothing" (*Writer as Artist* 124). To Harry in "The Snows of Kilimanjaro," death is an "evil-smelling emptiness," which he names "Nothing" (*CSS* 47). In *The Disasters of War*, Goya depicts a corpse pointing to the word "Nada," agreeing with Hemingway's nomenclature. For more discussion on this topic, see Cirino, *Thought in Action* (27–29).

See also entries at 145:19–20 and 210:11.

NOTES

1. For a differently edited version, see *Letters 2,* 391.
2. Thanks to James H. Meredith for alerting me to this aspect of Hemingway's military experiences.

CHAPTER 13

140:4–5 as lovely as a good horse or as a racing shell: These two similes have resonance in Hemingway's work. In *The Sun Also Rises,* the curves of Brett Ashley's body are likened to those of "the hull of a racing yacht" (30). Cantwell believes that Renata will "hold the pace and stay the course" (226:9–10), a horse-racing metaphor. Renata is also compared to a horse at 262:30. Hemingway frequently compared Adriana Ivancich to a horse and even wrote a story called "The Black Horse," which was his nickname for her. The ship comparison continues on 140:11–12.

140:6–7 What hand or eye framed that dark-ed symmetry? In the anarchy of his stream of consciousness, Cantwell misquotes William Blake's "The Tyger": "What immortal hand or eye / Could frame thy fearful symmetry?" (ll. 3–4, ll. 23–24).

140:14–15 Bois . . . Armenonville: Bois de Boulogne is a commune in southwestern France. In *The Sun Also Rises,* Count Mippipopolous asks Brett and Jake if they'd like to "ride out to the Bois for dinner" (64). Armenonville is a commune in northern France (see the entry at 132:16–17).

141:12 U.S.O.D.: This acronym stands for United States Olive Drab.

141:20 moglie and the bambini: *Moglie* is Italian for "wife"; *bambini* means "babies."

142:3 our home: As Carlos Baker points out (*Writer as Artist* 282), Cantwell is at "home" in Harry's Bar (77:28), here in the gondola, and also at the Gritti (153:1). To figuratively call Venice his "hometown," albeit adopted, means Cantwell also has comfort, intimacy, and familiarity in these three settings as well.

143:6–7 he ran his bad hand through her hair once, twice, and three times: That is, the right hand that stimulates Renata is going through the hair that stimulates Cantwell. That it occurs three times only emphasizes the importance of that number in this scene and in the novel.

143:7–8 **worse than desperation:** This moment heightens the description from 142:6–7, in which nothing was left of the kiss "but desperation." Later, Renata kisses Cantwell "kind, and hard, and desperately" (202:1).

143:14–15 **the island in the great river with the high steep banks:** Presumably a strained metaphor to describe Renata's clitoris, to which Cantwell's right hand may not be sensitive. For this reason, he is described as "finding it and losing it, and then finding it for good" (143:17–18). Whether readers respond to this scene as Hemingway intended or not, Renata and Cantwell's gondola ride has attracted much critical attention. The most provocative and ultimately convincing reading of this scene is Carl P. Eby's important article, "He Felt the Change So That It Hurt Him All the Way Through: Sodomy and Transvestic Hallucination in Hemingway" (especially 80–81). Eby argues that—perhaps because of Renata's menstruation, but perhaps not—Renata and Cantwell have inverted gender roles and she is penetrating him. The menstruation is a catalyst in that it provides a justification for sexual experimentation that Hemingway would not believe he needed in later work, such as *The Garden of Eden*.

Cantwell later asks, "Where is the island now and in what river?" (145:7).

144:9–11 **when the great bird had flown far out of the closed window of the gondola:** This objective correlative is a Hemingway favorite for sexual climax. In an earlier story, "Fathers and Sons," Hemingway signifies an orgasm by describing "the great bird flown like an owl in the twilight" (*CSS* 376).

144:21–22 **You're in the lee:** Renata is literally sheltered from the wind, but there's something more to this—Cantwell is also speculating that she is safe and prepared to continue sexual activity. However, she is not ready or "in the lee" until a moment later (145:6, 145:14).

144:26 **Thank you for the you:** Renata notices Cantwell's shift from identifying her as "a woman" to "you."

144:30–31 **reaching accurately and well:** This phrase is occasionally lampooned as an idiotic or quintessentially self-parodic sentence (e.g., Young, *Reconsideration* 119), but in Hemingway's defense, Cantwell has a crippled hand, and he is by nature and trade hyperconscious of accuracy. He has also been drinking, is in bad health, and his hand is insensitive to touch. Later, he recorks a bottle of wine "carefully, precisely, and lovingly" (153:17). The fastidiousness that is a psychological necessity in "Big Two-Hearted River" reemerges here, even if more consciously.

145:5–6 **doing whatever it is she should not do:** This sexual licentiousness was precisely Adriana Ivanchich's objection, that a young girl of her refinement would engage in drinking and sex in this manner. Discussion of the Hemingway-Adriana relationship often succumbs to a juvenile "did they or didn't they?" breathlessness, but it is virtually certain that they did not.

145:8–9 You are making the discovery. I am only the unknown country. Renata's exhortation to Cantwell, to which he responds with a rude and awkwardly mistimed rejoinder, is a mangling of the "to be or not to be" speech in Shakespeare's *Hamlet*, the reference to the afterlife as "The undiscovered country from whose bourn / No traveller returns" (3.1.81–82).

145:19–20 stopped thinking and he did not think for a long time: This pattern of nonthinking, which we see frequently in Hemingway's work, is seen the most often in this novel during chapter 13. For this reason, although nonthinking often accompanies moments of action in Hemingway's work, in *Across the River and into the Trees* it accompanies love, sex, and peak emotion. See 144:2 and 143:34 earlier in this chapter. Aspects of not-thinking are also suggested on 148:9–10, 148:11–12, 149:8, and 105:14–15. See entry at 210:11.

145:21 The gondola now was in one of the secondary canals: Hemingway is clearly putting forth another coy erotic metaphor.

146:8 for a little while: There should be a closing quotation mark after "while." The first edition has neither a period nor a closing quotation mark.

146:10 Couldn't I be you? Recalling 134:13–14, this trope of merging identity is a constant in Hemingway. When Renata claims that she has just taken Paris and is riding with Marshal Ney (146:12–13, 146:26–27), she has effectively assumed his identity. The same might be true of gender roles; this is what is meant by Eby's "transvestic hallucinations" ("He Felt the Change" 80–81). See *For Whom the Bell Tolls*, *A Farewell to Arms*, and most especially *The Garden of Eden* for the persistence of this theme. Rose Marie Burwell also makes a convincing argument that Hemingway's desire to merge identities was never stronger with any other person than it was with Adriana, calling it "the most potent instance of his attempting to experience the feminine aspect of his own creative imagination through love for a woman" (130). As Burwell points out, Hemingway would routinely address letters to her as "Adriana Hemingway" and sign those letters "Ernest Ivancich," blending their identities.

146:16 twenty-eighth division: This division, under Omar Bradley, invaded Normandy and fought in Hürtgen Forest. The 28th Infantry Division paraded through Paris on 29 August 1944. See 228:13–17 for a further mention of the 28th Division at Hürtgen Forest.

146:21–22 T.S. division: Slang meaning "tough situation" or "tough shit" (Dunlap 148). The phrase is repeated on 161:21.

146:26–27 when I think of you taking it, then, it is as though I were riding in this gondola with Maréchal Ney: In Shakespeare's *Othello,* Desdemona was similarly titillated by her husband's war achievements. In this case, the sex scene has merely interrupted Cantwell's storytelling. Is Renata ministering to Cantwell for his psychological welfare, her sexual satisfaction, or some combination of the two? In what would be a particularly maddening suggestion to Cantwell, she actually says, "I would love it if you were a General" (222:28–29).

Michel Ney (1769–1815), a marshal of France, fought during the French Revolutionary Wars and the Napoleonic wars. In *The Sun Also Rises,* Jake Barnes sees a statue of Ney, "in his top-boots, gesturing with his sword among the green new horse-chestnut leaves" (37).

147:1–3 Quatre Bas . . . Waterloo: Cantwell's criticism of Ney stems from the slow attack of Wellington at Quatre Bas. A French general, d'Erlon, abandoned Napoleon at Ligny in order to support Ney, thus robbing France of a complete rout of the Prussians.

147:6 Moskova: Cantwell is referring to "Moskva," the Russian word for Moscow. The Italian word for Moscow is "Mosca." Ney's command of the rear guard during the retreat from Moscow led him to be known as "the last Frenchman on Russian soil" (Leggiere 345). Just as Renata suggests (147:7), Napoleon referred to Ney as "the bravest of the brave" when he rejoined the army (Leggiere 345).

Cantwell will refer to his ex-wife as being more ambitious than Napoleon (195:32). Any mention of Napoleon is pointed in the context of this novel, since Napoleon and his army conquered the Venetian republic in 1797.

147:17–18 once more if it would not hurt you: Renata is inviting Cantwell to perform for a third time. Of course, we're not sure if she is wondering if his heart can take it physically or emotionally, or both. If Renata's first orgasm occurred when the great bird was released, it seems the second one occurs before Cantwell asks her how she is (145:30).

147:19–20 When the hell was I ever hurt? Apparently, the third sexual encounter occurs between Cantwell's blustering response and Renata's response, in the chapter division between chapters 13 and 14.

CHAPTER 14

148:1 Please don't be bad: Renata begins chapter 14 with a salvo of requests—albeit polite—to Cantwell about his behavior: "Please don't be bad . . . Please don't pretend to be stupid . . . please let's not think of anything . . . Please be good and kind" (148:1, 148:9, 148:9–10, 148:14). After their torrid lovemaking, Renata is careful to preserve their loving, affectionate mood and not to have Cantwell sabotage it with his gruffness or brutality.

149:15 Can I stay at the Gritti? Cantwell rebuffs Renata's request to spend the night, on account of "them," which likely refers to her family and her community, and also "you" (149:18), which is her psyche, her reputation. For such an occasionally forceful character, Renata is dissuaded quite easily in this instance, reconciled to go home. The Ivanciches lived in the Calle de Rimedio, near Piazza San Marco.

149:31 business habit: This phrase reminds one of Count Mippipopolous in *The Sun Also Rises*, who also is wounded during a war that he considers a "business trip" (67). That Cantwell views his military life as his "business" extends the theme of his "trade."

149:32–33 I wish . . . that you were not going to die: This admission is Renata's explicit acknowledgment of his impending death, talked around previously.

150:3–4 we go to Rome and get the clothes: Renata refers back to their fantasy that when Cantwell retires and must wear civilian clothes, she knows a tailor who would supply them and they could drive to Rome together (121:15–16).

150:16 unknowing, yet knowing all: What a beautiful phrase about the discretion of the gondolier; in Henry James's articulation, the Venetian gondolier has the "happy art of being obsequious without being, or at least without seeming, abject" (19). In Byron's "Beppo: A Venetian Love Story" (1817), the poet sees the advantage of activities in the gondola, "Where none can make out what you say or do" (616). Peter Ackroyd's recent history of Venice points out that the gondola was "designed for secrecy." They were not canoes, but rather "little cabins draped by blinds or black cloth" (85).

See also when the *Gran Maestro* exhibits the same professional graciousness, "observing, without observing" (entry at 247:14–15).

150:17–18 the Piazzetta and then across the great, cold, wind-swept square: The Piazzetta San Marco, the "little piazza" is a smaller extension of Piazza San Marco that sits on its southeast corner. San Marco is also mentioned at 63:7 and 116:29.

150:21 where the German shot the pigeons: For the second time, Renata is remembering the German troops who shot pigeons in San Marco, a symbolic desecration of Venice. At the first mention, she also recalled them killing her father (116:27–29).

150:25 C.I.D.: "Criminal Investigation Division."

151:3 Cinema Palace: The Cinema Palace is the theater on the Lido where the International Venice Film Festival takes place, as it has since 1932; however, since the setting of *Across the River and into the Trees*, the Cinema Palace underwent an expansion in 1952 and has been rebuilt.

151:12–13 anyone's gonococci brought from Schio: Schio, about sixty-five miles northwest of Venice, is hugely important in Hemingway's life, beginning with his stay in what he and his colleagues called the Schio Country Club, the residence of the American Red Cross unit in Italy in 1918. Hemingway revisited Schio with Hadley, his first wife, in July 1922. In his fascinating article for the *Toronto Star* that chronicles the trip, "A Veteran Visits the Old Front," he writes that Schio "was the finest town I remember in the war . . . one of the finest places on earth" (*DLT* 177).

Cantwell later compares Schio to Sheridan, Wyoming, "up against the mountains" (243:7–8).

See entry at 61:31.

151:22 when you said it about unpopular guest: Cantwell has just referred to himself as "the last man to leave the party" (151:17–18). It seems Renata has vacillated on her decision to leave based on her realization that Cantwell stayed and fought for Italy despite vast desertions in the Italian army.

152:2 they ought to take you out and hang you: Adriana Ivancich committed suicide by hanging in 1983. This thought is repeated toward the portrait, when Cantwell mentions that he tells it to "go out and hang yourself" (160:3). He will also tell the ex-Fascist hall porter to hang himself (164:2).

CHAPTER 15

154:6–7 **I'm not going to talk to a picture:** Cantwell's incessant interior monologue becomes a spoken one, as he directs his thoughts and emotions toward this portrait. It would be a misreading of this quirk of Cantwell to refer back to Jackson's opinion of him as "slug-nutty" (34:33); he is simply using this portrait as a prop to express his thoughts. In *The Old Man and the Sea,* Santiago also expresses his thoughts out loud to a marlin, the moon, the sharks, and so on, understanding that people would consider it crazy.

154:25–26 **What I would make in four hundred years:** Cantwell is being somewhat self-deprecating, or else his math is sloppy; if he would make a quarter of a million dollars in four hundred years, his salary would only have to be $625. As detailed in the entry at 49:3, Cantwell's salary would have been about $7,000 in 1949, so it would have taken him thirty-five years to earn $250,000.

155:4–5 **the hell with the pills:** Cantwell decides not to take his medicine.

155:7 **Red Smith:** At the time of this novel's publication, Red Smith (1905–1982) was the most widely read sportswriter in the English language. Cantwell continues reading Smith the following morning (and the following chapter) in the bathroom (156:9–10). In Hemingway's life and writing, the number of instances in which a contemporary, living writer receives unqualified praise is low indeed. Around the time of this novel's publication, Hemingway, in a *New York Herald Tribune* blurb entitled "Books I Have Liked" gave a public endorsement of Smith's collection of *Tribune* columns, *Out of the Red* (1950).

CHAPTER 16

The action of chapter 16 is consumed by Cantwell waking up and going to the bathroom and thinking. In this bathroom monologue, his consciousness is reported by "he thought" (156:6); "he thought" (156:12); "he thought" (156:18); "he thought" (157:1); "he said to himself" (157:3); "he thought" (157:6); "he considered" (157:7–8); "He was addressing no one, except, perhaps posterity" (157:12); "he thought" (157:21); "he said to himself" (157:25); "he asked himself" (157:27); "he said" (157:28); "he said to himself" (157:32); "he said" (157:32–33); "he thought" (158:19); "he said to himself" (158:23); "he said" (158:26); "he said to himself" (158:27); and "he thought" (158:29).

156:1 The Colonel woke before daylight: The opening of chapter 16 echoes the opening of the novel, in which Cantwell and the poler and the hunting party begin "two hours before daylight" on Sunday (11:1). Chapter 16 begins before daylight on Saturday. Cantwell confirms that this day is Saturday (250:15).

156:7 Probably flood the square: It is quite common for Piazza San Marco to become completely submerged by water, so Venetians would be used to this occurrence of what they call *acqua alta* (high water). When Cantwell and Renata arrange their breakfast at the Florian, which offers outside seating, Cantwell remarks that the square "should be flooded and it will be fun to watch" (182:33–34). Renata, however, does not like the square to be flooded, because, she tells Cantwell, "It is sad and the pigeons have no place to alight" (185:19–20); she does, however, enjoy watching the children play in the water.

156:14 He sat there: We are reading Cantwell's meditation while he is defecating. Of Hemingway's entire career, this earthy scene is the most striking tribute to the end of the Calypso episode in James Joyce's *Ulysses* (1922), in which Leopold Bloom also reads a newspaper as he moves his bowels. "A paper," Joyce writes, "He liked to read at stool" (55), with the pun clearly intended. Joyce's description is then graphic and scatological in ways Hemingway does not approach: "Asquat on the cuckstool he folded out his paper, turning its pages over his bared knees. . . . No great hurry. Keep it a bit. . . . . Quietly he read, restraining himself, the first column and, yielding but re-

136

sisting, began the second. Midway, his last resistance yielding, he allowed his bowels to ease themselves quietly as he read, reading still patiently that slight constipation of yesterday quite gone.... So. Ah!" (56). Joyce brilliantly allows the reader to determine which "column" Bloom is finishing, his newspaper or his excrement.

Cantwell's defecation should remind the reader of his memory of his failed tribute at his wounding site (26:16).

157:12 **addressing no one, except, perhaps, posterity:** Hemingway is playing with the word "posterity," which stems from the same etymology as "posterior," on which Cantwell is resting, from the French *posterus,* meaning "following."

This formulation echoes "Except, possibly, happiness" (69:19), Arnaldo's comment about the only thing that cannnot be found at Harry's Bar.

157:26 **your duty's not completed yet:** Is Cantwell playing on the word "doody"? If so, this is a truly crappy pun.

157:28 **Buy them new hats or shoot them:** This phrase attests to the rough humor of the protagonist and to the randomness of promotion, guilt, and even death, all being part of the "same process" (157:29).

158:4 **Joan of Arc:** Joan of Arc (ca. 1412–1431) was the spiritual leader of France during the Hundred Years' War, and she was burned at the stake for heresy after claiming divine guidance. Eby points out that Cantwell looking in the mirror and identifying with a young woman—perhaps the same age as Renata—continues the "transvestic impulse" that was prominent in the gondola in chapter 13 (*Fetishism* 209). Eby also reports that in the manuscript version of *The Garden of Eden,* a female character worries, after a haircut, that she, too, will look like "Jeanne d'Arc" (qtd. in *Fetishism* 231). Joan of Arc is also mentioned in Hemingway's "Banal Story" (*CSS* 275) and *The Torrents of Spring* (41). After his African plane crashes of 1954, Hemingway wrote in a letter that he had to take two breaths of fire, "which is something that never really helped anybody except of course Joan of Arc the reincarnation (admitted) of Gen. Charles de Gaulle" (*SL* 829).

158:4–5 **General (Brevetted) George Armstrong Custer:** A brevet is a proclamation assigning an officer to a particular rank, but not providing extra pay. Referred to as "that fool" (243:2–3) with "sawdust for brains" (158:7) by Cantwell, Custer (1839–1876) is mentioned in this context because of his notorious flowing, golden hair. Custer made his infamous "last stand" during the Great Sioux War at Little Big Horn on 25–26 June 1876. Hemingway included an excerpt from Frederic F. van de Water's history of Custer, *Glory Hunter,* in *Men at War.* As Cantwell mentions, Custer was renowned for his vanity, had a wife who published books about him, one of which Hemingway owned (Reynolds, *Hemingway's Reading* 115). When George Plimpton interviewed Hemingway for the *Paris Review,* a book on Custer's last stand was on Hemingway's desk.

In Eby's discussion of Hemingway's career-long consideration of Custer, he observes that Custer was demoted from general to colonel for disobeying the orders of his superiors, unlike Cantwell, who was scapegoated for the results after obeying orders (*Fetishism* 229).

In *To Have and Have Not* and *For Whom the Bell Tolls,* as well as a piece in *Esquire* called "He Who Gets Slap-Happy," Hemingway mentions a lithograph of Custer's Last Stand that was a painting for an Anheuser-Busch ad (19). For more on the Hemingway-Custer connection, see McLellan.

158:16–17 **they used to put in this same paper:** In other words, the reporting on the war in the *Herald Tribune,* which Cantwell is still reading during this reverie.

158:18–19 **complete with true handles:** This Hemingway joke-phrase, like "whatever that is," appears in connection to a joke about the atomic bombs he has in his car (45:9), to the jeep Cantwell will buy (51:10–11), Renata (206:31), and his farewell (246:15).

Hemingway frequently used this phrase in his correspondence during the late 1940s.

CHAPTER 17

159:1 **When it started to be light:** Chapter 16 begins "before daylight" (156:1), and as chapter 17 begins, we are beginning the day. We have "first and best light" (160:19) and then "good, or almost good" light (162:6).

159:3–4 **read and sign the forms he did not believe in:** Yet another example of the disconnect between Cantwell and the orders of his commanding officers, the great sadness in his life, and the ruination of his career. He will soon discuss politics in the army (170:9), which brings to mind the demotion that haunts him so severely.

159:6 **once they had ambition:** Cantwell, who will criticize his ex-wife's ambition (195:27, 195:32) and Leclerc's (200:23–24), confesses to the same quality himself.

159:6–7 **I have led my Ruffians:** Cantwell misquotes Shakespeare's *1 Henry IV*: "I have led my ragamuffins where they are peppered; there's not three of my hundred and fifty left alive, and they are for the town's end, to beg during life" (5.3.35–37). In the manuscript, Hemingway did his best to recall the exact quotation—he wrote "two hundred and fifty of them left alive"—but was sure to write himself a note to "correct quotation" (JFK 1).

Shakespeare's words served as the epigraph to Hemingway's incendiary *New Masses* article about the deadly 1935 Florida Hurricane, "Who Murdered the Vets?" Hemingway quotes Shakespeare correctly, and then issues the devastating rejoinder: "*Yes, and now we drown those three*" (43). Hemingway was brutally critical of governmental negligence that led to the deaths of 458 veterans sent down to the Keys to work during hurricane season.

159:10–11 **"Shakespeare. . . . The winner:** Hemingway, who in this novel quotes or paraphrases Shakespeare more frequently than he does any other writer, posits his common metaphor of writers as boxers. Hemingway wrote to his wife Mary on 2 October 1949 during the drafting of *Across the River and into the Trees*, "Also, in the stretch have decided to try and beat Mr. Shakespeare" (JFK, Outgoing Correspondence). The next day, he wrote to Al Horwits of Universal Pictures that his approach with the book was "to knock Mr. Shakespeare on his ass" (JFK, Outgoing Correspondence). Hemingway also saw himself as fighting Tolstoy, Turgenev, de Maupassant, and, in his never completed Land, Sea, and Air trilogy, Herman Melville.

The novelist John O'Hara wrote an bombastic, mostly positive review of *Across the River and into the Trees* in the *New York Times* in which he declared Hemingway to be "the outstanding author since Shakespeare" (1).

159:13 Did you ever read King Lear: In 1958, Hemingway declared that he read "some Shakespeare every year, *Lear* always" (Plimpton, "Art of Fiction" 119). When we first meet Renata, Cantwell describes her voice the same way Lear eulogizes his daughter Cordelia (79:6–7).

159:14 Mister Gene Tunney: Gene Tunney (1897–1978) was heavyweight champion of the world from 1926 to 1928 and retired with a career record of 81–1–3. Tunney and his wife visited Hemingway at the Finca Vigía in the late 1940s. George Plimpton recounts a story of Hemingway and Tunney sparring in Cuba when Hemingway broke the rules of sparring and threw a hard punch. Tunney responded by throwing "a whistling punch, bringing it up just a millimeter short of Hemingway's face" ("Ultimate Confrontation" 116). Tunney recollects that Hemingway cut him "across the lips" and thought, "What Ernest needs is a good little liver punch. . . . His knees buckled, his face went gray, and I thought he was going to go down. But he didn't, and for the next few hours Ernest was perfectly charming" (qtd. in Meyers, *Hemingway* 427). In a meditation about courage in the drafting of *Green Hills of Africa*, Hemingway once wrote, "Not all of the charming ones were cowards. Look at Tunney" (qtd. in Baker, *Life Story* 609). Thomas Hudson drinks to Tunney in *Islands in the Stream* (292). Tunney is also the source of an amusing anecdote in Adriana Ivancich's *La torre bianca*, in which she is introduced to Tunney at Hemingway's house in Cuba and asks him what he does for a living; she is mortified when her brother informs her that he was heavyweight champion of the world (133–34).

Hemingway also referred to the connection between Lear and Tunney in his 1954 article for *Look* magazine, "The Christmas Gift," in which he refers to small deer as "the animals on which Poor Tom in *King Lear* existed. Mr. Gene Tunney, the Shakespearean scholar, can provide the quotation" (*BL* 465). As Hemingway asserts, in *King Lear* Edgar says, "mice and rats and such small deer / Hath been Tom's food for seven long year" (3.4.117–18).

In the manuscript, Tunney's "lovely wife Polly" (JFK 1), Mary "Polly" Lauder (1907–2008), is also mentioned.

160:12 I have loved three and lost them thrice: As we have seen previously, the number three figures prominently in the novel. Three loves, three heart attacks, three battalions, Renata's three orgasms, three wars, and now three countries: Spain, Italy, and France. Cantwell is quoting Edmond Rostand's *Cyrano de Bergerac* (1897), where Roxane says, "I never loved but one man in my life, / And I have lost him—twice" (193). This formulation expresses for countries what Cantwell has previously lamented about women (91:20–21).

160:14 **General Fat Ass Franco:** General Francisco Franco y Bahamonde (1892–1975) was the prime minister of Spain and the Nationalist leader during the Spanish Civil War. Per Cantwell's allegation, Franco employed Moroccan mercenaries.

160:15 **shooting stick:** A cane or walking stick with an end that unfolds into a seat, this device was originally so named to ease the waiting during a hunt. In April 1949, *Life* magazine published a picture of General Franco sitting on a shooting stick, resplendent in a suit, poised with a rifle; it is a strikingly incongruous image, perhaps the Spanish version of then-presidential candidate Michael Dukakis wearing an ill-fitting combat helmet on a tank.[1]

161:4, 11 **you would eff-off . . . no eff-off in portrait:** In both instances, the manuscript says "fuck off." Later in the scene, when Cantwell and the portrait each say "the hell with you" (161:21, 161:24) to the other, those are each "fuck you" in the manuscript.
    Other instances of the euphemism "eff" appear on 87:30 and 154:21.

161:5–6 **Boy or daughter or my one true love or whatever it is:** For those still struck that Renata and Cantwell may have inverted gender roles during the gondola scene, it will be notable that Cantwell is so cavalier with gender designations as he addresses the portrait.

161:10 **third Wassermann:** The Wassermann is a test for syphilis, named after August Paul von Wassermann (1866–1925). Hemingway refers to "negative and positive Wassermanns" in his introduction to Elio Vittorini's *In Sicily* ("Introduction" 103).

161:17 **for now he had two stars:** Cantwell has become a two-star general in his reverie.

162:9 **I do not wish ever to be brutal:** Following his vow to be "the best Goddamned boy you ever witnessed" (161:13), this abiding self-exhortation ends chapter 17, the solitary meditation in his hotel room, shared only with the anthropomorphized portrait of Renata.

CHAPTER 17 · 141

NOTE

1. For alerting me to this image of Franco, I am indebted to Stacey Guill's paper, "'General Fat Ass Franco' and the 'Spanish Issue' in Ernest Hemingway's *Across the River and into the Trees*," delivered at the Hemingway Society's Sixteenth Biennial International Conference, San Servolo, Italy, 26 June 2014.

CHAPTER 18

163:1 **Gazzettino:** The local paper, *Il Gazzettino*, has various editions, depending on the town. In the manuscript, Hemingway wrote "the Gazzettino de Veneto" (JFK 1), along with a note to check the spelling. Although there has never been any such publication, Cantwell presumably would be receiving *Il Gazzettino di Venezia*, the paper of Venice. See 133:10 for the paper's other mention.

164:5–6 **a difficult trade being an ex-Fascist:** In the manuscript, Hemingway adds "and a shit" to this phrase (JFK 1). Cantwell continues to be conscious of the vestiges of the recently fallen Fascist regime (see 174:4–5).

164:10–11 **Do I have to hate the Krauts:** This theme is one of Hemingway's most prominent examinations of the metaphysics of war and violence. From Pedro Romero, the bullfighter in *The Sun Also Rises* to Santiago, the old fisherman in *The Old Man and the Sea,* Hemingway's stance was always that you should be able to execute a task—including killing game, a fish, a bull, or even a man—without personal acrimony. In *Islands in the Stream,* the young boy, David, has a long battle with the fish, which culminates with the statement "I don't hate him. I love him" (134), attesting to an emotional connection to one's enemy. Romero calls bulls his "best friends" (189), even though he tries to kill them. So, when Cantwell makes a distinction between the Germans "as soldiers and as human beings," he is stating that a soldier has a job to do and that personal emotions need not interfere. See also where the Russians are similarly described (70:29–31) and where Cantwell tells Renata he liked Rommel "Very much" (263:16).

In an unpublished World War II short story called "The Monument," Hemingway writes, "But at that time I had the true benignity of the non-believer and I wished everyone well including the Krauts we killed. If you have never killed anyone this may be difficult to understand. But it is a form of religion" (JFK 580a).

See entry at 38:25.

164:19 **as long as he lived:** This passage is another ironic moment; "as long as he lived" will only span one more day. Hemingway uses this same device in "The Short

Happy Life of Francis Macomber," in which—as the title suggests—Francis knows that after his moment of cowardice when hunting a lion, he merits his wife's scorn "for the rest of my life now" (*CSS* 7).

See entry at 76:16.

CHAPTER 19

166:1–3 **with the leisure of a fighter:** Since a fallen fighter is given ten seconds before he is counted out, Hemingway's hypothetical fighter would have come to, heard the referee count "four," and then known that he had five more seconds before being counted out. Particularly at this phase of Hemingway's life, metaphorical comparisons to sports were constant. For ample evidence of this, see Lillian Ross's 1950 *New Yorker* profile of Hemingway. In correspondence as he was writing this novel, Hemingway compared the act of writing to boxing, horse racing, and baseball. Cantwell has just referenced Gene Tunney and declared Shakespeare the undisputed champion (159:10–11, 159:14). He will later use an arcane college football simile to illustrate one of his anecdotes (214:17–19).

167:10 **Pin me no pin curls:** In her *Reading Hemingway* (335), Miriam Mandel finds in this construction an echo of Capulet's line in *Romeo and Juliet:* "Thank me no thankings, nor proud me no prouds" (3.5.153).

167:14–15 **he did not capitalize her now in his mind:** The conceit of the portrait as "Portrait," as its own character who may speak and listen, begins on 160:22. This self-reflective remark about capitalization is inane, since the capitalization of the word has been haphazard to this point. The novel has almost a dozen examples of portrait being addressed directly but not capitalized; see, for example, 161:21, 161:28, 161:32, 164:14, 164:18, 166:17.

167:29 **soldier-suit:** Cantwell is wearing his military uniform while he is in Venice. He wears a tunic (169:11, 194:31, 201:18); a raincoat with a belt (171:12–13; see also 172:8–11); "skirts well down" (171:14); and combat boots (174:10). When his uniform attracts the attention and possibly the scorn of some onlookers, Cantwell makes clear he is wearing is a uniform and "Not a costume" (43:12). Cantwell later makes a second gloss of the difference between a costume and a uniform (218:2–3).

The hyphen is incorrect; "soldier suit" is spelled properly at the end of this chapter (168:14).

167:31 **favoring his bad leg:** Cantwell's bad leg, we can be sure, is a result of the war injury that ruined his right kneecap (27:6–7). He admits to Renata that his head, legs, and feet still hurt him (82:31–32). Cantwell's gait recalls the beginning of Dante's *Inferno,* where the pilgrim recalls: "After I had rested my tired body a little, I again took up my way across the desert strand, so that the firm foot was always the lower" (I.28–30). Like Dante, Cantwell's walk is "slightly crooked" (174:8).

168:5–6 **Portrait. . . . Mirror:** Portrait is the past, Renata at sixteen; the mirror is the present, reflecting Cantwell at fifty. This scene recalls the moment in *The Sun Also Rises* when a naked Jake Barnes studies his wound in the mirror of the armoire in his Paris apartment. Cantwell looks at his face "in the glass of the long mirror" (75:24), a face that he will call "ugly" (75:26). The Colonel later tells Renata he doesn't much like to look at his wounded hand (83:3). He will also examine his face in the mirror and decide that it looks "as though it had been cut out of wood by an indifferent craftsman" (107:6–7). After defecating, he again looks at himself in the mirror, "set in the half closed door" (157:30–31).

168:9–10 **We are hung:** Cantwell puns about his genitalia, with reference to the hanging of the portrait of Renata.

168:14 **Today is another day:** This line is a change from the manuscript, which reads, "Today is today" (JFK 1).

CHAPTER 20

169:8 **the trouble," and he:** It appears that a speech tag is missing; either the dialogue should be attributed, or this sequence should be divided into two sentences.

169:16–17 **for he was lonely too:** The night porter replaces Portrait and Cantwell as the audience and interlocutor. This quality recalls the 1933 short story "A Clean Well-Lighted Place," in which the older waiter identifies with a lonely old man who recently attempted suicide.

170:1–2 **We were beaten and we have to wait a while now:** The night porter is referring to a relatively recent election. Luigi Einaudi (1874–1961) took office as president of Italy on 12 May 1948. He represented the Italian Liberal Party. In the first legislature after World War II, Alcide de Gasperi (1881–1954), representing the Christian Democratic Party, was the prime minister of Italy, beginning his term on 23 May 1948. Randolfo Pacciardi, incidentally, also became minister of defense on 23 May. This pivotal election, in which Italy transitioned from fascism to democracy, occurred on 18 April 1948.

170:25 **You've got a young party:** The night porter, then, seems to be a member of the Popular Democratic Front (*Fronte Democratico Popolare per la libertà, la pace, il lavoro*), a coalition of the Socialist and Communist Parties that joined together for the 1948 elections.

170:30 **Tito:** The night porter is asking about the then prime minister of Yugoslavia, Josip Broz-Tito (1892–1980), who was a Communist and earned praise for working toward the unity of the various states of Yugoslavia. Hemingway owned a book on Tito's life, *The Heretic: The Life and Times of Josip Broz-Tito*, published in 1957 (Brasch and Sigman 231). Cantwell refers to Tito as his "next door neighbor" (170:31); Yugoslavia bordered Italy on its western edge, the present-day Slovenia.

171:5 **Mister Tito has plenty problems:** Cantwell is referring to the split between the USSR and Yugoslavia in mid-1948; Joseph Stalin expelled Tito and Yugoslavia from

147

the Soviet Union, largely because Tito advocated Yugoslavia's independence from the Soviet Union.

171:9 any pearl of great price: Cantwell borrows from Matthew 13:46, which speaks of the merchant who finds such a pearl. The "pearl of wisdom" that Cantwell is dispensing also hints at Job 28:18, which states, "the price of wisdom is above pearls." In Nathaniel Hawthorne's *The Scarlet Letter,* Hester Prynne names her daughter Pearl, "as being of great price" (89).

171:11–12 ***Fa brutto tempo . . . Bruttissimo:*** The night porter says, "It's bad weather," to which Cantwell responds: "Very bad."

CHAPTER 21

172:2 **the usual dirty note:** Ten centesimi only came in the form of a note around the time of World War I and has since been produced as a coin. It would be unlikely that Cantwell would be carrying an antiquated bill for such a small sum of money, about two American cents.

172:2–3 **the crowd of those condemned:** Hemingway is at his most Dantesque in this image of the doomed clustered on the shores of the Grand Canal.

172:12 **water through a Burberry:** Burberry is an English clothing manufacturer. In a 15 September 1944 letter to his son Patrick, Hemingway writes that he has lost his Burberry "rain-coat" and instead is wearing "a battle jacket with the zipper broken held together by safety pins" (*SL* 572). Mary wears a Burberry rain coat in *Under Kilimanjaro* (112). In Hemingway's article about the D-Day invasion, "Voyage to Victory," he is also wearing a Burberry raincoat (*BL* 343).

172:13 **Groton:** Groton is a prestigious prep school in Massachusetts. Franklin Delano Roosevelt, the thirty-second U.S. president, is among its alumni.

172:13–14 **Canterbury:** Canterbury is a prep school in Connecticut. Hemingway sent his two youngest sons, Patrick and Gregory, there (Mandel, "Reading the Brusadelli Stories" 339). In a 1949 letter to A. E. Hotchner, the year of his youngest son's graduation from Canterbury, Hemingway refers to the "miserable, lace-curtain catholic education" that did not suit Gregory (*Dear Papa* 36).

172:17–18 **Benny Meyers of the ground forces:** Meyers was a World War II major general employed as a purchasing officer. He was convicted in 1948 of a felony for convincing someone else to lie about an investigation regarding Meyers's activities on behalf of Aviation Electric. He was sentenced to from twenty months to five years. Cantwell, therefore, is using Benny Meyers as a symbol of the *pescecani*, those who illegally or immorally profit from war. According to Dante's taxonomy, Meyers would be one of the Fraudulent, circle eight. Meyers was a major general of the air force, thus Cantwell wonders who the ground force equivalent is. Meyers is also mentioned as a man who is essentially Cantwell's antithesis (175:30–31).

The Senate War Investigating Subcommittee grilled Meyers for his approval of the $70 million contract with Howard Hughes's company for F-11 photo-reconnaissance planes, despite the crafts' technical issues. Hughes revealed that as reciprocation, Meyers asked for a postwar job. Meyers also profited illegally from buying stocks in the companies involved in military contracts ("Discomfited General" 26).

173:3–4 Is she a vehicle? In this random stream-of-consciousness aside, Cantwell can rest assured that a gondola is considered a vehicle, according to the *OED*: "Any means of carriage, conveyance, or transport; a receptacle in which anything is placed in order to be moved"; the word "vehicle" is derived from the Latin *vehere*, the verb "to carry."

173:6 penny for your thoughts: A bit later in this chapter, it will become "nickel for your thoughts now" (179:13). Hemingway critic Philip Young views this line as telling, snidely noting in his 1950 review of the novel: "But the reader is giving three dollars" (Review 56).

173:17 double Canfield: Named after the gambler R. A. Canfield, double Canfield is a game of solitaire similar to Klondike. Cantwell's game requires action. This reference recalls Steinbeck's *Of Mice and Men* (1939), in which George frequently plays solitaire to reinforce the theme of loneliness.

173:19 *trattorias*: Italian for small restaurants, the correct plural form of *trattoria* is *trattorie*. See also 49:2, where the word is not italicized.

173:22 *solitaire ambulante*: French for "walking solitaire."

173:27 game was to leave: This sentence would be clearer with a "the" before "game."

173:27–28 leave from the Gritti and make the Rialto by the *Fondamente Nuove*: A map is essential to explain the game Cantwell is playing. A *fondamenta* is a street adjacent to a canal. The Fondamente Nuove is the northern border of Venice, bordering the Canale delle Fondamente Nuove. As Zorzi and Moriani point out, Cantwell is certainly taking a circuitous route to the Rialto (35).

173:31 He liked the market best: Too much can be made of Cantwell's enjoyment of the market as a prophetic statement on 1950s consumerism. While it is true that Cantwell stays at a fancy hotel and dines heartily, the market at the Rialto is emblematic of Venice's cultural riches. It is somewhat surprising that Cantwell's walk does not take him, for instance, to the Accademia or the Scuola di San Rocco, where he might opine on masterpieces of art, rather than on prawns. Cantwell compares the market to the Prado or Accademia (178:29–30).

173:33–34 saying the things about him: In the manuscript, Hemingway wrote, "saying dirty things about him" (JFK 1).

174:5 former Fascists or maybe they are something else: In the manuscript, Hemingway wrote, "former fascists or present fascists" (JFK 1). Fascism would have been out of power in Italy for about three years, which makes its vestiges inevitable.

174:18 apse of the church of Frari: In the manuscript, Hemingway leaves a gap for the term "apse" here and on 174:19. He also leaves a gap for the name of the church, which is the Santa Maria Gloriosa dei Frari, built in 1338 and located in the San Polo district of Venice. Titian is interred in the Frari, which prominently features a monument to him.

174:25, 28–29 old and worn death smile . . . spat on the pavement: With his expression and by spitting, Cantwell expands on two behaviors that we have already seen. He has a brutal death glare (see entries at 42:7, 134:21–23, 197:6), and he is capable of spitting even in the most nerve-racking situations (see 39:16–17).

175:11–12 the simple odds of two to one: This near-confrontation against two men foreshadows the embedded narrative of Cantwell dispatching two men who are too forward in their admiration of Renata (261:7–17). It also reinforces Cantwell's criticism of General Montgomery, who waited until the odds were overwhelmingly in his favor, which Cantwell puts at fifteen to one.

175:14 badly educated youths: This odd putdown actually is a literal transposition of the Italian word *maleducato,* usually directed at anyone ignorant or boorish. Fernada Pivano's translation of this phrase is "*giovinastri maleducati*" (144), or "ignorant thugs."

175:20 they only saw my back and ass and legs: As with the remark about the 2:1 odds, this comment also prefigures the embedded narrative in chapter 40, when Cantwell instructs Renata: "Let's walk so we make even the backs of our legs look dangerous" (262:5–6).

175:26 Ten thousand dollars: Ten thousand dollars was the life insurance coverage for enlisted military during World War II.

175:32–33 **lost them at the Chateau that time at ten G's a head:** Cantwell is referring to the heavy shelling Colonel Buck Lanham's command post received on 9 August 1944 at Château Lingeard, resulting in severe casualties. Hemingway was invited to the Château that day but refused, later telling Lanham that the Château "stank of death" (Beistle 5).

176:12–13 **you had a lot of money on you:** It might be forgotten that Cantwell is carrying around Renata's emeralds, which would be quite a bounty for a street mugging, perhaps a quarter of a million dollars (154:24–25). In fact, in the manuscript, Hemingway had written "a quarter of a million dollars" in place of "a lot of money" (JFK 1).

176:18 **hardly noticing:** Cantwell's vigilance as a soldier corresponds to Hemingway's vigilance as an observer for writing, from scenes of violence, to details that render reality in new and more vivid ways. This impulse corresponds to the vindictive game he plays with the hall porter in the Gritti, in which he is determined to snatch the newspaper from his hand before he can release it (163:18).

CHAPTER 22

177:1 **He loved the market:** Venice's Rialto market, located at the center of the city, has lasted centuries. Excellent photographs of Hemingway's visit to the market are in Moriani (98–100). These three pictures depict Hemingway with a notepad, jotting down details about the fish market and interviewing a fishmonger. This effusive praise expands on "He liked the market best" (173:31), it being "the closest thing to a good museum" (178:29). Cantwell arrives at the fish market at 178:31.

177:5 *îlot de résistance:* French for "island of resistance"; Cantwell, for the umpteenth time, thinks in military metaphors and imagines his fellow shoppers as part of the "morning attack" (177:6).

177:8 **the great sausages:** Cantwell begins shopping for sausage for Bobby, the hunting dog, one of several gestures of generosity that mark Cantwell's final days, including the jeep engine for the boatman (48:11) and the ebony moor for Renata (100:22). These threads to the narrative give the reader a sense of anticipation, to wait for things that may happen, not just nostalgia or regret about things that have already happened. Cantwell also promises to send Cipriani a check for the statue of the little negro (244:21), although it is not evident that he ever does. We learn that Bobby never receives the sausage (272:14), which registers as one of Cantwell's final explicit laments (281:1–2).

177:8–9 **People at home think *mortadella* is a sausage:** Cantwell's claim here is a bit odd and understandable only if he is making an argument for the superiority of the Italian sausage to the American sausage, as if to say Americans think *they've* eaten sausage, but nothing like this. According to the *OED*, mortadella is "any of several types of Italian sausage." In *Tender Is the Night*, F. Scott Fitzgerald's characters "ate sandwiches of mortadel sausage" (59).

177:15 **the hogs that ate acorns in the mountains:** Cantwell's palate is apparently refined enough to recognize this common way to raise pigs for sausage.

177:16, 178:10 **quarter of a kilo . . . eighth of a kilo:** Cantwell orders 8.81 oz. for himself, the poler, and the man who will pick him up; he orders 4.4 oz. for Bobby, the dog.

178:29 **A market is the closest thing to a good museum:** Following Cantwell's consciousness in this moment is illuminating. Cantwell is not making some kind of resigned argument for crass commercialism, a prophecy for the 1950s. Instead, he is gushing about how holy he considers the open market at the Rialto. He is able to see art and beauty in the food and ritual of this famous Venetian tradition. His reference to the Prado, the famous art museum in Madrid, echoes a mention in *For Whom the Bell Tolls,* in which seeing Mantegna, El Greco, and Brueghel at the Prado equates to his commitment to the Republic, a "religious experience," a "part in something that you could believe in wholly and completely and in which you felt an absolute brotherhood with the others who were engaged in it" (235).

See entry at 173:31.

179:1–2 **presaged their death:** In addition to the warm, nostalgic tones of this scene, Cantwell also identifies with the lobsters, who are condemned—as with those waiting at the dock—and the nobility of the already dead small fish (179:7). The shrimp, too, are "awaiting their turn" (179:19–20); a man like Cantwell, who has dealt with death his whole life, and particularly this weekend, would be especially attuned to the metaphysics of the fish market.

Marina Gradoli has offered an ingenious connection between this passage and a sequence in Walt Whitman's *Leaves of Grass,* "A Song of Joys," which anticipates some of Hemingway's descriptive language:

> The work of fishermen, the work of the eel-fisher and clam fisher;
> I come with my clam-rake and spade . . .
> I have a small axe to cut holes in the ice . . .
> the dark green lobsters are desperate with their claws as I take them out, I insert
>   wooden pegs in the joints of their pincers . . .
> There in a huge kettle of boiling water the lobsters shall be boil'd till their color
>   becomes scarlet.
> Another time mackerel-taking,
> Voracious, mad for the hook, near the surface, they seem to fill the water for
>   miles (ll. 35–36, 38, 45, 47–49)

Gradoli notes the uncanny recurrence of "voracious," the instance of Cantwell cutting holes in the ice, and the coloring of the lobsters.

179:8 **pelagic:** Pelagic fish live in the open sea, far from the shore.

179:17 ***scampi brochetto:*** Hemingway means to write "*scampi brochette*"; a "brochette" is a skewer, the "rapier-like instrument" (179:17–18) to which Cantwell will refer. *Brochetto* might sound like an Italian word, but it is not correct. Hemingway wrote a note in the typescript to check the spelling of this word, but it was never fixed.

179:24 **the mustaches of that old Japanese admiral:** Togo Heiachiro (1848–1934) was a famous Japanese navy admiral, most notably in the Russo-Japanese War (1904–05). The German writer Frank Thiess's (1890–1977) 1936 novel *Tsushima*'s account of one of the battles of this war, the Battle of Tsushima on 27–28 May 1905, is included in Hemingway's *Men at War* anthology. Admiral Togo wore a dignified goatee with a long gray moustache. Hemingway made the same comparison in *Islands in the Stream*, when Thomas Hudson sees the antennae of prawns and "remarked that they were longer than those of a Japanese admiral" (205).

In the manuscript to *Across the River and into the Trees*, Hemingway wrote, "correct this" over the word "tentacles" (179:23), which he apparently concluded he did not need to do.

179:25–26 **Oh Christian shrimp:** Cantwell might be thinking of Leviticus 11:10 and Deuteronomy 14:10, which forbid the eating of fish without fins and scales. Cantwell is also satirizing the nineteenth-century hymn "Onward, Christian Soldiers," to which Hemingway also alludes in his 1944 poem, "Poem to Mary (Second Poem)." In that sprawling, desperate poem, he replaces, "Onward Christian soldiers, marching as to war / With the cross of Jesus going on before" with "Onward Christian soldiers / Marching to a whore / With the cross of Mary Welsh / Going on before" (*Poems* 111).

180:6 **Colonel cut closer to the shell:** Of course, those who would accuse Hemingway of constructing an omnipotent protagonist alongside an omniscient narrator would point to this unlikely scenario, whereby this dying army colonel with a crippled hand is more precise with a fish knife than a man who does it for a living. Compare the actual inspiration of this scene, in which Hemingway carried a notepad to learn, to gain information. When transmuting it into fiction, his character becomes the unequivocal expert.

As a comparison, see the scene in *The Sun Also Rises* when Jake Barnes orders a rum punch in Burguete and then shows the innkeeper how to make it (116).

CHAPTER 23

181:1 **Hotel Gritti-Palace:** This establishment does not hyphenate its last two words, as here, which is the only such error in the novel. Otherwise, when it is not referred to as simply the Gritti, the hotel is referred to as the Gritti Palace Hotel (76:1–2, 102:2, 202:27–28), the Gritti Hotel (60:29), or the Hotel Gritti (282:31).

181:6 **paid them what it was worth, and some more:** Just as chapter 22 ends with the payment of the seafood, chapter 23 begins with the payment of the gondoliers. As is the case with every other Hemingway protagonist, for Cantwell, payment of the just amount must be ethics as much as economics—knowing the value of something, and even when you do overpay, being aware that you are overpaying and the reason for it. When a character has about twenty-four hours to live, he cannot be consumed with wasting a few lire here and there; it must be a deeper ethic than that. Earlier, Cantwell debates whether or not to overpay a boatman, ultimately deciding to give him the money (47:7–8).

181:9 **The concierge:** During Cantwell's long walk, the concierge, Domenico, or Ico, has taken over for the night porter (169:2–3).

181:13–14 **An officer and not a Gentleman:** This phrase borrows from Title 10, Article 133 of the U.S. Uniform Code of Military Justice, which states, "Any commissioned officer, cadet, or midshipman who is convicted of conduct unbecoming an officer and a gentleman shall be punished as a court-martial may direct" (Rush, G. 90). Hemingway borrows this wordplay from his early story, "The Mercenaries," in which Captain Graves admits, "I was an officer, but not a gentleman" (qtd. in Griffin 108).

181:20 **Cripps will probably ration it:** Sir Stafford Cripps (1889–1952) served as the chancellor for the exchequer from 1947 to 1950, the position in the British cabinet in charge of all financial and economic matters. After World War II, he advocated a rigorous policy of austerity and rationing, to which Cantwell sarcastically refers.

182:16 **like ski-ing in the dark:** Renata describes sleep in this way here and at 186:18.

182:32 **Florian:** Il Caffè Florian opened in 1720 at Piazza San Marco 56 in Venice. Caffè Florian is Italy's oldest café. Cantwell refers to the "right hand side of the square" (182:32–33), recalling Cantwell's own injured right hand. The Florian is on the right side of the piazza (the south) from the perspective of Cantwell entering from the west. The Florian is to the south of the piazza, closer to the water, directly north of Riva degli Schiavoni. For a picture of Hemingway dining *al fresco* at the Florian during his last trip to Venice in 1954, see Moriani (164).

183:3–4 **did not feel good:** Cantwell has another spell with his heart, his most serious episode thus far in the current action of the novel.

183:10 **rested lightly and without illusion:** That is, the illusion of immortality; see earlier entry (39:5–6). In Hemingway's introduction to *Men at War,* a volume of war writing he selected and edited in 1942, he writes: "When you go to war as a boy you have a great illusion of immortality. Other people get killed; not you. It can happen to other people; but not to you. Then when you are badly wounded the first time you lose that illusion and you know it can happen to you" (xii). Cantwell soon challenges the concierge: "But what about you, boy? You're not immortal, are you?" (183:21–22). Cantwell's coming-of-age experience, like Hemingway's, occurred after World War I, when "he had been quite confident of his personal immortality" until his the first major wound disabused him of that notion.

The first wound represented "the loss of the immortality" (39:10–11). "Well, in a way," Cantwell wryly concludes, "that is quite a lot to lose" (39:11–12).

In an extraordinary letter to Mary during the battle at Hürtgen Forest, Hemingway wrote: "just like a gift . . . I get the old feeling of immortality back I used to have when I was 19—right in the middle of a *really* bad shelling" (qtd. in Mellow 539).

183:13 **as lightly as a hawk rests:** Cantwell is compared to a hawk, as opposed to a marsh bird or a heron or a curlew, as were the intimidated ex-Fascists (174:32–175:1). Hemingway used the word "hawk" to describe Zelda Fitzgerald's invidiousness (*MF* 186) in the vignette "Hawks Do Not Share" and also in "In Another Country" to describe the true warriors in World War I (*CSS* 208).

183:20 **It would be unnecessary:** Domenico's comradely assurance that a contingency will be in place to grant Cantwell's final wishes should be contrasted with the end of the novel, when Cantwell does not afford Jackson the same trust (282:29–283:2).

183:28–29 **change of life hotels:** "Change of life" is a reference to menopause, so Cantwell is referring to old-age homes. In the manuscript, Hemingway added the phrase "rocking away their dregs of life" after "women."

184:1 **energy crackers:** These pemmican biscuits, high in fat, were developed by Native Americans and later eaten by soldiers. The only truth to these crackers causing impotence, it seems, is the notion that foods high in fat inhibit blood flow to the extremities.

184:8, 10 **botulism, anthrax:** Hemingway told *Time* magazine that he was "ill with . . . anthrax infections in Cortina d'Ampezzo" during the writing of the novel ("Hemingway Is Bitter about Nobody" 110). See entry at 45:11.

184:14 **you can hear Margaret:** Cantwell seems to be referring to Margaret Truman, the president's daughter, who was an aspiring singer. However, Margaret Woodrow Wilson (1886–1944), the daughter of the twenty-eighth president of the United States, made several recordings during World War I, including at least one of the national anthem in 1915.

184:27 **twelve and one half minutes:** The walk from the Gritti to the Florian is fairly straight, and about a third of a mile northeast, most of it on Calle Larga XXII Marzo. After making this walk to meet Renata, he will pick her up at the Florian, and then they will decide to return to the Gritti for breakfast.

CHAPTER 24

185:4 **Are you all right?** Renata can evidently see the physical manifestation of his ailing heart.

185:10 **For nothing:** Hemingway is transposing Cantwell's Italian response, which is "per niente" or, as Pivano translates it, "Di niente" (153). See Cirino, "You Don't Know" (45–46).

185:16–17 **and pondered that for two seconds:** Cantwell, who values quick decisions, spends two of the novel's most important seconds considering what emerges as the single most crucial subplot to the novel: Alvarito and Renata's future relationship. It is clear that Renata understands Alvarito's interest in her and also his respect for Cantwell.

187:5–6 **obliquely . . . oblique:** This kind of descriptive neurosis or grammatical fussiness at this point in the plot is bizarre. Why would the adverb not be correct? Is he referencing Ovid's *Metamorphoses* "His side unguarded, with a blow oblique" (XII, l. 588:) or Horace's Ode to Diana: "Of a young boar with tusky cheek / that meditates the blow oblique" (III, Ode XXII) or Virgil, "blow oblique impell'd" (I, l. 301). The ancient poets are describing the blows received in battle, not the blowing of the wind, so Cantwell is correct to use the adverb.

See also the "family" or "tribe" controversy (258:3, 258:4). Hemingway was fond of these cute debates: in *The Sun Also Rises*, he is sure to clarify that they are not eating toast, but "bread toasted" (119).

187:9–10 **chest upstanding in the black sweater:** The portrait is also mentioned as having a black sweater (193:11).

CHAPTER 25

188:1–3 **At the Gritti:** This chapter begins in classic Hemingway fashion, with an accumulation of four prepositional phrases in one sentence.

189:14 *fabricar rognons:* According to Craig Boreth's *Hemingway Cookbook,* they are eating Rognons Grilled with Champignons, consisting of veal kidneys, mushrooms, butter, salt, and pepper (35). "*Fabricar*" is Spanish for "to make" or "to fashion." So, Cantwell, an American, is speaking to Renata, an Italian, about a French dish, and sprinkling in a little Spanish for good measure.

189:18–28 The dialogue that concludes chapter 25 is somewhat ambiguous, due to the paucity of Hemingway's dialogue attribution. It is a three-way conversation among Renata, Cantwell, and the *Gran Maestro;* six lines are quoted, with the speaker clearly indicated three times, the first, second, and sixth line. The other three lines are ambiguous, but it seems that the *Gran Maestro* speaks the third and fifth; he suggests that they order and then confirms that the couple doesn't want any more food. The fourth line, with the signifying word "unmaidenly" (189:24), must be Renata. "Maidenly" (or "un-maidenly") is a word Renata uses twice (142:30, 182:20) and which she claims to have learned from her governess. Cantwell uses the word, too, when addressing the portrait (167:27), so "maidenliness" is always associated with Renata.

CHAPTER 26

At the beginning of chapter 26 in the manuscript, Hemingway writes: "Found my typewriter ribbon fucked up and jammed at 0520. Why can't people find their own god-damned air-plane?"

190:1 **at the table:** The first sentences of chapters 24, 25, and 26 each establish a table at the Gritti: Renata is waiting at the table to begin chapter 24; the *Gran Maestro* sits them both at a table by the window to begin chapter 25, and here, the couple is able to watch the emerging storm over the Grand Canal.

190:14 **horse-chestnut:** In this discussion of trees, including the Lombardy poplar, or the "Italica," Cantwell's reference to the horse chestnut tree anticipates *A Moveable Feast,* in which "For luck you carried a horse chestnut and a rabbit's foot in your right pocket" (91).

191:3 **check the oil, Mac:** This episode, perhaps too cute on Hemingway's part, explores the not-that-funny aspect of Renata adopting American parlance, an episode that would probably only be charming if you adored someone, but is not as universal as Hemingway might have hoped. Although the humor falls flat, and we see how this moment might mean more to Hemingway and Cantwell than it would to the reader, the theme of language is furthered by this moment, as Cantwell teaches Renata the American vernacular, his version of Dante's *De vulgari eloquentia.*

Another phrase, "You hired out to be tough, didn't you?" (192:10–11) was apparently a Hemingway favorite. In a scathing May 1950 letter, his wife Mary proposed ending their marriage, writing: "About your work, you scoffed at others who couldn't go the distance on a book. You reiterated your phrase 'You hired out to be tough, didn't you?' You affirmed that you knew how to handle yourself in a long tough bout" (*How It Was* 263).

192:13 **Ida Lupino:** Lupino (1918–1995) was a legendary English-born actress who appeared most famously in *They Drive By Night* (1940) and *High Sierra* (1941). By adopting Lupino's gravely voice, Renata is apparently being tough, sexy, like a femme fatale.

192:15 **Gran Maestro!** Hemingway uses only three exclamation points in *Across the River and into the Trees:* here, when he calls the *Gran Maestro;* while duck hunting, when he calls Bobby, the dog (273:22); and earlier, when he says, "I will!" to the possibility of marrying Renata and having five sons (105:22).

192:24 **straighten up and fly right:** Cantwell is alluding to Nat King Cole's 1943 hit song, "Straighten Up and Fly Right". The Andrews Sisters recorded a version of this song the following year. Hemingway also used this phrase in a 1950 letter to Chink Dorman-Smith (qtd. in Greacen, "Irish Soldier" 9), simply to mean being tough and uncomplaining and to behave properly. In *Under Kilimanjaro,* G.C., too, asserts that he will "straighten up and fly right" (255).

CHAPTER 27

193:17–194:7 Hemingway unintentionally leaves an ambiguity in dialogue attribution. Renata begins the dialogue by asking if Cantwell closes the windows. After a brief response, it seems that Cantwell asks, "How much alike are we?" (193:20). Renata observes that they haven't had an opportunity to find out. Then, it is unclear who speaks the next two lines: it is likely that Cantwell agrees: "We never had a fair chance. But we've had enough of a chance for me to know" (194:3–4), but it is just as likely that Renata would say that as a continuation of her original statement. The next statement—"And when you know what the hell have you got?" (194:5)—is clearly Cantwell, to which Renata tries to offer a definition. And then, with Cantwell's remark about "limited objectives" (194:9–10), the dialogue regularizes. The glitch, then, is the sixth statement that follows their lying on the bed. The "fair chance" remark should either be appended to Renata's previous statement or attached to the Colonel's fatalistic one that follows.

194:1–2 **We never had much of a chance to find out:** A comment like this is an appropriate moment to wonder how long Cantwell and Renata have known each other. How brief has their relationship been? At some points, she does not know whether he has a son or not; at others, it seems they have experienced quite a lot together. One wonders if the "several months" that the Colonel has known the Anarchist bartender in Venice is also the same amount of time that he has known Renata (44:7).

194:9–10 **I don't believe in limited objectives:** The rejected title for Hemingway's unpublished World War II short story "Indian Country and the White Army" was "The Limited Objective."

194:12 **Other people's orders:** This line is one of the novel's most important: it reveals Cantwell's lingering resentment from the war, his obedience to an unwise order that got many of his men killed. As Cantwell ruefully said earlier, "you get the orders, and you have to carry them out" (176:7–8). He will later say, "it was a beautiful regiment until I destroyed it under other people's orders" (222:18–19). And "it was all the regiment I ever could have hoped for in this life until I lost it. . . . Under orders, of course" (213:29–30).

194:19 **I'm so ashamed about how things are:** Renata's statement reads as a general lament for the various sorrows and anxieties of the situation: her condition, her promiscuity, her tacit relationship with Alvarito, and Cantwell's impending death. In the next chapter, Renata will—again vaguely—say she is "sorry about things" (199:11). In both instances, "things" is a catchall.

195:4 ***Per piacere:*** Italian, as Cantwell says, for "for pleasure." In an odd twist, Cantwell seems to be translating this phrase for a native Italian speaker. (See Cirino, "You Don't Know" 51–52). After Cantwell asks to be taken to the Gritti, the boatman responds, "*Con piacere*" (47:18).

195:8 **I love you my last true and only love:** The punctuation of these paragraphs may make the meaning unclear, but Renata speaks both paragraphs, both imagining speaking Italian in the dark and commenting on the two languages (195:6–7). She goes on to quote the titles of two poems from later editions of Walt Whitman's *Leaves of Grass* (first published in 1855), "When Lilacs Last in the Dooryard Bloom'd" (1865) and "Out of the Cradle Endlessly Rocking" (1859).

See entry at 91:1 for a chart of such Homeric epithets.

195:27 **She was an ambitious woman:** A clear reference to Hemingway's third wife, Martha Gellhorn (1908–1998); Cantwell will continue to say that this ex-wife "had more ambition than Napoleon" (195:32). In the manuscript, "ambitious bitch" was written and later replaced by "ambitious woman" (JFK 1). The several remarks about Martha amount to, in Jeffrey Meyers's phrase, "a tasteless and transparent attack" (*Hemingway* 461).

195:34–196:1 **let's not speak about her:** In this sequence, Cantwell and Renata continually promise to avoid the topic of his ex-wife. Beginning with Renata's plea here, they continue: "Let's talk about something nice" (196:12); "let's skip it" (196:16); "Please let's skip it" (196:17); "Let us forget her" (197:13). And then, when she was "forgotten" (197:14), it is an example of the confessional quality of this dialogue. Through her questioning, Renata has taken Cantwell through anger, sadness, regret, and violence, until the bad memory is gone. As Cantwell tells his extended narrative of the liberation of Paris, we read that "he was not lecturing; he was confessing" (204:22–23). Renata tells him, "Don't you see you need to tell me things to purge your bitterness?" (220:2–3). See also "until you are purged of it" (207:8). Renata urges Cantwell to sleep, telling him that she believes that "if you slept you might get rid of them" (223:1–2), meaning the bad memories. Thinking of Hürtgen Forest, Cantwell believes that if he thinks of two things, he might "get rid of them" (234:11).

196:25–26 in another country and besides the wench is dead: The "other country" Gellhorn wrote about is presumably Spain, where she and Hemingway traveled together during the Spanish Civil War. The phrase alludes to Christopher Marlowe's (1564–1593) play, *The Jew of Malta* (1592). T. S. Eliot beat Hemingway to this reference in his "Portrait of a Lady" (1915), although Hemingway's short story "In Another Country" (1927) and *The Sun Also Rises* (1926) also make use of it. In *The Dangerous Summer* (1960), Hemingway writes that a bull has been stabbed "in aorta country" (117).

196:28 Phoebus the Phoenician: Cantwell's reference is to Eliot's "Phlebus the Phoenician, a fortnight dead" from the "Death by Water" section of *The Waste Land*. "Phoebus" is another name for Apollo, the god of the sun. "Phlebus" is a character in a Platonic work. A "Phoenician" is someone from Phoenicia, an ancient Semitic civilization.

When Cantwell vindictively declares that his ex-wife is dead, "But she doesn't know it yet" (196:28–29), it echoes Addie Bundren's monologue in *As I Lay Dying*, during which she says of her husband, "And then he died. He did not know he was dead" (174).

197:18 He knew about panics: In *Men at War,* Hemingway writes, "Cowardice, as distinguished from panic, is almost always simply a lack of ability to suspend the functioning of the imagination" (xxiv). In one of Hemingway's greatest dramatizations of this phenomenon, Francis Macomber tries to find the courage to finish off a wounded lion, but when it charges, begins "running wildly, in panic in the open" (*CSS* 17).

197:21–22 act of divorcement: Hemingway and Gellhorn divorced in December 1945, which makes the enduring quality of this vitriol somewhat striking. Cantwell has homicidal fantasies, and Renata guides him through an exorcism of these impulses. When Cantwell suggests that perhaps his ex-wife will hang herself (197:31–32), it has tragically ironic resonance; Adriana Ivancich hung herself from a tree on the Mediterranean coast town of Orbetello in 1983 (see 152:1–2).

After reading *Cosmopolitan*'s first installment of *Across the River and into the Trees,* before getting to the part featuring Hemingway's unpleasant portrait of her, Gellhorn remarked that the novel made her feel "quite sick . . . it has a loud sound of madness and a terrible smell as of decay" (204).

197:28–29 **she is why we cannot marry:** In other words, Renata is not allowed to marry a divorced man. Hemingway's second wife, Pauline Pfeiffer, had a similar hesitation. Renata distinguishes her beliefs with "cinema people" who are married multiple times and still blessed by the Pope. Cantwell's previous marriages, she explains, prevent her from marrying him (121:26–27). Cantwell will later tell Renata that he understands that they cannot marry, "although I do not approve" (238:25). Adriana Ivancich recalled that Hemingway once told her, "I would ask you to marry me if I did not know you would say no" (qtd. in Reynolds, *Final Years* 219).

198:5 **For keeps and for always:** The inside joke phrase "for keeps" is repeated (86:23–24, 269:21). "*Para siempre*" (198:6) is Spanish for "for always."

CHAPTER 28

199:11 **I'm sorry about things:** "Things" must mean that she is sorry that Cantwell is dying and that they are not able to have traditional sex. She might also be apologizing about Alvarito's presence in their lives and his inevitable role as Cantwell's replacement. This iteration picks up Renata being "so ashamed" (194:19).

199:12 **Never discuss casualties:** Cantwell relies on one of Hemingway's favorite slogans, which he employed constantly in his correspondence; in a 1938 letter, he writes to Max Perkins about Tom Wolfe's death, but "it never does any good to discuss casualties" (*SL* 473); in a 1952 to Harvey Breit of Charles Scribner's death: "There's no use ever discussing casualties" (*SL* 755); to Chink Dorman-Smith in 1954, "You know we never discuss casualties" (*SL* 843). In *A Moveable Feast,* when discussing the writing that has been stolen from him in Paris, he attributes the same phrase to Chink: "Chink had taught me never to discuss casualties" (*MF-RE* 70). Similarly, after David Bourne's writing is destroyed in *The Garden of Eden,* he tells his wife, "Let's not discuss casualties" (227).

201:23 **Doges:** A doge was a chief magistrate in ancient Venice; this position ended when Napoleon conquered Venice in 1797. So Renata is tracing her lineage back at least one hundred and fifty years.

201:31 ***Domenica del Corriere* or *Tribuna Illustrata?*** *La Domenica del Corriere,* featuring an illustration on the front cover, was the Sunday supplement to the *Corriere della Sera* daily newspaper, and it was published from 1899 to 1989. *La Tribuna Illustrata* was also an illustrated weekly, published from 1890 to 1969.

In the manuscript, Hemingway wrote: "Il Secollo [*sic*] or La Semana del Popolo?" Then he wrote: "(check) (Coloured covered bad taste weekly)." Hemingway was thinking of *Il Secolo XIX,* an Italian paper printed in color since 1886 and perhaps *L'illustrazione del Popolo* (1838–1945), which was inspired by *La Domenica del Corriere* with its focus on illustrations. However, that paper was not in existence while Hemingway was writing the novel. *Semana* is Spanish for "week"; in Italian, it would be "settimana." *La Settimana Incom Illustrata,* a periodical founded in 1948, also belongs to this genre and may have been in Hemingway's mind.

These are the "illustrated papers" that Renata has been saying she reads (128:13–14, 134:8, 200:33, 201:1, 201:30).

202:4–5 how close life comes to death when there is ecstasy: The best example of ecstatic death in Hemingway is "The Snows of Kilimanjaro," which fuses life and death because of the vision of the pinnacle of Mount Kilimanjaro. Cantwell's death is handled realistically rather than metaphysically; one of Hemingway's strategies, in fact, in much of his war writing is to demystify death. Think of the odd line, for example, in *A Farewell to Arms* when Frederic Henry describes the death of his good friend Bartolomeo Aymo: "He looked very dead" (214).

202:10 sleep's other brother: As opposed to a sensation of ecstasy, this letdown expresses the anticlimactic reality of death. With this phrase, Cantwell references T. S. Eliot's "death's other Kingdom" from "The Hollow Men" (l. 14, l. 46). Hemingway drew more explicitly on this line during a draft of the scene in *A Farewell to Arms* depicting Frederic Henry being anaesthetized: "They only choke you. It is not like . . . it is just a chemical choking" (*FTA,* Hemingway Library 299). Hemingway refers to "Love's dark sister Hate" in "Poem to Mary (Second Poem)" (*Poems* 109), as well as "Love's lovely sister" (110).

In *The Grapes of Wrath* (1939), in a related description of the anaesthetizing effects of alcohol for the migrant worker John Steinbeck writes: "Death was a friend, and sleep was death's brother" (327).

202:11 Death is a lot of shit: This paragraph-long meditation on death echoes a similar articulation about love in "The Snows of Kilimanjaro," written more than a decade earlier. In the manuscript of the short story, Hemingway originally wrote, "Love is a pile of shit" (JFK 702), which became "Love is a dunghill" (*CSS* 43).

The connection to "The Snows of Kilimanjaro" continues as Cantwell thinks about the various ways death can "come"—he gives ten examples (202:11–24)—just as in the story, "death had come and rested its head on the foot of the cot" (*CSS* 54).

202:32 Here goes: One of the litmus tests of Hemingway's narrative is whether this "here goes" will cause readers to shift excitedly in anticipation, or rather groan—here he goes again. Chapters 29 through 35 consist almost entirely of Cantwell's memories, which memories continue even after Renata has fallen asleep (227–36). Cantwell, in fact, sleeps in between chapters 31 and 32 (223–24). While most novels would be approaching a climax, *Across the River and into the Trees* invests the next seven chapters, more than ten percent of the novel, in Cantwell revealing his war memories.

CHAPTER 29

203:1 Just as the first sentences of chapters 24, 25, and 26 establish the characters at a table in the Gritti (see entry at 190:1), chapters 28, 29, and 30 all begin by locating Cantwell and Renata on the bed in the Gritti Palace Hotel. The first sentence of each chapter is "They lay together now and did not speak and the Colonel felt her heart beat" (199:1–2); "They lay on the pleasantly hard, new-made bed with their legs pressed tight against one another, and her head was on his chest, and her hair spread across his old hard neck; and he told her" (203:1–3); and "The Colonel and the girl lay quietly on the bed and the Colonel tried to think of nothing; as he had thought of nothing so many times in so many places" (211:1–3).

203:8 **we took Cherbourg:** Cantwell refers to the 25 June 1944 capture of Cherbourg. He and the rest of the 4th U.S. Infantry Division linked up with the "airborne divisions that had landed beyond the beaches" (Giangreco 131). The ETO document on the event, *The Famous Fourth,* states that on 14 June 1944, the Cherbourg "beachhead was firmly in American hands" (8) and by the 25th, the 4th "occupied the entire city except forts along the waterfront and in the harbor" (10).

Cherbourg is mentioned upon Cantwell's arrival in Venice (52:25).

203:13–14 **I took nothing but an Admiral's compass:** Although there is no evidence that Hemingway actually took such a compass, H. R. Stoneback makes the plausible speculation that this detail "has the feel of untransmuted fact, of compulsive personal confession that serves the narrative in no obvious fashion, of Hemingway's—not Cantwell's—confession of theft" (193). This compass is one of many aspects of the novel that give the impression of "compulsive personal confession."

203:15–16 **all the Wehrmacht stamped Martell:** The Wehrmacht was the complete fighting force of Nazi Germany—the army, navy, and air force—from 1935 to 1945. Martell is a brand of cognac. In other words, the Allies appropriated some of the stock that the Nazis had plundered. A hyphen between Wehrmacht and stamped would make this sentence clearer. Cantwell will continue discussing the Martell cognac on 204:3.

203:20–21 **through his Esses, or sometimes his G's:** Cantwell means a member of his staff (at the level of battalion or brigade), or a staff member (at the level of division or corps).

204:6–7 **more wire strung than there are cunts in Texas:** According to James Sullivan's biography of the late comedian George Carlin (1937–2008), Carlin's lawyer included this line in an appendix to the appellate court as proof that the "seven dirty words" also appeared in literary works such as the Bible and *Across the River and into the Trees* (Sullivan 156). Earlier, Cantwell had speculated that if an American girl is beautiful, she is probably from Texas and might possibly be able to name the correct month (166:12–14).

204:14 **make it fifty:** In 1950, the Wyoming population was 290,529, and in 2012 it was 576,412, according to the U.S. census; approximately 50 percent of each number are women.

204:21 **the mucking break-through:** The manuscript reads: "the fucking break-through" (JFK 1).

204:25 **Christmas tree ornaments:** Cantwell uses slang for "chaff," or metal foil that was released by planes to confuse the radar of the Allies. According to the *OED*, chaff is "strips of metal foil or similar material released in the atmosphere to interfere with radar detection."

204:26 **it was called off:** Cantwell is describing the miscommunication that led to what he calls the "Valhalla Express," the short bombing that led to a disastrous friendly fire incident on 25 July 1944.

204:28 **like I love the pig's you know:** In the manuscript, "ass-hole" is in place of "you know." *Islands in the Stream* contains a similar sentiment, in which to the notion of *dulce et decorum est*, that it is sweet and fitting to die for one's country, Thomas Hudson responds: "In the pig's asshole" (258).

204:31 **the second day we were for it:** Following the Valhalla Express on July 25, the breakthrough at Normandy was 25–27 July 1944.

205:10 **S-2:** An S-2 is the security officer for the military unit.

205:10–11 **Valhalla Express:** The Valhalla Express occurred on 25 July 1944, when six hundred American troops were accidentally bombed due to a misunderstanding between General Bradley and Montgomery, leading to 136 deaths (Reynolds,

Final Years 101). Historian John C. McManus pins the blame for the fiasco squarely on Bradley, having in his judgment "failed to understand the limitations and perils of strategic bombers in support of ground troops" (297). Hemingway refers to the Valhalla Express as a synonym for the breakthrough in a 25 August 1950 letter (*SL* 710) to fellow writer Bob Cantwell (1908–1978), the conspicuously surnamed author of *The Land of Plenty* (1934). The Colonel continues to discuss this traumatic episode on 206:3–14, 207:10–12, 228:33–229:2, and 230:18–19.

In Norse mythology, Valhalla was the hall of the slain. Cantwell imagines a kind of Valhalla where he would be able to chat with Rommel and Udet, who died in 1944 and 1941.

205:30–31 **Sixth Parachute Division:** This 1944–45 German airborne division took serious losses during the Normandy breakthrough, when it was opposed by General Collins's VII Corps. The Sixth Division surrendered to Allied forces in May 1945.

206:8 **no one need ever worry about hell:** This articulation recalls Hemingway's famous 18 August 1918 letter to his parents after his World War I wounding: "there have been about 8 times when I would have welcomed Hell. Just on a chance that it couldn't come up to the phase of war I was experiencing" (*Letters 1,* 130). Hemingway elaborates on this notion in his early story "The Woppian Way," in which a character, Pickles McCarty, says, "the Carso was hell. Not the Sherman hell—the 1915 type" (JFK #843). This articulation is true to the modernist ideal that twentieth-century fiction had to treat war in a new way to accommodate the advancement that technology, communication, and warfare had made since the U.S. Civil War.

206:28 **Phillipines:** Hemingway visited Manila in the Phillipines in May 1941 with his then-wife Martha, and, according to Peter Moreira, "couldn't stand" it (180).

207:8 **until you are purged of it:** As his own *Purgatorio*, part of Cantwell's journey is exorcising his horrible memories of war. Dante's second canticle begins with Dante singing of "that second realm where the human spirit is purged and becomes fit to ascend to Heaven" (1.4–6). This extended telling of his World War II experiences from chapters 29–35 is a central part of this purgation. Renata's function in the novel, then, may be more active and strategic than readers first imagine. She says, "Don't you see you need to tell me things to purge your bitterness?" (220:2–3) and urges his need to, by speaking about his memories, "get rid of them" (223:1–2). However, Renata tries to be judicious; she also says that speaking of the Valhalla Express "is not good for you" (207:23).

207:13 **Pete Quesada:** Elwood Richard "Pete" Quesada (1904–1993) was an air force general who innovated the attachment of bombs to Spitfires to convert British planes into "a ground-support fighter-bomber" (Weigley 165). Quesada was the commander of the IX Fighter Command in England, which provided air cover for the invasion of Normandy.

207:30 and stroked his head: One of the most common romantic and/or sexual acts in Hemingway; see particularly *For Whom the Bell Tolls*, *The Garden of Eden*, and *The Sun Also Rises*.

208:11 The hell with sorrows: The manuscript says, "Fuck sorrows" (JFK 1).

208:18–20 bow tie . . . haberdasher: Harry S. Truman often wore bow ties when he was a senator from Missouri (1935–1945). He worked as a haberdasher from 1919 until 1921. The manuscript mentions Truman's relationship with Kansas City political boss Tom Pendergast (1873–1945).

208:21 opposition: Cantwell refers to the five-foot, eight-inch Thomas E. Dewey (1902–1971), lampooned as "the little man on the wedding cake," whom Truman defeated in 1948 to become thirty-third U.S. president.

208:23 no-fight general: Whether this barb is aimed at Eisenhower or Walter Bedell Smith, it does continue Cantwell's revulsion over his superiors who are desk generals, more comfortable in the office and in the safety of SHAEF headquarters than on battlefields.

209:3 There is at least one in every town: At this point in the manuscript, Cantwell explicitly mentions Truman as the current president: "He is President. I know he did not want to be at one time. But he wants to be now" (JFK 1).

209:5 Arlington: In addition to holding the tombs of the unknown soldiers from several wars, Arlington National Cemetery in Arlington, Virginia, is also where Presidents Taft and Kennedy are interred.

209:12 where we beat them: In the manuscript, Cantwell says, "where we kicked the shit out of them" (JFK 1).

209:22 Père Lachaise: Père Lachaise Cemetery in Paris, founded in 1804, is perhaps the most visited cemetery in the world. Among those interred there are Gertrude Stein and Alice B. Toklas.

209:23 what we have here: This reference suggests San Michele Cemetery in Venice, an island of tombs north of the Fondamente Nuove, where, among others, Ezra Pound is buried.

209:27–28 **I will go with you if you like:** This melodramatic statement of devotion mirrors Horatio's offer to Hamlet, or Juliet's suicide over Romeo's body. This almost mythological gesture is made the more morbid when we recall that Adriana Ivancich committed suicide in 1983, although there is absolutely no suggestion that Hemingway's death was even the slightest factor.

Just as Cantwell refers to dying as "the one thing we do alone" (209:29), in Hemingway's previous novel, *For Whom the Bell Tolls,* Robert Jordan tells Maria of his death, "What I do now I do alone. I could not do it well with thee" (463). However Jordan does not go on to compare death to "going to the bathroom" (209:30), as Cantwell does.

210:2 **You get married:** In this important moment, Cantwell assures her that her life will go on even if his does not. Cantwell also gives his explicit blessing, perhaps for her pending relationship with Alvarito. The five sons, then, will not be his. Adriana had two sons; Hemingway had three.

In Hemingway's letters of this period, in the same letters in which he would rave about his love for Adriana, he would tell others that he only wished she would have a happy marriage with a man who would be good to her.

210:4, 7 **The lion-hearted . . . The crap-hearted:** A reference to King Richard I of England (1157–1199), known as Richard the Lion-Hearted. In the manuscript, the self-deprecating phrase was "the shit-hearted" (JFK 1). The winged lion, poised atop a column in Piazza San Marco, is symbolic of Venice.

210:10 **And member you speak worst:** Apparently a typographical error. In the first edition, "member" is "remember," which it clearly should be.

210:11 **think about nothing:** This enormous trope in all of Hemingway both concludes chapter 29 and begins chapter 30, as the "Colonel tried to think of nothing" (211:2). Hemingway's overstressed protagonists typically wish to have a respite from traumatic memory, an urgent situation, a dire future by concentrating on a pleasant sensation. His heroes understand how difficult such an act is and how temporary such a victory might be. "Big Two-Hearted River" is an excellent example of an entire narrative in which the protagonist attempts to shield himself from thought. As Henri Bergson discusses (see entry at 139:20), thinking about "nothing" cannot really mean that your mind is erased; it is an impossible objective.

See entries at 145:19–20, 268:4.

CHAPTER 30

211:1 **lay quietly on the bed:** Chapter 30 is the third consecutive chapter that establishes Renata and Colonel Cantwell in bed. The declaration that "it was too late" (211:4–5) marks another progression in Cantwell's knowledge of his own mortality.

211:6 **Othello and Desdemona:** Although this is the novel's only explicit mention of the most famous Venetian couple in all of literature, the tragedy resonates throughout this novel. In a scholarly article with a title that promises much: "*Othello* as a Key to Hemingway," Ernest Lockridge sweeps aside *Across the River and into the Trees*, mentioning only this single reference and ignoring its subtextual pervasiveness, to say nothing of the setting.

One wonders, further, how Cantwell can with a straight face refer to anyone else as "garrulous" (211:9–10)—excessively talkative or rambling—given his own chronic loquaciousness. Othello is a war hero whose precise experiences are unknown, and Cantwell would only be guessing about his own war experience in relation to Othello.

211:14 **final Moroccan campaign against Abdel Krim:** The Rif War, or the Second Moroccan War, was fought from 1920 to 1926 between France and Spain forces against the Moroccan Rif Berbers. Abdel Krim (1882–1962) was the leader of the Moroccan troops against the Spanish and later the French occupiers. John Dos Passos went to Morocco in 1925; according to Dos Passos's biographer, Hemingway also considered going but instead stayed in Paris to finish *The Torrents of Spring* (Carr 212). Although Hemingway had no experience in Morocco, one of his sources for Cantwell, Charlie Sweeny, met up with him in Paris and told him he was on his way to fight. According to Michael Reynolds, Hemingway then told Gertrude Stein he was ready to join Sweeny. Reynolds observes that Hemingway wrote the scene in *The Sun Also Rises* when Bill Gorton and Jake Barnes joke about the ongoing conflict, on 20 August 1925, right after his meeting with Sweeny ("Putting on the Riff" 31).

211:16 ***Einheit:*** This military concept taking the German word for "unity" was devised by Heinz Guderian (1888–1954) from 1933 to 1939 and aimed to enhance communication and cooperation between disparate components of the military.

This notion of unity had artistic implications for Hemingway. In an unpublished letter to Mike Ward, a former colonel, on 11 October 1949, he wrote: "It is about an old colonel worse than me or you. Read in anything you want between the lines. I have done it on the old Einheit system and there is always plenty of space between the lines" (JFK, Outgoing Correspondence). Hemingway also had fun with this phrase; in describing a weather system to A. E. Hotchner on 29 September 1949, he spoke of some "small and worthless cyclones, hurricanes rather, being einheited [squeezed out] by the other characters" (*Dear Papa* 44). In a later unpublished letter to German writer Fritz Habeck (1916–1997), Hemingway attempted to clarify the term, comparing it to a channel in which water is able to seep through a pile of pebbles. This metaphor suggests Cantwell is distinguishing between the mass attack of the World War I and the more modern tactics of World War II.

212:7 **RAF:** The Royal Air Force, the air force of the British military.

212:27 **Napoleon:** The second of three mentions (195:32, 213:1). It is a popular belief that Napoleon once stated that he preferred lucky generals to good ones. When George Plimpton interviewed Hemingway in 1958, Eugene V. Tarle's *Napoleon's Invasion of Russia, 1812* was on Hemingway's desk ("Art of Fiction" 111). Any mention of Napoleon has significant thematic impact, since Napoleon conquered Venice in 1797.

213:25–215:13 This sequence is the closest we get to an explanation about Cantwell's backstory: he unnecessarily assaulted a town, lost a regiment under other people's orders, and then was scapegoated and then demoted. This information may answer Malcolm Cowley's charge that the weak point to the novel was that Hemingway never dramatized why Cantwell lost his stars.

214:8 **Spa, by a correspondent:** Spa is a town in the Ardennes in Belgium. SHAEF set up headquarters there, in which it detained and interrogated Nazi officers.

In the manuscript, "by a correspondent" is "by Hank Gorrell," a reference to the UPI journalist whom Hemingway knew in Spain and France. Gorrell (1911–1958) authored, among other works, *Soldier of the Press,* which contains an anecdote about Hemingway, clad in a nightgown, waking him up at the Hotel Florida in Madrid to see a battle that had broken out in the street. Gorrell describes Hemingway as being "so excited that he was prepared to go to the front with his nightgown on" (46).

214:18–19 **Minnesota . . . Beloit, Wisconsin:** One wonders how Renata would possibly understand this strained David-and-Goliath analogy to American college football. Minnesota was 7–2 in both 1948 and 1949 and led by future hall of famer Bud Grant. The only record of Beloit ever playing Minnesota in football was in 1930, a 39–20 Minnesota victory (Owens).

Hemingway's paternal grandfather, Anson, was a member of the Beloit College Trustees in 1888. The following year, he also contributed $500 worth of real estate to the college. Hemingway's favorite high school English teacher, Frank Platt, graduated from Beloit College in 1908 (F. Burwell).

This strained simile recalls Frederic Henry's articulation in *A Farewell to Arms* that while he was in Switzerland, "the war seemed as far away as the football games of some one else's college" (291).

214:24 **some handsome jerk:** In the manuscript, Cantwell's rant is even more searing: "and some relation to some politician, or his most favoured boy, because naturally such a General is not awake yet, having slept late with the blondest lady correspondent that was available, puts an air mission on you (JFK 1). The manuscript reveals that Cantwell is alluding to Hoyt S. Vandenberg (1899–1954), a "senator's nephew," as he is mocked there. Vandenberg contributed to the planning of the Normandy invasion and was an air force general during World War II. His uncle was Arthur H. Vandenberg (1884–1951), U.S. senator from Michigan during World War II and the writing of *Across the River and into the Trees*.

215:6 **Figure him as our next President:** The manuscript refers to a "nylon-smooth Captain in the Navy writing a daily diary of their doings" (JFK 1), a mocking reference to Harry C. Butcher's *My Three Years with Eisenhower*. See a similar reference to Butcher on 129:26.

215:23 **1335:** It is striking that Renata and Cantwell only see each other for a few hours on this day, Saturday. They meet for a relatively late breakfast after her long sleep, and Cantwell has agreed to meet Alvarito at the garage at 2:30 P.M., or 14:30, to depart for their hunting trip, to be held on Sunday. Cantwell rebuffs Renata's offer to spend the night at the Gritti, and then Renata sleeps late the next morning; for two people who are more or less conscious that they are seeing each other for the last time, they spend far less time together than they could have.

215:25 **Then I will have it:** Renata's desire to listen to Cantwell is not purely altruistic. She does want him to confess for his own soul and conscience, but she also gets a thrill of listening to his stories of the past, both sexually and emotionally.

216:3 **Schnee-Eifel:** The 4th Infantry Division attacked the Siegfried Line at Schnee Eifel on 14 September 1944, and the battle lasted until 17 September. This barrier, a "steep, thickly wooded ridge" (*Famous Fourth* 20), made up Hitler's vaunted Western Wall, which he claimed to be impregnable. In Hemingway's article for *Collier's*, "War in the Siegfried Line," he described Schnee Eifel as "the dark forest wall . . .

where the dragon lived" (*BL* 393). Hemingway was not an observer during those days, remaining in the division headquarters due to illness (Beistle 10).

216:6 **General Walter Bedell Smith:** Smith was Eisenhower's chief of staff at SHAEF from 1944 until 1945. Cantwell condemns Smith for his errors and essentially consigns him to hell. Cantwell considers Smith ignorant and obtuse (225:20) and then "wrong as hell" (228:3). The Colonel recalls Smith giving the fateful orders of the attack (227:7–8). See entry at 118:32.

216:9 **Hurtgen Forest:** The site of on the German-Belgium border of the epic Battle of Hürtgen Forest between the U.S. and Germany, 19 September 1944 to 10 February 1945. The 1st Army lost more than thirty-three thousand men at this battle.

216:10 **Stadtswald:** Actually spelled Stadtwald, it would describe the Aachener Stadtwald. Hemingway used it as another name for Hürtgen Forest (Greacen, "Irish Soldier" 9). In German, *Stadt* means "city" and *Wald* means "forest."

216:11 **Aachen:** The United States and Germany fought the Battle of Aachen from 2 to 19 October 1944. Aachen was surrounded by the U.S. 1st Infantry Division and 3rd Armored Division with the 2nd Armored Division and 30th Infantry Division. Germany surrendered on 21 October 1944. Aachen is also mentioned at 219:9.

In Hemingway's short story "Black Ass at the Cross Roads," the protagonist and his band of irregulars kill Germans who are trying to escape into Aachen to fight.

216:22 **Sad stories of the death of kings:** Renata quotes from Shakespeare's *King Richard II*. Her literary allusion is astute, referring to Richard's (the king's, not the colonel's) magnificent speech about the discourse of war. "For God's sake, let us sit upon the ground, / And tell sad stories of the death of kings— / How some have been deposed, some slain in war, / Some haunted by the ghosts they have deposed" (3.2.151–54). According to Carlos Baker, Hemingway used this phrase in 1949 to characterize his conversation with Leopoldina, his favorite Cuban prostitute (*Life Story* 475).

216:26–27 **The Stars and Stripes:** *Stars and Stripes*, in existence since the Civil War and based in Washington, D.C., reports on issues affecting the U.S. military.

216:30 **I will not name names:** In the manuscript, Cantwell declares that he "will name names" and lists Drew Middleton (1913–1990) of the *New York Times*, Harold Peters of United Press International, and Duke Shoop (1904–1957) of the *Kansas City Star* as among the "fine ones." When the novel was serialized in *Cosmopolitan*, Cantwell also acknowledged Herbert Clark (*Cosmopolitan*, May 1950 134). Clark

(1907–1964), whom Mary refers to as her "beloved old boyfriend from Chicago" (*How It Was* 111), worked for the Paris *Herald Tribune*.

217:3 telephone racers: Cantwell is deploring the habit of journalists whose priorities were to rush off and phone in a story, as opposed to staying in the danger zone and observing the entirety of the action.

217:3–7 There were a few deads . . . : The last five sentences of this paragraph are not in the manuscript. It is amazing that Hemingway maintained Renata's subsequent question—"But how did you ever marry one?" (217:8)—because, as it stands, it seems that Renata is asking Hemingway how he ever married a woman. In the draft, before the five sentences were added, Renata is responding to the sleazy aspects of war journalism; Hemingway's third and fourth wives (and Cantwell's most recent wife) were war correspondents.

217:24 perpetuate ignominy: In the manuscript, Hemingway wrote "perpetrate ignominy" (JFK 1), which is actually more logical. Hemingway changed these words in the typescript (JFK 2), likely out of confusion. "Perpetuate" means "to continue something indefinitely"; "perpetrate" means "to perform an immoral or unlawful action."

217:29 But don't you ever write one word of this: In the manuscript, Cantwell tells Renata not to write "one fucking word" of this (JFK 1).

218:3, 4 the weapon: In the manuscript, "the weapon" is specified to be a Colt .45.

218:20 the great General: In the manuscript, Cantwell names the target of his mockery: General Walter Bedell Smith, whom he calls "Chief of Staff to all the Epworth Leagues of Kansas." Smith was born in Indianapolis, Indiana, but was stationed at Fort Leavenworth in Kansas in 1933 (see entry at 216:6). Cantwell does recall Smith giving the orders (227:7–8).

218:24–25 Chautauqua lecture: Organized in 1874, this program was part of an adult education movement involving lecturers, entertainers, preachers, and educators. William Jennings Bryan, namedropped in *The Sun Also Rises* and alluded to in this novel (45:20–21), is the figure most commonly associated with these lectures.

219:8 Versailles: SHAEF was based in Versailles, about fifteen miles southwest of Paris, beginning on 20 September 1944.

219:12 Rheims: Rheims, about ninety miles northeast of Paris, was where Eisenhower received Germany's unconditional surrender on 7 May 1945.

CHAPTER 31

221:2–3 **high brass, even from Kansas:** As per the entry on 126:33, Kansas is a reference to Eisenhower, who was reared in Abilene, Kansas.

221:3–4 **higher than osage-orange trees:** The Maclura pomifera is a small tree, which reaches nine to thirteen yards in height. See entry at 33:5.

221:8 **C Rations:** Field Ration, Type C, these provisions were three canned meals and were almost uniformly despised for their lack of variety. Cantwell does not like them either (see Streeter).

221:12, 15, 16 **S-3:** An S-3 is an operations officer on a military staff. See also 225:4.

221:14 **1305 (that is one o'clock and five minutes after:** It is unclear why Cantwell would need to explain military or twenty-four hour time to an Italian, who would be accustomed to such a designation. See also Cantwell's gratuitous explanation of "*per piacere*" to Renata (195:4).

222:6 **light on the ceiling:** Picking up from the "play of the light on the ceiling" (215:16–17) and Renata's exhortation to look at "the light on the ceiling" (219:2), this mysterious trigger ultimately leads to a devastating reminiscence, the loss of his battalion, a memory that makes Cantwell "completely desperate at the remembrance" (222:6–7). Although the narrator characterizes the emotional intensity of Cantwell's memories, he does not explicitly confide to Renata the power of his feelings. See also "the strange play of the light on the ceiling" (226:3), "the wonder light on the ceiling" (232:12), "the magic spots and changes of light" (249:7) that are even in Harry's Bar.

Henry James once referred to the light in the Veneto "a mighty magician" and "the greatest artist of all" (52).

Cantwell naps between chapters 31 and 32.

CHAPTER 32

225:2 **986342:** These digits represent the location on a map reference grid that would provide the location of the object in question. Hemingway takes this exact sequence from the 18 November 1944 Unit Journal for the 22nd Infantry Regiment, which would place them in Hürtgen Forest (Boice 67).

225:4, 5, 7, 10 **S-6:** An S6 is a military staff member who serves as a communications officer.

225:29 **I am Mister Dante . . . For the moment:** Just like Dante, both the writer and the adjudicator, Cantwell has condemned some of these figures to hell, most particularly General Walter Bedell Smith. He knows he is being at least partially "unjust" (225:31), just as earlier he is the "unjust bitter criticizer" (210:7–8). Cantwell, then, draws the circles as in Dante's conception of hell, but he also alludes to Giotto's perfect circles (57:3–7).

CHAPTER 33

226:2 **sleepy:** Following Cantwell's nap, Renata speaks "sleepily" (224:7, 225:28), and is sleepy on 226:2, 226:19, which leads to her nap on 227:3 and her waking up and speaking on 229:26, and then going back to sleep on 229:32. Cantwell admires the way she sleeps like a cat—"when it sleeps within itself" (226:19–20)—and then deeply because of her youth and beauty (156:17–18, 165:3). She also sleeps "as though she had not gone to sleep" (158:28). Renata compares sleep to skiing in the dark (182:16–17, 186:18, 186:20–22).

226:8 **knocker's shop:** Like "knocking shop," this phrase is slang for a brothel (Partridge 1167).

226:15 **it was Schultz. Or Schlitz:** A girl who worked at a soda counter would know her grandfather's name as Schultz because Carl H. Schultz was the designer of seltzer bottles, which would have been used in the soda shop. Schlitz is the name of a Milwaukee-based brewing company that, along with Anheuser-Busch, dominated U.S. breweries for the first half of the twentieth century.

227:6–229:25 This interior monologue, where Cantwell tells Renata without speaking out loud, recounts the narrative of his experiences at the Ardennes with the 4th Infantry Division, beginning on 16 December 1944.

227:9 **the Big Red One:** The nickname for the 1st Infantry Division, which during World War II fought at the D-Day invasion, the Battle of Hürtgen Forest, and the Battle of the Bulge.

227:10 **Ninth:** The 9th Infantry Division fought in Normandy, Northern France, the Ardennes, Rhineland, and Central Europe during World War II.

227:11 **us:** Cantwell is referring to the 4th Infantry Division. In the Battle of the Bulge, there were the 1st Army (commanded by Courtney Hodges), the 12th Army

181

(commanded by Omar Bradley), and the 3rd Army (commanded by Patton), which were all supported by the British (Montgomery).

Cantwell's 4th Infantry Division participated in the Normandy Invasion at Utah Beach on 6 June 1944 and the capture of Cherbourg on 25 June and assisted with French forces in liberating Paris. Cantwell then was among the 22nd Infantry Regiment when it went from Paris to Belgium and into Germany. In an interview, Hemingway listed the destruction of the 22nd at Hürtgen Forest as one of the things *Across the River and into the Trees* was about (Breit 62). According to historian Edward G. Miller, the 22nd suffered "103 officer and 2,575 enlisted casualites" out of "3,257 officers and men" (161).

227:24 Calypso singing PRO: Cantwell refers to Captain Marcus O. Stevenson, the PRO who supervised Hemingway's activity beginning in late July 1944. According to scholar Steve Newman, Stevenson "looked like a Texas Ranger, with an accent to match." Stevenson brought Hemingway to the 22nd Infantry Regiment, effectively introducing him to Colonel Buck Lanham. Hemingway mentions Stevenson in his responses to the inspector general's interrogation (Meredith, "Inspector General Interview" 100), referring only to his presence as his chauffeur and the division's public relations officer.

227:30 I can detect it at over one thousand yards: Cantwell's sensitivity to "horseshit" anticipates Hemingway's assertion that the "most essential thing" for a writer is to have a "built-in, shock-proof shit detector . . . the writer's radar" (Plimpton, "Art of Fiction" 128).

228:11 Passchendaele with tree bursts: Cantwell compares the Hürtgen Forest campaign with the Second Battle of Flanders (63:31). Cantwell blames the destruction of his regiment, in part, on "Tree burst wounds" (222:14). Cantwell repeats this phrase at 232:11. The tree bursts, Hemingway wrote in "War in the Siegfried Line," were "*like javelins in the half-light of the forest*" (*BL* 396, emphasis in original). Colonel Lanham once recalled that in Hürtgen Forest, "you could just as easily get killed with a tree sliver as a bullet" (qtd. in E. Miller 161).

228:13 poor bloody twenty-eighth: The 28th and 9th Divisions fought together in Hürtgen Forest, unsuccessfully opposing the 275th Volksgrenadier Division. The 28th Division was relieved by the 22nd, which sustained the most serious losses of the entire campaign.

229:11 section-eighted: The military term for a discharge due to being mentally unfit to serve.

229:18–19 **for around twenty-eight years:** The Battle of the Piave was in 1918; the Battle of Hürtgen Forest ended in February 1945.

229:21 **the three towns:** The three towns to which Cantwell refers are Grosshau, Kleinhau, and Strass. The 22nd Infantry Regiment, led by Colonel Lanham, was ordered to attack these cities from late November to December 1944. When Hemingway refers to *Across the River and into the Trees* being about the destruction of the 22nd Regiment, it is accurate with respect to the Hürtgen Forest campaign (see entry at 227:11).

229:29–30 **The war is over and forgotten:** An ironic remark, given that Cantwell has immersed himself in his war memories. It echoes Frederic Henry in *A Farewell to Arms,* who deserts the Italian army during the retreat of Caporetto and right before his "separate peace" declaration, says, "I was going to forget the war" (243).

230:12–13 **five and ten and twenty percenters:** Cantwell uses this as a derogatory phrase for the elite, who are safe, as opposed to the common soldiers, who are in great danger.

230:15 **killed several men from the academy at Gettysburg:** Cantwell's snide joke suggests that the last time officers were killed in action was during the Battle of Gettysburg, in July 1863. In a more serious parallel, Hemingway routinely compared the Battle of Hürtgen Forest to the killing fields of Gettysburg.

230:18 **They killed General McNair by mistake:** General Lesley James McNair (1883–25 July 1944) was killed by heavy bombs by the 8th Air Forces near Saint-Lô, in what Cantwell calls the Valhalla Express. General McNair was the highest-ranking U.S. officer killed in action during the war (Gilmore 293). McNair's legacy rests largely in his responsibility for training soldiers in World War II; in 1940 he was in charge of all army troop training, and by the time of his death, his methods had trained 7.7 million troops (Craf 30). General McNair's training philosophy contradicts Cantwell's, as illustrated by his 11 November 1942 radio address: "Our soldiers must have the fighting spirit. If you call that hating our enemies then we must hate with every fiber of our being. We must lust for battle; our object in life must be to kill; we must scheme and plan night and day to kill. There need be no pangs of conscience, for our enemies have lighted the way to faster, surer, and crueler killing, they are past masters" (qtd. in Craf 31).

CHAPTER 34

231:10 *motoscafo:* Italian for "motorboat." See also the beginning of chapter 39 (252:16), when Cantwell and Jackson actually do get on the boat.

231:13 **will not ever see one another again:** At this point, Cantwell is all but certain that he will not live long enough to see Renata again; this is the last time. Goodbye will, indeed, be forever.

232:7 **old Hieronymus Bosch really painted:** The manuscript has "old Breughel" [*sic*] instead of Bosch (JFK 1). Bosch (1450–1516) was a Dutch painter whose triptych *The Garden of Earthly Delights* plays a prominent role in the manuscript of Hemingway's *The Garden of Eden*. When Hemingway names Bosch in his lengthy list of influences (Plimpton, "Art of Fiction" 118), his interviewer questions the inclusion because of the apparent disparity in themes, an objection that Hemingway dismisses (119).

232:10 **scythe:** Hemingway also uses and undoes this traditional image of death in "The Snows of Kilimanjaro," implying that it is antiquated, a symbol for some obsolete, clichéd rendering of death. As Harry tells his wife: "Never believe any of that about a scythe and a skull . . . It can be two bicycle policemen as easily, or be a bird" (*CSS* 54).

CHAPTER 35

233:1 **The first day there:** The first day in Hürtgen Forest for the 22nd Infantry Division would have been 16 November 1944. Similar to Cantwell's declaration, three battalion commanders were "lost" (one killed and two wounded) on 17–18 November (22nd Infantry Regiment Society). Regarding Cantwell's later query about the loss of company commanders (233:6–7), historian Robert Sterling Rush gives a statistical outline of the decimation of the 22nd Infantry Division at Hürtgen Forest: "Between 16 and 24 November," he writes, "351 NCOs [non-commissioned officers] and officers were killed our wounded badly enough to be evacuated, which means that more than one in every four soldiers who fell during this period was either an officer or an NCO" (301).

233:5 **Christmas trees:** Hürtgen Forest was populated with towering fir trees, often 150 feet tall.

233:6–7 **company commanders:** In the first four hours of the first day of attack at Hürtgen Forest, 16 November 1944, the 22nd suffered casualties to forty-six enlisted men and nine officers (Boice 66). As historian Robert Sterling Rush writes of the regiment, "Attrition among company commanders was so high that no fewer and quite possibly more than thirty-one officers commanded the regiment's nine rifle companies during the battle—reflecting a casualty rate greater than 300 percent" (3), as each position would have been replaced more than three times. The entire Battle of Hürtgen Forest led to casualties of 2,575 enlisted men and 103 officers, including twelve officers killed in action (E. Miller 161).

234:13 **Grosshau:** Hemingway visited Grosshau on 30 November 1944 and witnessed the "grisly spectacles" described in *Across the River and into the Trees* (Beistle 14). Hemingway saw a German that had been roasted by phosphorous, to which he referred mordantly in a letter to Lanham four years later, and which would appear in *Across the River and into the Trees* (235:3–4). This moment actualizes the beginning of Homer's *Iliad*, in which Achilles's rage ends up "leaving so many dead men—carrion for dogs and birds" (1.5–6).

Colonel Buck Lanham led the attack against Grosshau; the 22nd Infantry Regiment reached Grosshau on 27 November 1944 (*Famous Fourth* 25).

234:16 howitzer: A short-barreled artillery that launches projectiles at soaring trajectories.

234:31–32 how he had been flattened and the strangeness of his flatness: Hemingway used a biographical experience for this incident; entering Grosshau on 30 November 1944, he found an American soldier "so flattened by the passage of many vehicles that he was hardly recognizable as human" (Baker, *Life Story* 437).

235:1 white phosphorus: American mortar rounds frequently used white phosphorus, including during the liberation of Cherbourg, where the 87th Mortar Battalion fired almost twelve thousand white phosphorus rounds into the city.

235:13–14 my brother Gordon: Hemingway's brother, Leicester (1915–1982), fought in France and Germany during World War II. He also committed suicide via gunshot.

235:15 deliquesced: According to the *Oxford English Dictionary*, the second meaning of the word is "*gen.* To melt away (*lit.* and *fig.*). (Mostly *humorous* or *affected.*)" In *Islands in the Stream*, Thomas Hudson's knife probes "into the charred deliquescence that the land crabs were feeding on" (325). In *Under Kilimanjaro*, Hemingway theorizes that baboon bait soured "after it had reached its first full bloom of decay and begun to enter deliquescence" (253).

235:24 I can hang and rattle: This cowboy phrase refers alternately to the stick-to-itive-ness necessary to ride a bronco. Although he cannot do much to change your situation, or the inevitability of a hung-up cowboy helplessly twisting in the wind, a true cowboy endures. In a 20 November 1948 letter to Mary, Hemingway asked about Martha Gellhorn's recent novel, *The Wine of Astonishment*, "How come Marty never used [the phrases] Black-Ass nor hang and rattle or I'll wind your clock in her book. Guess she must have been figureing [*sic*] on shareing [*sic*] the wealth and left that for me" (*SL* 654). Hemingway also uses the phrase during the climactic scene in *Islands in the Stream*, when Hudson says, "We can let these sons of bitches hang and rattle . . . Or we can go in now and finish it" (439). In this sense, the phrase is reminiscent of how Cantwell allows towns or people to "fall of their own weight."

Cormac McCarthy uses the phrase in his great 1992 novel, *All the Pretty Horses* (103).

235:26 your opposite number: Cantwell is addressing the portrait, whom he will call "canvas girl" (235:33), so the portrait's opposite number is Renata herself.

CHAPTER 36

Just as Renata and Cantwell step into the refreshing "sharp, cold bright day" (237:1), the reader might at this point also welcome a breath of fresh Venetian air. The characters have been in Cantwell's hotel room from page 193 to page 236, 43 pages and more than ten thousand words of almost total inaction beyond Cantwell recounting military exploits of the past, napping, and sipping the occasional Valpolicella. This sequence takes up about fifteen percent of the novel.

237:15 you are a rich American: Renata is teasing, suggesting to proprietors that this worldly man would appear to be richer than this Italian teenager, while the opposite is true. Cantwell will later confess that all his "worldly goods" are practically nonexistent (267:9).

237:16 Et toi, Rimbaud: A humorous restatement of Caesar's dying words to Brutus in Shakespeare's *Julius Caesar:* "*Et tu, Bruté?*—Then fall Caesar" (3.1.76). Arthur Rimbaud (1854–1891) was a precocious French poet who stopped writing verse by the age of twenty. Rimbaud as a referent at this point is striking: he was born in Charleville in the Ardennes, the site of the Battle of the Bulge, which has just occupied so much of Cantwell's attention.

237:17 an awfully funny Verlaine: Paul Verlaine (1844–1896) was a French symbolist poet who became Rimbaud's mentor and lover. In 1873, during their tumultuous affair, Verlaine shot Rimbaud with a pistol, wounding the younger poet's hand, in another connection to Cantwell's wound. Verlaine and Rimbaud have become almost synonymous with volatile relationships; in "You're Gonna Make Me Lonesome When You Go," Bob Dylan laments, "Situations have ended sad / Relationships have all been bad / Mine've been like Verlaine and Rimbaud."

Verlaine's "Chanson d'automne" (1866) was the signal for the French Resistance that the beginning of Operation Overlord, the invasion of Normandy, was imminent.

238:1 Louis Sixteenth: Louis XVI (1754–1793) was the king of France from 1791 to 1792, before he was executed alongside his wife, Marie Antoinette. See 131:19–20, 254:24, 265:15–17.

238:3–4 **still be able to spit:** Hemingway, who spent much of his career focused on the behavior of people who knew they might die, has Cantwell assert that he would go to his execution stoically, his mouth not dry at all. Cantwell is also able to spit as he prepares for a possible street fight (174:28–29; see also 27:14–15 and 39:17).

238:22–23, 24–25, 26, 31–32, 239:3 **to make her understand truly . . . I understand that . . . I understand . . . I think I begin to understand . . . I understand it now very well:** By divesting himself of the stones, Cantwell is informing Renata that he will not live much longer. He says "No" in a manner that is "not rough" but perhaps has definitive, matter-of-fact finality. This sequence, then, brings to an undeniable level of clarity what both characters frequently hint at or even try to avoid, but say rarely.

238:29–30 **the portrait has value." "That is different:** While the stones have objective value—perhaps a quarter of a million dollars—the portrait is "different"; it is priceless even if it may not be a valuable commodity as a work of art.

CHAPTER 37

240:5–6 **the tide coming in at Mont St. Michel:** Cantwell refers to Mont-Saint-Michel in lower Normandy, an island noted for its volatile tides from the Cousenon River.

241:4 **Ft. Riley:** Fort Riley, a barracks in northern Kansas, was the training grounds for the 9th Armored Division, which would go on to fight, among other places, in Normandy and at Bastogne in the Battle of the Bulge.

241:4–5 **polo at the Country Club:** Cantwell refers to the Kansas City Country Club, founded in 1886. Steve Paul suggests that the highlighting of this area might stem from its proximity to Hemingway's cousins (message to author, 24 October 2012). Cantwell's affinity for polo is also mentioned (18:30); apparently, some of his concussions came from polo.

241:11 **Muehlebach Hotel:** Currently named the Kansas City Marriott Downtown and located at 200 West 12th St. in Kansas City, the Muehlebach hosted the elite, including many former presidents, since its construction in 1915.

As a young journalist for the *Kansas City Star*, Hemingway wrote his family of the hotel, "You feel like a million bucks to have a private room at the Muelebach [sic]" (*Letters 1*, 65). Cantwell now reiterates the young Hemingway's exultation, because he and Renata will "pretend that we are oil millionaires" (241:12–13).

241:16–17 **the big Buick Roadmaster, with the Dynaflow Drive:** This model was also Hemingway's. Dynaflow is a transmission, which was new to the 1948 Buick Roadmaster. Moriani's *Hemingway's Veneto* includes a picture of Hemingway's car (72). In Adriana Ivancich's autobiography, she remembers seeing Hemingway's car pull up, a car "so big that it had to be American" (*La torre bianca* 9). See entry at 28:2.

241:24 **St. Joe:** Cantwell is referring to St. Joseph, Missouri, about fifty miles north of Kansas City. Per the 2010 census, it was the eighth largest city in Missouri, with a population just over 125,000. Jesse James (1847–1882) was killed in St. Joseph, and the Jesse James Home Museum now marks the site of his death. When Cantwell fantasizes that he and Renata will "cross the river and go west" (241:25–26), he is referring to the Missouri River.

241:25 **Roubidoux:** Actually spelled Robidoux, this hotel in St. Joseph, Missouri, was opened in 1908. The bar is the Pony Express Bar'n Cocktails, so named because the Pony Express began in St. Joseph. The Robidoux Hotel was imploded in 1976.

241:31–32 **Chimney Rock ... Scott's Bluff ... Torrington:** In Cantwell's scenario, he and Renata are driving southeast to northwest: from St. Joseph to Chimney Rock, the state park in Bayard, Nebraska, more than 500 miles away. They then proceed to Scott's Bluff, Nebraska, another 20 miles. Next, they go to Torrington, Wyoming, 37 miles. The entire trip is more than 550 miles long. Scottsbluff, Nebraska, is in a county called Scott's Bluff, so it is impossible to know which one Cantwell intends here. Hemingway stayed in Scottsbluff in July 1932.

Hemingway wrote a strikingly similar letter to his son Patrick in 1958, describing such a trip: "Drove north of Scott's Bluff and Torrington which are on U.S. N. 30 and into Casper then north through Buffalo and Sheridan and over the Big Horns to Cody" (*SL* 888).

242:31 **Sheridan:** A town in northern Wyoming, near the Montana border, which Cantwell will describe as being "wonderful" (242:33) and "right up against the mountains" (243:7–8); that is, the Bighorn Mountains. Hemingway finished his draft of *A Farewell to Arms* in Sheridan in August 1928 (Reynolds, *1930s* 3). As Hemingway writes in his 1948 introduction to *A Farewell to Arms*, the first draft was finished "near Big Horn in Wyoming" (*FTA*, Hemingway Library vii). Sheridan is also the setting of Hemingway's short story, "Wine of Wyoming," published in *Winner Take Nothing* (1933).

243:1 **Wagon-Box Fight:** The Wagon Box Fight was a 2 August 1867 episode of Red Cloud's War between the United States Army and the Sioux Native Americans (including Crazy Horse), just south of Sheridan.

243:2 **Billings:** Billings is the largest city in Cantwell's home state of Montana. It is about 130 miles northwest of Sheridan, Wyoming.

243:13 **Cloud's Peak:** At an elevation of 13,167 feet, this is the highest point of the Big Horn mountains in Wyoming,.

243:16 **hydromatic drive:** Hydramatic was an automatic transmission, introduced in 1940 Cadillacs and Oldsmobiles. Hemingway's Buick Roadmaster had Dynaflow transmission.

243:28 **It was no feat for a man:** That is, "It was no mean feat for a man."

244:9 **figlia:** Italian for "daughter."

CHAPTER 38

246:14 **Farewell, a long farewell:** Cantwell is referencing a speech by Cardinal Wolsey in Shakespeare's *Henry the Eighth:* "Farewell, a long farewell, to all my greatness!" (3.2.352).

247:4 **and she had said to herself:** Here is another brief glimpse into someone else's consciousness; we gain access into Renata's thoughts, coaxing herself to be strong and not to dwell on this painful goodbye.

247:13 **Wirtschaft:** A German word for "inn" or "pub." In the page and a half since chapter 38 began, Cantwell has spoken German, French, Spanish, and English, and remarked inanely on the beauty of the Italian language. He is clearly feeling goodbye jitters.

247:14–15 **observing, without observing:** This gracious professional characteristic of the *Gran Maestro* recalls the gondolier during Cantwell's dalliance with Renata, who was "unknowing, yet knowing all" (150:16).

247:31–32 **They have confiscated everything he owns:** As Mandel reports, all of Brusadelli's property was impounded in early November 1948 ("Reading the Brusadelli Stories" 336).

248:10–11 ***Por merito di guerra:*** Italian for "for merit of war." Although the Order is given a Spanish name and Cantwell seems to maneuver liberally between languages, "por" is Spanish for "for"; in Italian, the *Gran Maestro* would have said "per." In Pivano's translation, the error is noted and allowed to remain (206).

248:26–28 **Love is love and fun is fun. But it is always so quiet when the goldfish die:** Hemingway quoted this line in various correspondence during the period. In a letter to Charles Scribner on 19 August 1949 from Cuba, Hemingway wrote, "riding is riding and fun is fun and as old Blicky [Baron von Blixen] used to say, 'It's always so quiet when the goldfish die'" (*SL* 665). Von Blixen (1886–1946) was an African big game hunter and purportedly the model for the safari guide Robert Wilson in Hemingway's "The Short Happy Life of Francis Macomber." Hemingway also mentions him in *A Moveable Feast,* during an episode where a barman forgets having met F. Scott Fitzgerald but not Baron Von Blixen, who is "not a man that you forget" (193). Carlos Baker speculates that Von Blixen might be referencing a W. H. Auden line from *The Sea and the Mirror:* "It's madly ungay when the goldfish die" (*SL* 665).

249:1 **crab *enchillada*:** Hemingway misspells *enchilada.*

249:24–25 **that *vino secco,* from Vesuvius:** In addition to the martinis and Valpolicella, this "vino secco" or "dry wine" from Vesuvius in southern Italy will also conjure up the famous eruption of the volcano of Mount Vesuvius that decimated the southern Italian city of Pompeii in 79 A.D.

250:3–4 *fraîche et rose comme au jour de bataille*: Cantwell is quoting French historian Edgar Quinet (1803–1875), who actually wrote: "fraîches et riantes comme au jour des batailles" (367). Cantwell's quotation tells Renata that they should be "fresh and rosy like on the day of battle." Quinet's original means "fresh and cheerful like on the days of the battles." Hemingway also uses this quotation in *Green Hills of Africa,* his 1935 account of his safari: "And that last night, drunk, with [James] Joyce and the thing he kept quoting from Edgar Quinet, 'Fraîche et rose comme au jour de la bataille'. I didn't have it right I knew. And when you saw him he would take up a conversation interrupted three years before. It was nice to see a great writer in our time" (71).

Quinet's original reads:

Aujourd'hui, comme aux jours de Pline et de Columelle, la jacinthe se plaît dans les Gaules, la pervenche en Illyrie, la marguerite sur les ruines de Numance; et pendant qu'autour d'elles les villes qui ont changé de maîtres et de nom, que plusieurs sont rentrées dans le néant, que les civilisations se sont choquées et brisées, leurs paisibles générations ont traversé les âges et se sont succédé l'une à l'autre jusqu'à nous, fraîches et riantes comme au jours des batailles. (367)[1]

Joyce parodies this same Quinet quotation in *Finnegans Wake* (281), except he quotes it more accurately.

Even though Cantwell says he hasn't "the slightest idea" who said it (250:6), in *Green Hills of Africa* Hemingway does attribute the words to Quinet. After a romantic interlude with Renata on his bed in the Gritti, Cantwell washes up in the bathroom and then feels "as young as at his first attack" (107:24). Hemingway's fourth wife, Mary, lists this quotation as one of his favorite phrases, which he might apply to "a girl, a book, a wine, an aphorism" (*How It Was* 134).

In a letter to Harvey Breit in 1956, Hemingway also employs this Quinet phrase to express his excitement over an impending trip to Africa (*SL* 873).

See also when the narrator explains that one reason Renata loved Cantwell was his cheerfulness in the morning, "attack or no attack" (266:6).

250:7 **Collége des Maréchaux**: Cantwell claims to have attended a class at l'École des marechaux, an informal name for the Centre des hautes études militaires (CHEM), a school for French officers.

250:21 ***A Pâques ou à la Trinité:*** Literally: "on Easter or on the trinity"; it is a French vernacular phrase akin to "when hell freezes over." This humorous reference has been mistaken for Hemingway's placing the setting of the novel on Easter, although the reference is not to be taken literally.

The phrase appears in the eighteenth-century French ballad, "Marlbrough s'en va-t-en guerre" [Marlbrough has left the war], the lyrics of which suggest that the Duke of Marlborough will come home, per the cliché, "when hell freezes over."

250:27 **the woman that I pay alimony to:** The manuscript has "bitch" instead of "woman."

250:27–28 **who could not even make a child:** This outrageous attack applies to Hemingway's fourth wife, Mary, more than it does to Martha, his third. In August 1946, Mary suffered an ectopic pregnancy that rendered her unable to bear a child. Martha would not produce a child; Mary could not (see entry at 94:11). For Cantwell to compare his ex-wife's fallopian tubes to the inner tubes of major American tire companies represents the ugly depths of his hatefulness.

Martha had abortions in 1930, 1933, 1942 (which would have been Hemingway's child), and 1948 (Moorehead 42, 59, 198, 262).

NOTE

1. "Today, as in the days of Pliny and Columella, the hyacinth thrives in Wales, the periwinkle in Illyria, the daisy on the ruins in Numantia, and while around them the cities have changed masters and names, while some have ceased to exist, while the civilizations have collided with each other and smashed, their peaceful generations, one after another, have passed through the ages and have come up to us, fresh and cheerful like on the days of the battles."

CHAPTER 39

253:20 It's easy if you're bad: Here is the key to Cantwell's attitude, and perhaps anyone's: if you do not allow yourself to be affectionate or emotionally attached, goodbyes are easier. One can imagine how many friends Cantwell has had to say goodbye to in battle, and the hard shell of emotionlessness might be the only way to get through such heart-wrenching moments. The same phenomenon is demonstrated in "The Snows of Kilimanjaro," where Harry's wife challenges his rudeness, asking him, "is it absolutely necessary to kill off everything you leave behind?" (*CSS* 43).

In this goodbye scene stretching over chapters 38 and 39, Cantwell has certainly not become a nice, sweet man, but the fragile victory the novel has captured is that around Renata, he is conscious of his behavior and he tries desperately to be kind. Trying, as Renata will tell him, is "all the hope we have" (254:27).

253:21 go over and sit on the bench there under the tree: A loose allusion to the title, as is the later, "They . . . walked across the gravel and sat on a bench under the trees" (253:28–29) and possibly even "across the stretch of gravel and down the stone steps" (254:30–31).

When Renata says "Good-bye" (255:6), her story is over, the flashback to Friday and Saturday. She is physically present between pages 78 and 255, about two-thirds of the narrative.

CHAPTER 40

256:1 **sunken oak hogshead:** We are back on Sunday morning, in the "shooting barrel" (12:21), the "oaken staved hogshead sunk in the bottom of the lagoon" from chapter 1 (13:4–5).

256:2–4 **A blind is any artifice . . . :** An unusual moment of exposition in the narrative, in which the narrator is explaining something to the reader, rather than Cantwell lecturing to another character.

256:9–257:8 Cantwell makes the distinction between harmless, amusing lying in civilian life and the lying that costs lives in the military.

257:31 **Then they saw it was ice:** In the manuscript, Hemingway wrote a note to himself: "This is what the Colonel thinks when the duck flight slows up because, with the good light, the birds see the ice and no longer come in and go out to the open sea to raft up" (JFK 3).

257:33–258:1 **not a Colonel now, nor anything but a gun handler:** Cantwell has gone back to the identity of a "shooter" (11:5), as he was when we first met him. Compare this moment to a similar articulation in *For Whom the Bell Tolls:* "You're a bridge-blower now. Not a thinker" (17).

258:13 **the sullen boatman:** This Charon figure returns; Cantwell places him in the fifth circle of hell, populated with the sullen and the wrathful. The boatman is also referred to as a "sullen character" (270:23).

259:3 **he said to himself:** This awkward construction makes it seem like he is calling himself "beauty," but he is talking about Renata, just not speaking out loud.

260:8–11 **So he had no shooting and he thought without intention . . . :** This two-sentence sequence is one of the finest passages in the novel, with Hemingway using the word "it" both allusively and also specifically. Cantwell thinks "without intention," which is to say that his involuntary memory acts upon him, rather than him trying to select a specific recollection through effort. Instead, his mind carries him back to a street fight in the indeterminable past. Although we could strain to replace a specific noun for "it," Hemingway himself does, as chapter 41 begins: "the miracle" (265:2), which again, he claims was not "consciously implemented" (265:3–4).

For a similarly extraordinary moment where Hemingway utilizes this technique, see "The Snows of Kilimanjaro," where when the writer Harry realizes he will certainly die before he exhausts his talents: "There wasn't time, of course, although it seemed as though it telescoped so that you might put it all into one paragraph if you could get it right" (*CSS* 50). Hemingway is challenging the reader to substitute something specific for all four instances of the word "it." While "life" might fit for the first three and "the story" for the fourth, the reader might also provocatively substitute "life" for all four instances (see Cirino, *Thought in Action* 64, 118).

260:12–264:6 In a novel filled with mostly vague allusions to Cantwell's exploits during World Wars I and II, this specific extended recollection is a rare window into a particular part of his past, possibly the moment that caused Renata to fall in love with him, the episode that "made it" (260:9) or "made the miracle" (265:2). Dramatically, it serves a similar purpose as the arm-wrestling episode in *The Old Man and the Sea* (69–70) and the recollection in "Big Two-Hearted River" of arguing about coffee with Hopkins (*CSS* 168–69), a specific random recollection from the past as a break from the urgency of the present.

This anecdote, roughly 1,150 words, is not in the manuscript.

260:13 **the girl:** It is strongly implied that the girl in the anecdote is Renata, although this only becomes certain at the beginning of the next chapter, when this incident is pointed to as a new phase of intimacy in their relationship. Any information about the history of their relationship is valuable; if Renata is nearly nineteen, how old was she when they started their romance?

260:27 **Or look away:** A character's decision to view violence or to look away is one of the central themes to Hemingway's work. Jake Barnes gives Brett Ashley the same choice—albeit one she ignores—when they are watching the bullfight in *The Sun Also Rises*. Dr. Adams allows a young Nick Adams to decide to watch or look away from a Caesarean operation in "Indian Camp." But here, after the conflict, when Cantwell asks her if she watched, Renata's response is "Yes" (261:27). Hemingway and his characters notice such a willingness, and they respect the acceptance of violence as a byproduct of modern life. (For a more complete treatment of this topic, see Cirino, "Beating Mr. Turgenev" and *Thought in Action* 101–15).

Cantwell walks away after landing the final left hook of the fight, because he does "not want to hear the head hit the pavement" (261:17), sparing himself a similar detail of violence. This notion of—in James Joyce's phrase—"the ineluctable modality of the audible" (*Ulysses* 31) is present in a powerful moment in the manuscript of Hemingway's *The Garden of Eden,* in which the protagonist recalls witnessing an execution: "I've seen the guillotine on the Boulevard Arago at 0500 and heard the thud" (JFK 64). In other words, if he was there at five in the morning, he wasn't there by accident. And ultimately, he was close enough to see and stayed long enough to hear the beheading.

260:31 **shore patrol:** The shore patrol is responsible for sailors during their shore leave.

261:7 **left from nowhere:** This description echoes the duck hunt itself, in which "a pair of pin-tails came, suddenly, from nowhere" (257:11). We must also remember that Cantwell has already instructed us about street fighting and "the simple odds of two to one" (175:11–12).

262:19 **that thing:** An ambiguous comment; it must mean more than "that fight." This undefined quality goes back to the "it" that was the cause of speculation on 260:9–11, which justifies the drift into retrospective reverie. In a relationship that defies logic, it is just as illogical that a street fight was a catalyst. This street fight, for whatever reason, is what Cantwell can retrospectively point to as deepening their love.

263:12 **If you ever fight, then you must win it:** Although Cantwell is referring to street fisticuffs, his experience suggests that this mindset also applies to foreign policy. In his introduction to *Men at War,* Hemingway makes the same claim: "once we have a war," he writes, "there is only one thing to do. It must be won. For defeat brings worse things than any that can ever happen in a war" (xi). Despite Hemingway's professed hatred of war, he asserts again in the introduction, "there are worse things than war; and all of them come with defeat. The more you hate war," he goes on, "the more you know that once you are forced into it . . . you have to win it" (xxvii). See the telling exchange in *A Farewell to Arms,* where one of Frederic Henry's ambulance drivers says, "There is nothing worse than war," to which Frederic replies, "Defeat is worse." Passini responds: "I do not believe it . . . What is defeat? You go home" (50).

In Hemingway's *Ken* magazine piece, "Treachery in Aragon," he writes, "War is a hateful and dirty business but when one has become involved in a war there is only one thing to do: win it" (26).

263:13 **All the rest is cabbage:** Rommel's complete quotation, according to war correspondent Drew Middleton, is "in war it is only winning, all the rest is cabbage" (142).

263:27 **Anche io:** Italian for "me too," although an Italian would elide the first of the consecutive vowel sounds to say "*Anch'io.*" See the entry at 62:31.

CHAPTER 41

265:2 made the miracle: This ambiguous reference picks up "it" (260:9–11) and "that thing" (262:19), which essentially depicts Cantwell meditating in the duck blind about his love for Renata and how it came about. "The great miracle" is nothing less than the mystery of love, as improbable as Cantwell and Renata's relationship might be. Hemingway described the meeting with Adriana as "something that struck me like lightning" (qtd. in Meyers, *Hemingway* 440).

265:7–8 abandoned treachery: The treacherous duck emerges as a minor theme as the novel concludes. Back at the Rialto market in chapter 22, Cantwell remarks that the lobsters "have all been captured by treachery" (179:2–3). This treachery is continued by the duck, who calls to the flying widgeon (257:24), who "came in well, with treachery speaking to them" (257:29). The dejected hen "quacked hard in her loyal treachery" (267:1–2), a slick oxymoron.

The word "treachery," insisted upon at this late stage of the novel, further deepens Hemingway's allusion to Dante, who placed the treacherous, the fraudulent, and the traitorous in his ninth and final circle of hell. In Hemingway's *Ken* article, he writes a surreptitious attack on John Dos Passos: "There are some very politically naïve people in America who do not believe there is any such thing as treachery . . . there are all sorts of treachery just as there are all sorts of heroism in war" ("Treachery in Aragon" 26).

266:5–6 never been sad one waking morning of his life: Mary's memoirs, *How It Was*, describes Hemingway as typically waking "cheerful and with budding plans, as he did three hundred and sixty mornings a year in the seventeen years I shared with him" (136). He was, on the morning following their wedding-day dispute, "refreshed and cheerful as always" (184). In *The Garden of Eden*, David Bourne "had never known a morning when he had not waked happily until the enormity of the day had touched him" (148). See also *Under Kilimanjaro*, where Hemingway "never knew of a morning in Africa when I woke that I was not happy at least until I remembered unfinished business" (16). This idea also refers back to the Quinet line about the glee on the morning of battle (250:3–4) and Renata's love of Cantwell "attack or no attack" (266:6).

266:23 **chamois shooting patch:** Leather made from the chamois, a type of antelope; it is nonabrasive so it would not stick, as Cantwell prefers.

266:27–28 **Boss over and unders:** Boss & Co. has been a gun manufacturer since 1812, and it pioneered the over-and-under model in 1919. The double barrels of an over-and-under are arranged one on top of the other, rather than side by side. Hemingway killed himself on 2 July 1961 with a double-barreled Boss shotgun.

267:4 **I never give her anything:** Cantwell might be correct, but he did have an extremely thoughtful idea to make her a vest from the plumage of the mallard drake he killed (259:26–33).

267:13 **With all my worldly goods I thee endow:** Cantwell is quoting from the wedding sacraments in the *Book of Common Prayer* (279). As the novel ends, Cantwell does bequeath to Renata the painting and his two shotguns (282:29–30). In his hastily scribbled will, he makes no note of his uniform, medals, or books, which are mentioned here (267:10–11).

267:16 **V.M.I.:** An abbreviation of the Virginia Military Institute, located in Lexington, Virginia. Cadets receive class rings and combat rings during their junior year. In the manuscript, Hemingway had written "from the Point" instead of "from V.M.I." (JFK 3).

267:18 **D.S.C. with cluster:** The Distinguished Service Cross is the second highest military honor given in the American armed forces, for valor and gallantry in confrontation of the enemy; Colonel Buck Lanham received it for his actions in the Hürtgen Forest campaign. In World War II, approximately five thousand such awards were given, and only about fifty military personnel received two or more. A cluster is an oak leaf cluster that signifies an additional honor.

267:18–19 **silver stars:** The silver star is the third highest military honor; as does the DSC, it rewards valor and gallantry in confrontation of the enemy.

268:4 **think about your girl:** Here in chapter 41, we progress from "Now don't think of her. Don't think of Renata" (265:13) to "think about your girl"—Cantwell decides that even painful thoughts of Renata are preferable to murderous thoughts of the sullen poler.

268:6–7 **You going to run as a Christian?** Cantwell realizes that after a lifetime of "killing armed men" (65:21), it is disingenuous to believe that "Thou shalt not kill" (Exodus 20:13, Deuteronomy 5:17), the sixth commandment, applies to him. However, when he says "Maybe I will get Christian toward the end" (268:10), he echoes Count Greffi from *A Farewell to Arms,* who expected to get religious as he grew closer to death: "I had always expected to become devout. All my family died very devout. But somehow it does not come" (263).

Hemingway and Lanham enjoyed telling the anecdote that Hemingway asked the company chaplain if he believed there were no such thing as atheists in foxholes. The chaplain responded, "No, sir, Mr. Hemingway . . . not since I met you and Colonel Lanham" (qtd. in Baker, *Life Story* 435).

268:32–270:8 He remembered how . . . : This 399-word anecdote about a "moment in action" with his "best friend," George, refers to an early fall engagement in the Ardennes. Hemingway wrote an autobiographical short story, never published, called "Indian Country and the White Army" centered on the Allied army in the Ardennes. "The Ardennes, contrary to previous military thought, is not an impassable obstacle," Hemingway writes. "It is a four-lane highway if you know how to use it" (JFK 496B).

269:18 he said to his best friend: By all accounts, particularly his own, Hemingway's best friend during World War II was Buck Lanham. He did, however, refer in subsequent correspondence to George Wertenbaker as among his best friends during the war. Wertenbacker was a young colonel who commanded a P47 group, and Hemingway stayed in his headquarters. Another possibility among Hemingway's war friends is George Bickel, who commanded a P51 group.

269:33 Geneva Convention: Although we are not sure what Cantwell might have done to violate it, the 1932 Geneva Convention protects against, for instance, the torturing of prisoners to acquire information. Cantwell did learn the readiness of the enemy from a German, even though his later prediction about its behavior is not ascertained from a "kraut" (270:4). In a letter to his son John, Hemingway asserted that he was planning on having the Geneva Convention tattooed in reverse on his ass (Coté 98).

270:7–8 and that was the end of that story: In a novel consumed with Cantwell's anecdotes about war, usually told to Renata, or even Jackson, this story comes while he is in meditation in a duck blind and possibly prevents painful and unproductive thoughts about Renata. In fact, after he tells himself the story, he wonders if Renata would have enjoyed it.

270:14 over ninety-five percent: The manuscript reveals that Hemingway contemplated giving Cantwell a 90–10 success rate, before crossing it out and deciding on better than 95–5.

270:25 **The shooting's over:** One wonders if the novel might not have productively ended at this point, with another farewell to arms. This line refers not simply to the immediate matter of the duck hunt but to a lifetime of killing and hunting and firing guns. This moment is a beautiful end to chapter 41 and resonates with the same melancholy, elegiac tone as in Fitzgerald's *The Great Gatsby*, when Nick sees a random visitor expecting a party at Gatsby's house, who did not realize "the party was over" (179).

CHAPTER 42

As he began drafting this chapter, Hemingway wrote "Next to Last Chapter," even though that claim would be incorrect.

272:3–4 **they worked together in complete co-ordination:** We see an unexpected harmony between these two adversaries, the sullen and the wrathful (see 184:24, for Cantwell as wrathful). We will soon see Cantwell back up this new thaw in their relationship with generous offers from his flask (272:28, 274:3).

272:24 **earliest days:** A curious reference, because how early would these earliest days have been? Was this flask purchased, engraved, and given to Cantwell in secrecy because Cantwell was married, or because she was a minor? At the age of eighteen, had they been romantically involved for more than a year? More than two? How long ago did the street fight take place? See entry at 260:13.

272:26–27 **From R. to R.C.:** From Renata to Richard Cantwell.

CHAPTER 43

275:15 **The Barone killed forty-two:** It might be expected that Hemingway would have made his alter ego the "top gun" (275:14), but in this sense, *Across the River and into the Trees* is consistent with *Green Hills of Africa,* when Hemingway is defeated in a hunting competition with Karl, a loss that leaves him, as he says, "cold in the pit of my stomach" (291). The Barone Alvarito kills forty-two to Cantwell's four. This lopsided contest prefigures the next way Alvarito will supersede Cantwell, taking his place with Renata.

This exchange about Venice, which leads to Alvarito "looking at nothing" is a coded, tacit agreement about Renata, in which Renata embodies Venice and Venice is code for Renata. Cantwell tells Alvarito, "And I love Venice" (277:6–7), clearly implying a love for Renata. Alvarito cannot meet Cantwell's eyes and then confesses, "We all love Venice. Perhaps you do the best of all" (277:9–10). Cantwell's unnecessarily repetitive yet emphatic rejoinder is, "I love Venice as you know" (277:11–12), which Alvarito acknowledges, "Yes. I know," and then "looked at nothing" (277:13). That brief, pointed, yet entirely unstated transfer of power is the most profound transposition in the novel. Even if this dialogue is too opaque for the reader, Cantwell believes the necessary connection was made: "Alvarito understands" (281:22).

Alvarito's smile goes from "shy" (276:15) to "shy, dark" (277:20).

CHAPTER 44

This penultimate chapter is slight, only 176 words. In the manuscript, Hemingway does not make a division between chapters 44 and 45, but calls 44 "Last Chapter" and 45 "Last Chapter—(continued)." Chapter 45 has 754 words.

278:1 **a villa with great gates:** Nanuk Franchetti had a villa in Treviso, north of Venice.

279:1 **unforeseen contingencies:** The contingencies, of course, are foreseen. Cantwell has no illusions of immortality and knows that his goodbye to Alvarito, like his earlier farewell to Renata, is forever.

CHAPTER 45

280:1 **early darkness:** Cantwell dies and the novel ends on Sunday evening, at dusk.

280:5 **I ordered you:** Cantwell explodes with his last burst of temper and then an immediate apology, followed by a justification. This tension that has dogged Cantwell throughout the novel, just as it has defined the narrative, continues to the end. What particularly galls Cantwell is that his authority was questioned and his command was not immediately and unquestioningly obeyed.

280:17–281:2 **I sent four of the ducks:** In this extraordinary gesture, Cantwell's life ends with an inventory, making sure that he reconciles debts and has fulfilled promises. Despite this awkward phrasing—"of the ducks I promised to those I promised them to" (280:17–18)—we understand how important seeing through that promise was to him. He laments that there will not be feathers for the waiter's wife, as he had hoped (70:23–26), or the sausage for the dog, as he had planned (178:14).

281:22 **Alvarito understands:** Not that Alvarito understands that he has shot well but that he understands the significance of Cantwell's last shoot and that he understands that the Colonel approves of Alvarito as a worthy successor to Renata's heart.

281:29 **Three strikes is out:** Cantwell is having his fourth heart attack.

281:32 **Do you know what General . . . :** Cantwell explains the motivation behind Hemingway's title. At this point in the manuscript, Hemingway wrote: "(Put in entire and correct quotation) from book by KIDD entitled "I Rode With Stonewall) ending with—Let us go across the river and rest under the shade of the trees" (JFK 1). See entry for Title.

282:3 **A. P. Hill:** Ambrose Powell Hill Jr. (1825–1865) was a Civil War general who served under Stonewall Jackson. Hill died shortly before the end of the war.

282:20 **carefully and well:** Cantwell's last action is proper, efficient, intentional, economical.

283:3 **through channels:** In a novel so conspicuously dominated by Cantwell's voice, by his speech and speeches, Hemingway's awarding of the final words to Ronald Jackson is surprising and even incongruous. Jackson, who prefers highways to anything off-road and unpredictable, will happily rely on the bureaucracy to manage Cantwell's possessions rather than deliver them himself. The channels of the military organization will no doubt prove as intricate and confusing as the labyrinthine canals of Venice.

In Hemingway's "Poem to Mary (Second Poem)," he writes: "All officers, warrant officers and enlisted men will be provided with a copy of their own true loves that they will never see again and all these copies will be returnable through the proper channels" (*Poems* 108).

Later in the same poem: "RETURN HER NOW THROUGH THE PRESCRIBED CHANNELS. RETURN HER" (*Poems* 111).

APPENDIX 1

TIME CHART

phrase	page	time	activity
two hours before daylight	11:1	Sunday morning	duck hunt
it was daylight	13:4	Sunday morning	duck hunt
day before he came down to Venice	17:3–4	Thursday	doc appt.
day before yesterday	21:1	Wednesday?	** *mistake* **
a few weeks ago	26:6	flashback	buries feces, $
Now	28:1	Friday	trip to Venice
late afternoon winter light	57:14–15	Friday	looking out window
eleven hundred tomorrow	60:14	Saturday	meets Jackson
day after tomorrow	70:22	Sunday	duck hunt
day after tomorrow	75:20	Sunday	duck hunt
the last sunlight of that day	76:2	Friday	Gritti to Harry's
meet at the garage at two-thirty	123:8–9	Saturday	with Alvarito
I go duck shooting tomorrow	133:23	Saturday	meets Alvarito
the shoot is on Sunday	134:6	Sunday	duck hunt
transport at noon tomorrow	135:23–24	Saturday	portrait
The Colonel woke before daylight	156:1	Saturday	Cantwell wakes up
When it started to be light	159:1	Saturday	Cantwell sees portrait
It is Saturday	250:15	Saturday	Renata speaks
early darkness was beginning	280:1–2	Sunday	trip to Trieste

a few weeks earlier—burying the 10,000 lire and feces at the spot of his wounding
Thursday—the doctor's appointment
Friday—the trip with Jackson from Trieste to Venice; meeting Renata; gondola
Saturday—solo walk to the marketplace; saying goodbye to Renata; meeting Alvarito to go hunting
Sunday—the duck hunt; death on the way to Trieste

ERRORS

Word/Phrase	page	should be
song writers	17	songwriters
seconal	18	Seconal
Then he said.	18	Then he said,
Johnston	25	Johnson
Sollingen	26	Solingen
San Dona	28	San Donà
Pilot Town	33	Pilottown
negronis	43	Negronis
Scuola San Rocco	49	Scuola di San Rocco
killed on Grappa	51	killed on the Grappa
Lysette	55	Lisette
Maitre d'Hotel	58 (2x), 66	maître d'hôtel
Caro	79	caro
Cavalry	92	cavalry
Gondoliere	92	gondoliere
The girl whose	107	The girl, whose
Assalone	115	Asolone
use to drink	124	used to drink
St. Lo	125	St. Lô
Perrier Jouet	126	Perrier-Jouët
Etoile	127	Étoile
cuerpo d'Armata	129	*corpo d'Armata*
Toussu le Noble	133	Toussus-le-Noble
Velasquez	137	Velásquez
for a little while	146	for a little while"
soldier-suit	167	soldier suit
brochetto	179	brochette
Gritti-Palace	181	Gritti Palace
member	210	remember
Schnee-Eifel	216	Schnee Eifel
Stadtswald	216	Stadtwald
perpetrate	217	perpetuate
Mont. St Michel	240	Mont.-St.-Michel
Roubidoux	241	Robidoux
Wagon-Box	243	Wagon Box
hydromatic	243	Hydramatic
enchillada	249	enchilada
Collége	250	Collège
Mallard	259	mallard

APPENDIX 1 · 209

APPENDIX 2

"IN HARRY'S BAR IN VENICE"
ERNEST HEMINGWAY

Ladies and Gentleman:
It is a great honor to be with you tonight and to discuss my new book. This is one of the things that I love to do most and it gives me great pleasure that I can share it with all of you.

The book came to me in a sort of a haze in Harry's Bar in Venice. Harry's Bar is a small place, but it is, in effect, a microcosm of all of that great and beautiful city which has been so well described by those writers Ruskin, Sinclair Lewis, Byron, and others.

The hero—if he can be called a hero—of this book is a young colonel, eighteen years old. He was made a colonel, no one knows quite how, and stationed in Trieste for his own sins. He is a fanatic at shooting at all things, including objects floating down the Grand Canal and he has come to Venice to practice his, shall we say, avocation. In Venice in Harry's Bar, which has become almost a sacred place for those of us who know it and who have enjoyed both the credit and the hospitality of Cipriani, he meets an Italian or rather, should we say, a Venetian countess aged eighty-six. In the corner of the room is a princess of Greece named Aspasia. The young colonel is mad about the princess of Greece, but still he has his countess and his obligations. The action of the book, ladies and gentlemen, only takes place during a period of forty-eight days, during which the colonel who is continuously in Harry's Bar—known to the local residents or *indigentes* as Cipriani's—is continuously drunk, due to his own efforts and his credit with Signor—speaking Italian—Cipriani.[1]

For forty of these forty-eight days, the colonel is unable to find his countess! She has taken refuge in the basilica. Naturally, she is given full facilities there and enjoys herself very much, looking out of the upper windows and studying the action of the pigeons during this time of indecision for the young colonel who is on indefinite leave by the request of his superior officers. He makes the acquaintance of a beautiful Venetian maiden, aged no one knows what—some say sixteen some say seventeen, others who are treacherous say eighteen. She, through her powers of seductiveness, induces him to visit the island of Tornicello.² The colonel is accompanied by his faithful black priest who is his spiritual advisor and can almost be regarded as his spiritual manager. Together they make a pilgrimage to this island, a very ancient part of the lagoon which surrounds Venice, a town which I shall describe later after consulting my Baedeker. It is love at first sight between the Colonel and Aftera.³ There is nothing to be done; it is a hopeless love, but much can come of it and the Colonel takes advantage of this situation in a manner which might be criticized in certain circles but which we will attempt to condone due to the presence of his faithful black priest who at this moment has passed out. Aftera or Afdera, as the name is pronounced by the local inhabitants, is indomitable—nothing like her has been seen since Attila the Hun sat in the sacred chair of Tornicello.⁴ The colonel, who is an extremely devout Catholic, having only been expelled from the church at the age of sixteen, loves Afdera as he has never loved anyone in all of his existence. Afdera loves him as she loves the front page of *Europeo*. What greater comparison can we make? God himself is absent for a time, probably on His own business, but he returns to Tornicello to bring happiness to these star-crossed lovers. Afdera and the Colonel marry, but, ladies and gentlemen, there is tragedy in all of this. There is a tragedy that one can hardly say without having his voice break. Afdera is the victim of a heart condition, a cardiac condition acquired during her youth. The colonel cannot stand to see her die, and so he himself swims off into the sunset, headed, as far as we know, toward Chioggia, a fishing port well down the coast. But the colonel can swim, and we hope that he can make it.

This, in a quick résumé, is the story of my new book and I hope that everyone will buy it, paying three dollars, and the twenty percent of each of these three dollars will go to me to pay Gagliaretta and other people first and then to go to the Fundación Afdera which is to commemorate that great soul who has brought us such happiness.⁵ I thank you, ladies and gentlemen, for your patience.

NOTES

1. An *indigente* is a poor, needy person. Unless he is making a strained joke, Hemingway seems to mean *cittadini*, which would mean "citizens."
2. It is unclear why Hemingway adds a syllable to "Torcello"; he is confused or else making a joke.
3. Afdera Franchetti was the sister of Nanuk, the inspiration of the Barone Alvarito in *Across the River and into the Trees*. She is being mocked, among other reasons, for giving a scandalous interview to *Europeo* magazine that suggested that she and Adriana Ivancich were the inspirations for Renata in the novel, which implied a romantic relationship between Hemingway and her. Hemingway's gibe about the pronunciation of her name—Afdera versus Aftera—must be an inside joke.
4. Attila the Hun ransacked northern Italy in the middle of the fifth century.
5. Hemingway uses the Spanish word for "foundation." An Italian organization would be *fondazione*.

WORKS CITED

Ackroyd, Peter. *Venice: Pure City.* New York: Doubleday, 2009.
Alighieri, Dante. *Text.* Vol. 1 of *Inferno.* Trans. Charles Singleton. Princeton, NJ: Princeton UP, 1970.
———. *Text.* Vol. 1 of *Purgatorio.* Trans. Charles Singleton. Princeton, NJ: Princeton UP, 1973.
Andrews, Robert, ed. *Columbia Dictionary of Quotations.* New York: Columbia UP, 1993.
Antongini, Tommaso. *D'Annunzio.* Boston: Little, Brown, 1938.
Baker, Carlos. *Hemingway: A Life Story.* New York: Scribner, 1969.
———. *Hemingway: The Writer as Artist.* 4th ed. Princeton, NJ: Princeton UP, 1972.
Barrie, J. M. *The Plays of J. M. Barrie.* London: Hodder & Stoughton, 1929.
Beach, Joseph Warren. "How Do You Like It Now, Gentlemen?" *Hemingway and His Critics: An International Anthology.* Ed. Carlos Baker. New York: Hill & Wang, 1961. 227–44.
Beegel, Susan F. *Hemingway's Craft of Omission: Four Manuscript Examples.* Ann Arbor: UMI Research P, 1988.
Beistle, Donald. "Ernest Hemingway's ETO Chronology." *Hemingway Review* 14.1 (1994): 1–16.
Bergson, Henri. *Creative Evolution.* Trans. Arthur Mitchell. Mineola, NY: Dover, 1998.
———. *The Creative Mind: An Introduction to Metaphysics.* Trans. Mabelle L. Andison. Mineola, NY: Dover, 2007.
Bidle, Kenneth E. "Rite de Passage à Mort." *Fitzgerald/Hemingway Annual* (1973): 259–70.
Blake, William. "The Tyger." *Songs of Innocence and Songs of Experience.* New York: Dover, 1992. 37–38.
Boice, William S., ed. *History of the Twenty-Second United States Infantry.* NP: 1959.
Book of Common Prayer and Administration of the Sacraments and Other Rites and Ceremonies of the Church. New York: Oxford UP, 1897.
Boreth, Craig. *The Hemingway Cookbook.* Chicago: Chicago Review P, 1998.
Bosworth, R. J. B. *Mussolini's Dictatorship: Life under the Fascist Dictatorship, 1915–1945.* New York: Penguin, 2007.
Brasch, James Daniel, and Joseph Sigman. *Hemingway's Library: A Composite Record.* New York: Garland, 1981.
Breit, Harvey. "Talk with Mr. Hemingway." *Conversations with Ernest Hemingway.* Ed. Matthew J. Bruccoli. Jackson: U of Mississippi P, 1986. 60–62.
Brian, Denis. *The True Gen: An Intimate Portrait of Ernest Hemingway by Those Who Knew Him.* New York: Grove, 1988.
Browning, Robert. "A Toccata of Galuppi's." *The Norton Anthology of English Literature,* 8th ed. Vol. E. *The Victorian Age.* Ed. Carol T. Christ and Catherine Robson. New York: Norton, 2006. 6 vols. 1262–64.

Bruccoli, Matthew J. "Hemingway 'Theft' Identified." *Hemingway Newsletter* 12 (June 1986): 4.
Burwell, Fred. "Fridays with Fred: The Hemingway Connections." *Terrarium*. 12 January 2012. Web. <http://www.beloit.edu/campus/news/fwf/?story_id=338898>.
Burwell, Rose Marie. *Hemingway: The Postwar Years and the Posthumous Novels*. Cambridge: Cambridge UP, 1996.
Byron, George Gordon Lord. "Beppo: A Venetian Love Story." *The Poetical Works of Lord Byron*. London: Oxford UP, 1930. 614–24.
———. *Childe Harold's Pilgrimage*. *The Poetical Works of Lord Byron*. London: Oxford UP, 1930. 174–244.
Caesar, Julius. *The Conquest of Gaul*. Trans. S. A. Handsford. New York: Penguin, 1951.
Camus, Albert. *The Rebel: An Essay on Man in Revolt*. Trans. Anthony Bower. New York: Knopf, 1956.
Carr, Virginia Spencer. *Dos Passos: A Life*. Garden City, NY: Doubleday, 1984.
Cassar, George H. *The Forgotten Front: The British Campaign in Italy, 1917–1918*. London: Hambledon, 1988.
Cavallaro, Gaetano V. *The Beginning of Futility*. Bloomington, IN: Xlibris, 2009.
Cirino, Mark. "Beating Mr. Turgenev: 'The Execution of Tropmann' and Hemingway's Aesthetic of Witness." *Hemingway Review* 30.1 (Fall 2010): 31–50.
———. "A Bicycle Is a Splendid Thing: Hemingway's Source for Bartolomeo Aymo in *A Farewell to Arms*." *Hemingway Review* 26.1 (Fall 2006): 106–14.
———. *Ernest Hemingway: Thought in Action*. Madison: U of Wisconsin P, 2012.
———. "You Don't Know the Italian Language Well Enough: The Bilingual Dialogue of *A Farewell to Arms*." *Hemingway Review* 25.1 (Fall 2005): 43–62.
Comley, Nancy R. "The Italian Education of Ernest Hemingway." *Hemingway's Italy: New Perspectives*. Ed. Rena Sanderson. Baton Rouge: LSU P, 2006. 41–50.
Comley, Nancy R., and Robert Scholes. *Hemingway's Genders: Rereading the Hemingway Text*. New Haven: Yale UP, 1994.
Concise Oxford Paravia Italian Dictionary. New York: Oxford UP, 2009.
Coté, William E. "Correspondent or Warrior? Hemingway's Murky World War II 'Combat' Experience." *Hemingway Review* 22.1 (2002): 90–106.
Cowley, Malcolm. "Hemingway Portrait of an Old Soldier Preparing to Die." *New York Herald Tribune* 10 September 1950: 1, 16.
———. "A Portrait of Mister Papa." *Ernest Hemingway: The Man and His Work*. Ed. John K. M. McCaffery. Cleveland: World Publishing, 1950.
Craf, John R. *Invasion Leaders: American Military Leaders, 1942–1944*. Philadelphia: McKinley, 1944.
Crane, Stephen. *The Red Badge of Courage*. 1895. New York: Norton, 2008.
Crosswell, D. K. R. *Beetle: The Life of General Walter Bedell Smith*. Lexington: UP of Kentucky, 2010.
D'Annunzio, Gabriele. *Notturno*. Trans. Stephen Sartarelli. New Haven: Yale UP, 2011.
de la Mare, Walter. *The Collected Poems of Walter de la Mare*. London: Faber & Faber, 1979.
Del Riccio, Luigi. *The True Story of Eleonora Duse's Love Affair with D'Annunzio*. Girard, KS: Haldeman-Julius, 1924.
"Discomfited General." *Time* 50.21 (24 November 1947): 26.
Donaldson, Scott. *Hemingway vs. Fitzgerald: The Rise and Fall of a Literary Friendship*. Woodstock, NY: Overlook, 1999.
Douglas, Henry Kyd. *I Rode with Stonewall*. 1940. Marietta, GA: Mockingbird, 1995.

Douglass, Frederick. *Narrative of the Life of Frederick Douglass*. New York: Signet Classics, 1997.

Doyle, N. Ann, and Neal B. Houston. "Ernest Hemingway's Letters to Adriana Ivancich." *Library Chronicle of the University of Texas at Austin* 30 (1985): 15–37.

"drag chain." *Merriam-Webster On-line*. Web. 18 March 2015. <http://www.merriam-webster.com/dictionary/drag%20chain>.

Dunlap, A. R. "G.I. Lingo." *American Speech* 20.2 (April 1945): 147–48.

Dylan, Bob. "You're Gonna Make Me Lonesome When You Go." *Blood on the Tracks*. New York: Columbia, 1974. LP.

Eby, Carl P. "He Felt the Change So That It Hurt Him All the Way Through: Sodomy and Transvestic Hallucination in Hemingway." *Hemingway Review* 25.1 (Fall 2005): 77–95.

———. *Hemingway's Fetishism: Psychoanalysis and the Mirror of Manhood*. Albany: SUNY P, 1999.

Eco, Umberto. *The Name of the Rose*. Trans. William Weaver. San Diego: Harcourt Brace Jovanovich, 1983.

Eisler, Benita. *Byron: Child of Passion, Fool of Fame*. New York: Knopf, 1999.

Eliot, T. S. *The Complete Poems and Plays, 1909–1950*. New York: Harcourt, Brace & World, 1971.

———. "Tradition and the Individual Talent." *Norton Anthology of Theory and Criticism*. Ed. Vincent B. Leitch. New York: Norton, 2001. 1092–98.

Euro-Mediterranean Regional Programme for Local Water Management. "Worksites: Italy." Web. March 18, 2015. <http://www.isiimm.agropolis.org/index.php?page=worksites&country=3>

Famous Fourth: The Story of the 4th Infantry Division. ETOUSA, 1945.

Faulkner, William. "Address upon Receiving the Nobel Prize for Literature." *The Portable Faulkner*. Ed. Malcolm Cowley. New York: Penguin, 2003. 649–50.

———. *As I Lay Dying*. 1930. New York: Vintage, 1990.

———. *Light in August*. 1932. New York: Vintage, 1990.

———. *Sanctuary*. 1931. New York: Vintage, 1993.

———. *The Sound and the Fury*. New York: Vintage, 1990.

Fitzgerald, F. Scott. 1925. *The Crack-Up*. 1945. Ed. Edmund Wilson. New York: New Directions, 1993.

———. *The Great Gatsby*. New York: Scribner, 2004.

———. *Tender Is the Night*. New York: Scribner, 2003.

Frye, Northrop. "Novels on Several Occasions." *Hudson Review* 3.4 (Winter 1951): 611–19.

Gellhorn, Martha. *Selected Letters of Martha Gellhorn*. Ed. Caroline Moorehead. New York: Holt, 2006.

Gerogiannis, Nicholas. "Hemingway's Poetry: Angry Notes of an Ambivalent Overman." *Ernest Hemingway: The Papers of a Writer*. Ed. Bernard Oldsey. New York: Garland, 1981. 73–87.

Giangreco, D. M. with Kathryn Moore. *Eyewitness D-Day: Firsthand Accounts from the Landing at Normandy to the Liberation of Paris*. New York: Union Square P, 2005.

Gilmore, Donald L. "McNair, Lesley James." *Historical Dictionary of the U.S. Army*. Ed. Jerold E. Brown. Westport, CT: Greenwood, 2001.

Gorrell, Hank. *Soldier of the Press: Covering the Front in Europe and North Africa, 1936–1943*. Columbia: U of Missouri P, 2009.

Greacen, Lavinia, ed. "Hemingway and the Irish Soldier." *Irish Times* 19 March 1983: 9.

———. "Letters From Cuba." *Irish Times* 21 March 1983: 10.

Greene, Philip. *To Have and Have Another: A Hemingway Cocktail Companion.* New York: Perigee, 2012.

Griffin, Peter. *Along with Youth: Hemingway, the Early Years.* New York: Oxford UP, 1985.

Hawthorne, Nathaniel. *The Scarlet Letter.* 1850. Oxford: Oxford UP, 1998.

Hazlitt, William Carew. *History of the Venetian Republic: Her Rise, Her Greatness, and Her Civilization.* Vol. 1. London: Smith, Elder, & Co. 4 vols. 1860.

Hemingway, Ernest. *Across the River and into the Trees.* 1950. New York: Scribner, 1996.

———. *Across the River and into the Trees. Cosmopolitan.* May 1950: 50–51, 130–39.

———. "Across the River and into the Trees." Manuscript. Unpublished Manuscripts. Folders 1–6. John F. Kennedy Library and Museum. Boston.

———. "The Art of the Short Story." *New Critical Approaches to the Short Stories of Ernest Hemingway.* Ed. Jackson J. Benson. Durham: Duke UP, 1990. 1–13.

———. *By-line Ernest Hemingway: Selected Articles and Dispatches of Four Decades.* Ed. William White. New York: Scribner, 1967.

———. *Complete Poems.* Ed. Nicholas Gerogiannis. Lincoln: U of Nebraska P, 1992.

———. *The Complete Short Stories: The Finca Vigía Edition.* New York: Scribner, 2003.

———. *The Dangerous Summer.* 1960. New York: Scribner, 1985.

———. "The Dangerous Summer." *Life* 5 September 1960: 78–109.

———. *Dateline: Toronto: The Complete "Toronto Star" Dispatches, 1920–1924.* Ed. William White. New York: Scribner, 1985.

———. *Dear Papa, Dear Hotch: The Correspondence of Ernest Hemingway and A. E. Hotchner.* Ed. Albert J. DeFazio III. Columbia: U of Missouri P, 2005.

———. *Death in the Afternoon.* 1932. New York: Scribner, 1960.

———. *Di là dal fiume e tra gli alberi.* Tr. Fernanda Pivano. Milan: Mondadori, 1997.

———. *A Farewell to Arms.* 1929. New York: Scribner, 1995.

———. *A Farewell to Arms: The Hemingway Library Edition.* 1929. New York: Scribner, 2012.

———. *For Whom the Bell Tolls.* 1940. New York: Scribner, 1995.

———. *The Garden of Eden.* 1986. New York: Scribner, 2003.

———. "The Garden of Eden." Manuscript. Unpublished Manuscripts. Folder JFK #422.

———. *Green Hills of Africa.* 1935. New York: Scribner, 2003.

———. "He Who Gets Slap-Happy: A Bimini Letter." *Esquire* (August 1935): 19, 182.

———. "In Harry's Bar in Venice." *The Ernest Hemingway Audio Collection.* New York: HarperCollins, 2001. CD.

———. "Indian Country and the White Army." Unpublished Manuscripts. JFK #496B.

———. "Introduction, *In Sicily.*" *Hemingway and the Mechanism of Fame.* Ed. Matthew J. Bruccoli. Columbia, SC: U of SC P, 2006. 102–03.

———. *Islands in the Stream.* 1970. New York: Scribner, 2004.

———. *The Letters of Ernest Hemingway.* Vol. 1. *1907–1922.* Ed. Sandra Spanier and Robert W. Trogdon. Cambridge: Cambridge UP, 2011.

———. *The Letters of Ernest Hemingway.* Vol. 2. *1923–1925.* Ed. Sandra Spanier, Albert J. DeFazio III, and Robert W. Trogdon. Cambridge: Cambridge UP, 2013.

———, ed. *Men at War: The Best War Stories of All Time.* New York: Bramhall House, 1952.

———. "The Monument." Unpublished Manuscripts. John F. Kennedy Library #580a.

———. *A Moveable Feast.* 1964. New York: Touchstone, 1996.

———. *A Moveable Feast: The Restored Edition.* New York: Scribner, 2009.

———. *The Old Man and the Sea.* 1952. New York: Scribner, 1995.

———. *The Only Thing That Counts: The Ernest Hemingway/Maxwell Perkins Correspondence, 1925–1947.* Ed. Matthew J. Bruccoli. New York: Scribner, 1996.
———. "Safari." *Look* 18.2 (26 January 1954): 19–34.
———. *Selected Letters, 1917–1961.* Ed. Carlos Baker. New York: Scribner, 1981.
———. "The Snows of Kilimanjaro." Unpublished Manuscript Folder #702. John F. Kennedy Library. Boston, MA.
———. *The Sun Also Rises.* 1926. New York: Scribner, 2003.
———. *To Have and Have Not.* 1937. New York: Scribner, 1996.
———. "Torcello Piece." Unpublished Manuscripts. John F. Kennedy Library #773.
———. *The Torrents of Spring.* 1926. New York: Scribner, 1998.
———. "Treachery in Aragon." *Ken* 1.7 (30 June 1938): 26.
———. *Under Kilimanjaro.* Kent, OH: Kent State UP, 2005.
———. "Who Murdered the Vets? A First-Hand Report on the Florida Hurricane." *Hemingway and the Mechanism of Fame.* Ed. Matthew J. Bruccoli. Columbia: U of SC P, 2006. 43–48.
———. "The Woppian Way." Unpublished Manuscripts. John F. Kennedy Library #843.
"Hemingway Is Bitter about Nobody—But His Colonel Is." *Time* 11 September 1950: 110.
Hemingway, Mary Welsh. "Harry's Bar in Venice." *Holiday* (June 1968): 62–63, 106.
———. *How It Was.* New York: Knopf, 1976.
Home Fronts: Technologies of War. Vol. 3 of *History of World War I.* New York: Marshall Cavendish, 2002.
Homer. *The Iliad.* Trans. Robert Fitzgerald. Garden City, NY: Anchor, 1975.
Horace. *The Odes of Horace.* Trans. Lord Ravensworth. London: Upham & Beet, 1858.
Hotchner, A. E. "Hemingway, Hounded by the Feds" *New York Times* 1 July 2011: A19.
———. *Papa Hemingway.* New York Carroll & Graf, 1999.
Howard, Deborah. *The Architectural History of Venice.* New Haven: Yale UP, 2002.
Hugo, Victor. *Les Misérables.* 1862. Trans. Lee Fahnestock, Norman MacAfee, and C. E. Wilbour. New York: Signet, 1987.
Hurston, Zora Neale. *Their Eyes Were Watching God.* 1937. New York: HarperPerennial, 2006.
Ivancich, Adriana. "I Am Hemingway's Renata." Trans. Mark Cirino. *PMLA* 129.2 (March 2014): 257–66.
———. *La torre bianca.* Milan: Mondadori, 1980.
Ivancich-Biaggini, Gianfranco. "Ricordo Personale di Hemingway." *Hemingway e Venezia.* Ed. Sergio Perosa. Firenze: Olschki, 1988. 219–31.
James, Henry. *Italian Hours.* New York: Penguin, 1995.
Jewiss, Virginia. "Preface." *Notturno.* Gabriele D'Annunzio. Trans. Stephen Sartarelli. New Haven: Yale UP, 2011. vii–xi.
Johnston, Kenneth G. "Hemingway and Mantegna: The Bitter Nail Holes." *Journal of Narrative Technique* 1.2 (May 1971): 86–94.
Joyce, James. *Finnegans Wake.* 1939. New York: Penguin, 1999.
———. *Ulysses.* 1922. New York: Random House, 1986.
Kendall, Mary Claire. "Hemingway on Hemingway & Hollywood." *Forbes* (21 July 2012): <http://www.forbes.com/sites/maryclairekendall/2012/07/21/hemingway-on-hemingway-hollywood/>.
Kert, Bernice. *The Hemingway Women.* New York: Norton, 1983.
La Bianca, Nicholas. *Growing Up Under Fascism in a Little Town in Southern Italy.* Philadelphia: Xlibris, 2009.

Lanier, Sidney. "The Dying Words of Stonewall Jackson." *Poems of Sidney Lanier*. Ed. Mary Day Lanier. New York: Scribner, 1906. 238–39.

Latham, Aaron. "Papa's Mother and Wives." *New York Times Book Review* 17 July 1983: Sec. 7: 8.

Lawrence, D. H. *Studies in Classic American Literature*. 1923. New York: Penguin, 1977.

Leggiere, Michael V. *The Fall of Napoleon*. Vol. 1. *The Allied Invasion of France, 1813–1814*. Cambridge: Cambridge UP, 2007.

Lewis, Sinclair. *Dodsworth*. 1929. New York: Pocket, 1949.

Lingeman, Richard. *Sinclair Lewis: Rebel from Main Street*. New York: Random House, 2002.

Lisca, Peter. "The Structure of Hemingway's *Across the River and Into the Trees*." *Modern Fiction Studies* 12.2 (Summer 1966): 232–50.

Lockridge, Ernest. "*Othello* as a Key to Hemingway." *Hemingway Review* 18.1 (Fall 1998): 68–77.

Lynn, Kenneth S. *Hemingway*. New York: Simon & Schuster, 1987.

Lyons, Leonard. "The Lyons Den." *New York Post* 10 March 1950: 30.

Macdonald, John, with Željko Cimprić. *Caporetto and the Isonzo Campaign: The Italian Front 1915–1918*. Barnsley, South Yorkshire: Pen & Sword, 2011.

Madden, Thomas F. Thomas F. *A History of Venice: Queen of the Seas*. Prince Frederick, MD: Recorded Books, 2010. CD.

Mandel, Miriam. "*Across the River and into the Trees*: Reading the Brusadelli Stories." *Journal of Modern Literature* 19.2 (Autumn 1995): 334–45.

———. *Reading Hemingway: The Facts in the Fictions*. Lanham, MD: Scarecrow, 2001.

———. "Reading the Names Right." *Hemingway Repossessed*. Ed. Kenneth Rosen. Westport, CT: Praeger, 1994. 131–41.

Mann, Thomas. *Death in Venice*. 1912. Trans. Stanley Appelbaum. New York: Dover, 1995.

———. *Death in Venice and Seven Other Stories*. Trans. H. T. Lowe-Porter. New York: Vintage, 1958.

McCarthy, Cormac. *All the Pretty Horses*. New York: Knopf, 1992.

McGeorge, Stephen C. "Ten-in-One Rations." *Historical Dictionary of the U.S. Army*. Ed. Jerold E. Brown. Westport, CT: Greenwood, 2001. 468.

McLaughlin, Robert L. "'Only Kind Thing Is Silence': Ernest Hemingway vs. Sinclair Lewis." *Hemingway Review* 6.2 (Spring 1987): 46–53.

McLellan, Davis. "The Battle of Little Big Horn in Hemingway's Later Fiction." *Fitzgerald/Hemingway Annual* (1978): 245–48.

McManus, John C. *The Americans at Normandy*. New York: Doherty, 2004.

Mellow, James R. *Hemingway: A Life without Consequences*. Reading, MA: Addison-Wesley, 1994.

Meredith, James H. "Calculating the Complexity in *Across the River and into the Trees*." *North Dakota Quarterly* 64.3 (1997): 96–104.

———. "Hemingway's U.S. 3rd Army Inspector General Interview during World War II." *Hemingway Review* 18.2 (Spring 1999): 91–102.

———. "The Rapido River and the Hürtgen Forest in *Across the River and into the Trees*." *Hemingway Review* 14.1 (Fall 1994): 60–66.

Meyers, Jeffrey. "Chink Dorman-Smith and *Across the River and into the Trees*." *Journal of Modern Literature* 11.2 (July 1984): 314–22.

———. *Hemingway: A Biography*. New York: Harper & Row, 1985.

Middleton, Drew. *Retreat from Victory: A Critical Appraisal of American Foreign and Military Policy from 1920 to the 1970s*. New York: Hawthorn, 1973.

Miller, Edward G. *A Dark and Bloody Ground: The Hürtgen Forest and the Roer River Dams, 1944–1945*. College Station: Texas A&M UP, 1995.
Miller, Paul W. "Hemingway vs. Stendhal, or Papa's Last Fight with a Dead Writer." *Hemingway Review* 19.1 (1999): 127–41.
Moorehead, Caroline. *Gellhorn: A Twentieth-Century Life*. New York: Holt, 1993.
Moreira, Peter. *Hemingway on the China Front: His WWII Spy Mission with Martha Gellhorn*. Washington, DC: Potomac Books, 2006.
Moreland, Kim. *The Medievalist Impulse in American Literature: Twain, Adams, Fitzgerald, and Hemingway*. Charlottesville: U of Virginia P, 1996.
Moriani, Gianni. *Hemingway's Veneto*. Crocetta del Montello: Antiga, 2011.
Nelson, Dorman. Message to the author. 16 May 2012. E-mail.
"The New Hemingway." *Newsweek*, 11 September 1950, 90–95.
The New Oxford Annotated Bible: Revised Standard Edition. New York: Oxford UP, 1973.
Newman, Steve. "Ernest Hemingway's Courts Martial During World War II." *Ernest Hemingway: Selected Articles and Features by Steve Newman*. Web. 9 April 2012. <http://ernestmillerhemingway.blogspot.com/search?q=ERnest+Hemingway+involvement+in+World+War>.
"Nitroglycerin for Angina: Using It Correctly." *Harvard Heart Letter* 7.6 (1997): 1.
Nuti, Elisabetta Zingoni. "The 'Honorable Pacciardi' Remembered." *Hemingway Review* 11.1 (Fall 1991): 56–57.
O'Hara, John. "The Author's Name Is Hemingway." *New York Times* 10 September 1950: 1, 30–31.
O'Neill, Molly. *New York Cookbook*. New York: Workman, 1992.
O'Shaughnessey, Margaret. "Painters and Paintings in *Across the River and into the Trees*." *Hemingway's Italy: New Perspectives*. Ed. Rena Sanderson. Baton Rouge: LSU P, 2006. 201–11.
Ovid. *The Metamorphoses*. Trans. Thomas Orger. London: Hodson, 1811.
Owens, Terry. Messages to the author, 4 and 7 May 2012. E-mails.
Panunzio, Constantine Maria. *The Soul of an Immigrant*. New York: Macmillan, 1921.
Partridge, Eric. *J–Z*. Vol. 2 of *The New Partridge Dictionary of Slang and Unconventional English*. New York: Routledge, 2006.
Paul, Steve. Message to the author. 24 October 2012. E-mails.
Plimpton, George. "The Art of Fiction: Ernest Hemingway." *Conversations with Ernest Hemingway*. Ed. Matthew J. Bruccoli. Jackson: U of Mississippi P, 1986. 109–29.
———. "The Ultimate Confrontation." *Sports Illustrated*, 17 October 1977: 100–06, 108, 112, 114.
Pound, Ezra. *The Cantos of Ezra Pound*. New York: New Directions, 1996.
Proust, Marcel. *The Captive & The Fugitive*. Vol. 5 of *In Search of Lost Time*. Trans. C. K. Scott Moncrieff and Terence Kilmartin. Rev. D. J. Enright. New York: Modern Library, 2003.
Quinet, Edgar. *Oeuvres complètes*. Vol. 2. Paris: Germer-Baillère, 1857.
Raab, David. *Battle of the Piave: Death of the Austro-Hungarian Army*. Pittsburgh: Dorrance, 2003.
Reed, Henry. "New Novels." *Listener* 44 (9 November 1950): 515.
Reynolds, J. A. "CARROLL, BENAJAH HARVEY." *Handbook of Texas Online* Uploaded on June 12, 2010. Modified on February 1, 2011. Published by the Texas State Historical Association. Web. <http://www.tshaonline.org/handbook/online/articles/fca63>.
Reynolds, Michael. *Hemingway: The Final Years*. New York: Norton, 1999.
———. *Hemingway: The Homecoming*. New York: Norton, 1999.
———. *Hemingway: The 1930s*. New York: Norton, 1997.
———. *Hemingway: The Paris Years*. New York: Norton, 1999.

———. *Hemingway's First War: The Making of* A Farewell to Arms. Princeton, NJ: Princeton UP, 1976.

———. *Hemingway's Reading, 1910–1940: An Inventory*. Princeton, NJ: Princeton UP, 1981.

———. "Putting on the Riff." *Hemingway Review* 5.1 (1985): 30–31.

———. *The Young Hemingway*. New York: Blackwell, 1987.

Ross, Lillian. *Portrait of Hemingway*. New York: Avon, 1961.

Rostand, Edmond. *Cyrano de Bergerac*. Tr. Brian Hooker. New York: Bantam, 1982.

Rush, George E., ed. *U.S. Military Justice Handbook*. San Clemente, CA: LawTech, 2001.

Rush, Robert Sterling. *Hell in Hürtgen Forest: The Ordeal and Triumph of an American Infantry Regiment*. Lawrence, KS: UP of Kansas, 2001.

Ruskin, John. *The Stones of Venice*. Vol. 3. *The Fall*. New York: Cosimo Classics, 2007.

Russo, John Paul. "'To Die Is Not Enough!" Hemingway and D'Annunzio. *The Italian in Modernity*. Ed. Robert Casillo and John Paul Russo. Toronto: U of Toronto P, 2011. 393–433.

Sanderson, Rena. "Hemingway's Italy: Paradise Lost." *Hemingway's Italy: New Perspectives*. Ed. Rena Sanderson. Baton Rouge: LSU P, 2006. 1–37.

Saxon, Wolfgang. "Lady Diana Cooper Is Dead: A Beloved British Eccentric." *New York Times* 18 June 1986: B10.

Scafella, Frank. "'Nothing' in 'Big Two-Hearted River.'" *Hemingway: Up in Michigan Perspectives*. Ed. Frederic Joseph Svoboda and Joseph J. Waldmeir. East Lansing: Michigan State UP, 77–90.

Shakespeare, William. *The Norton Shakespeare*. 2d ed. New York: Norton, 2008.

———. *Shakespeare's Sonnets*. New Haven: Yale UP, 2000.

Shirer, William Lawrence. *The Collapse of the Third Republic: An Inquiry into the Fall of France in 1940*. New York: Simon & Schuster, 1969.

Smith, Paul. *A Reader's Guide to the Short Stories of Ernest Hemingway*. Boston: G. K. Hall, 1989.

Stein, Gertrude. *The Autobiography of Alice B. Toklas*. In *Selected Writings of Gertrude Stein*. Ed. Carl Van Vechten. New York: Vintage, 1962. 1–237.

Steinbeck, John. *The Grapes of Wrath*. 1939. New York: Penguin, 2002.

———. *The Red Pony*. 1937. New York: Penguin, 1994.

Stoltzfus, Ben. "The Stones of Venice, Time, and Remembrance: Calculus and Proust in *Across the River and into the Trees*." *Hemingway Review* 22.2 (Spring 2003): 19–29.

Stoneback, H. R. "Hemingway's Happiest Summer—'The Wildest, Most Beautiful, Wonderful Time Ever Ever'; or, The Liberation of France and Hemingway." *North Dakota Quarterly* 64.3 (1997): 184–220.

Streeter, Tim. "U.S. Army Field Rations." *Modeling in the U.S. Army in WWII*. 2002–2007. Web. <http://www.usarmymodels.com/ARTICLES/Rations/krations.html>.

Sullivan, James. *Seven Dirty Words: The Life and Crimes of George Carlin*. Cambridge, MA: Da Capo, 2010.

Tanner, Stephen L. "Wrath and Agony in *Across the River and into the Trees*." *Hemingway's Italy: New Perspectives*. Ed. Rena Sanderson. LSU P, 2006. 212–21.

Thompson, Mark. *The White War: Life and Death on the Italian Front, 1915–1919*. New York: Basic Books, 2010.

Tintner, Adeline R. "The Significance of D'Annunzio in *Across the River and into the Trees*." *Hemingway Review* 5.1 (Fall 1985): 9–13.

Twain, Mark. *Adventures of Huckleberry Finn*. 1884. New York: Norton, 1999.

---. "The Diary of Adam and Eve." *The Complete Short Stories of Mark Twain*. New York: Bantam, 1964. 273–95.

22nd Infantry Regiment Society. "The 22nd Infantry Regiment's Experience in the Hürtgen Forest." *22nd Infantry Regiment Society*. Web. <www.22ndinfantry.org/wwii.htm.>

Vasari, Giorgio. *The Lives of the Most Excellent Painters, Sculptors, and Architects*. Trans. Gaston du C. de Vere. New York: Modern Library, 2006.

Virgil. *The Aeneid*. Trans. Robert Fitzgerald. New York: Vintage, 1984.

Wade, Gary, transc. *Conversations with General J. Lawton Collins*. Fort Leavenworth, KS: Combat Studies Institute, U.S. Army Command and General Staff College, 1984.

War of the Rebellion: A Compilation of the Official Records of the Union and Confederate Armies. 128 vols. Washington, DC: GPO, 1891.

Weigley, Russell Frank. *Eisenhower's Lieutenants: The Campaign of France and Germany, 1944–1945*. Bloomington: Indiana UP, 1981.

Westerbeke Corporation. Message to the author, 2 April 2013. E-mail.

Whitman, Walt. *Leaves of Grass and Other Writings*. New York: Norton, 2002.

White, E. B. "Across the Street and Into the Grill." *New Yorker* 14 October 1950: 28.

Wickes, George. "Where Did Cantwell Steal the Passage?" *Hemingway Newsletter* 16 (June 1988): 3.

Williams, Tennessee. *The Glass Menagerie*. 1944. New York: Signet, 1987.

Wylder, Delbert E. *Hemingway's Heroes*. Albuquerque: U of New Mexico P, 1969.

Yellin, Emily. *Our Mothers' War: American Women at Home and at the Front during World War II*. New York: Free P, 2004.

Young, Philip. "The Assumptions of Literature." *College English* 24.5 (February 1963): 352–57.

---. *Ernest Hemingway: A Reconsideration*. University Park: Pennsylvania State UP, 1966.

---. Review of *Across the River and into the Trees*. *Tomorrow* 10 (Nov. 1950): 55–56.

Zorzi, Rosella Mamoli and Gianni Moriani. *In Venice and in the Veneto with Ernest Hemingway*. Venice: U Venezia Ca' Foscari, 2011.

INDEX

Aachen, 177
Abdel Krim, 174
Abilene, Kansas, 120, 179
Ackroyd, Peter, 31, 48, 84, 133
Across the River and into the Trees (ARIT). See specific headings
Adventures of Huckleberry Finn, The (Twain), 55, 74, 88
Alberto in *ARIT*, 40, 79
Alighieri, Dante. *See* Dante Alighieri
Alvarito in *ARIT*, 117–18; and boater, 6; and hunting, 204; importance of, 52–53; and Latisana, 16; and Renata, 119, 125, 159, 164, 173, 204, 206
Antongini, Tommaso, 51
Antony and Cleopatra (Shakespeare), 121
Ardant du Picq, Jean Jacques Joseph, 32, 122
Ardennes, 7, 32–33, 175, 181, 187, 201
Arezzo, 18
ARIT (Across the River and into the Trees). See specific headings
Arlington National Cemetery, 172
Armenonville, 129
Artists in *ARIT*: Bosch, 184; Botticelli, 20, 96; Brueghel, 19, 34, 154; Cézanne, 73; Degas, 73; Giotto, 17, 18, 19, 20, 59–60, 180; Goya, 89, 128; El Greco, 154; Mantegna, 18, 19, 112, 154; Masaccio, 18; Michelangelo, 18, 20; Piero della Francesca, 18, 20, 34; Tintoretto, 35, 45, 48; Titian, 20, 48, 96, 151; Velázquez, 127; Veronese, 84
"Art of the Short Story, The" (Hemingway), 127
As I Lay Dying (Faulkner), 165
Asolo, 56
As You Like It (Shakespeare), 22
Auchinleck, Claude, 111, 116
Auden, W. H., 193

Bach, Johann Sebastian, 89, 107
Baedeker, 112–13
Bainsizza, 51
Baker, Carlos: as biographer, 3, 22, 49, 74–75, 177; as editor, 51, 193. *See also specific works*
Balzac, Honoré de, 79–80
"Banal Story" (Hemingway, short story), 137
Barco de Avila, 41
Barman in *ARIT*, 58
Barrie, J. M., 106
Bassano, 23, 50, 69
Basso Piave, 63, 64, 111
Battle of the Bulge, 7–8, 27, 52, 181, 187, 189
Battle of Caporetto, 21, 27, 32, 49, 51, 63, 111; in *A Farewell to Arms*, 24, 30, 37, 183
Battle of Flanders, 66, 182
Battle of Gettysburg, 183
Battle of Hürtgen Forest, 131, 177, 180, 181, 185; and *ARIT*, 182, 183; and Cantwell, 27, 117, 165, 182; Hemingway on, 34, 39, 157, 183; and Lanham, 182, 200
Battle of the Little Big Horn, 137
Battle of Monte Grappa, 50, 51, 54, 63, 110
Battle of Normandy, 28, 121, 181; breakthrough at, 109, 170, 171; invasion of, 27, 29, 119, 131, 172, 176, 182, 187
Battle of Passchendaele, 66, 182
Battle of the Piave, 22, 27, 37, 110, 116, 183
Battle of the Vittorio Veneto, 21, 37, 49, 50, 51, 63, 110, 111
Battles of the Isonzo, 14, 55, 68, 116; and boatman, 51, 98; Cantwell on, 51, 64
Baum, Richard T., 118
Bayard, Nebraska, 190
Beach, Joseph Warren, 40
Beistle, Donald, 27
Bergamo, 66, 91

221

Big Horn Mountains, 190
"Big Two-Hearted River" (Hemingway, short story), 98, 128, 130, 173, 197
Belloc, Hillaire, 33
Berenson, Bernard, 41, 84
Bergman, Ingrid, 126
Bergson, Henri, 128, 173
Bible, 44, 79, 148, 155, 170, 200
Bickel, George, 201
Bidle, Kenneth E., 18
Billings, Montana, 190
Bismarck, Otto von, 24
"Black Ass at the Cross Roads" (Hemingway, short story), 107, 177
Blake, William, 129
Boatman in *ARIT*: background of, 6, 98; and Cantwell, 7, 9, 63, 203; Charon compared to, 5, 9, 90, 196; introduction of, 5
Bois de Boulogne, 125, 129
Bologna, 42, 91
Book of Common Prayer, 101–2, 200
Boreth, Craig, 160
Borgatti, Renata, 107
Bosworth, R. J. B., 44
Bradley, Omar Nelson, 115, 116, 119, 131, 170–71, 181–82
Brasch, James Daniel, 51
Breckenridge, John C., 94
Breda, Ernesto, 40
Breit, Harvey, 34, 167, 194
Brenta River, 31, 40, 111
Brescia, 67, 75
Browning, Elizabeth Barrett, 53
Browning, Robert, 53–54, 67, 112
Bruccoli, Matthew J., 39–40
Brusadelli, Giulio, 62, 66, 192
Bryan, William Jennings, 45, 178
Buffalo, Wyoming, 20, 190
Bulge, Battle of the, 7–8, 27, 52, 181, 187, 189
Burano, 31, 35
Burnham in *ARIT*, 14, 19
Burwell, Rose Marie, 131
Butcher, Harry C., 45, 123, 124, 176
Byron, George Gordon Lord, 20, 56, 118, 133; on Venice, 46, 53. *See also specific works*

Caesar, Julius, 66
Cahn, Sammy, 12
Cambronne, Pierre Jacques Étienne, 49
Camus, Albert, 45

Canfield, R. A., 150
Canterbury, 149
Cantwell, Bob, 171
Cantwell, Richard in *ARIT*, 5; age of, 11, 34, 58, 65; age difference with Renata, 4, 83, 197; and alcohol, 43, 44, 60–61, 66, 68, 72, 81, 98, 100, 109, 110, 118, 120, 122, 130, 193; animals compared to, 73, 106, 157; baby of, 92, 97; Buick of, 26–27, 189, 191; childhood of, 14–15, 190; and civilian vs. soldier, 8, 67, 68, 73–74, 84, 86, 90, 110; confession/purgation of, 28, 29, 33, 113–14, 164–65, 171, 176; daughter of, 24, 97, 103–4; and death, 69, 156, 174, 184, 188; and defecation, 22, 23, 135, 136–37; demotion of, 7–8, 11, 12, 34, 94, 111, 139, 175; efficiency of, 9, 59, 69, 130, 207; enemies of, 38, 72–73, 143; and ex-Fascists, 6, 73, 151, 157; glare of, 151; and Gordon, 186; hand injury of, 9, 61–62, 69, 85, 86, 129, 130, 155, 157; happiness of, 10, 33, 67, 71; health of, 9, 11–13, 24, 38, 70, 79, 100, 102, 108, 124, 130, 132, 135, 146, 157, 159, 206; and Hemingway, 121–22; inspiration for, 6; and jeep engine, 47; killing by, 112; knowledge of, 52, 71; memory of, 52; salary of, 48, 101, 102n2, 135, 187; sausage purchase by, 153–54; and spitting, 24, 151, 188; temper of, 10, 33, 42, 56–57, 84, 127, 133, 141, 195, 206; vigilance of, 98, 109, 152; and war stories, 28–29; will and testament of, 200
Caorle, 14, 26, 34
Caporetto, Battle of, 21, 27, 32, 49, 51, 63, 111; in *A Farewell to Arms*, 24 30, 37, 183
Carlin, George, 170
Carroll, Benajah Harvey, 76
Carso, 51, 55, 64, 116, 117, 171
Casals, Pablo, 107
Casanova, Giacomo, 126
Casper, Wyoming, 41, 190
Cather, Willa, 123
Ceggia, 20, 21
Characters in *ARIT*. *See specific characters*
Château Lingeard, 152
Cherbourg, 54, 116, 119, 169, 182
Cheyenne, Wyoming, 41
Chicago, Illinois, 41, 42
Childe Harold's Pilgrimage (Byron), 41, 126
"Christmas Gift, The" (Hemingway), 13, 140
Churchill, Winston, 8
Cipriani, 31, 43, 58, 74, 92

222 INDEX

Cities, American. *See specific cities*
Cities, international. *See specific cities*
Clamart, 124
Clark, Herbert, 177
"Clean Well-Lighted Place, A" (Hemingway, short story), 128, 147
Codognato, 100, 102
Codroipo, 91
Cody, Wyoming, 190
Cole, Nat King, 162
Collins, "Lightning" Joe, 81, 115–16, 171
Comley, Nancy R., 51, 106, 108
Condottieri, 62, 66, 68
Cook in *ARIT*, 65
Cooke City, Montana, 41
Cooper, Diana, 85–86
Cooper, James Fenimore, 107
Cortina d'Ampezzo, 14, 107, 111, 158
Coté, William E., 27
Cousenon River, 189
Coward, Noel, 106
Cowley, Malcolm, 79, 97, 175
Crane, Stephen, 70n2
Cripps, Stafford, 156
Crosby, Bing, 12
Custer, George Armstrong, 137–38

Dalmatia, 110
Dandolo (Contessa) in *ARIT*, 51, 52, 56, 70, 81
Dangerous Summer, The (Hemingway, book), 16–17, 111, 121, 165
D'Annunzio, Gabriele, 6; burial site of, 56; daughter of, 57, 107; and Duse, 56, 101, 102n1; eye injury of, 51, 54–55, 57, 71; home of, 54, 56; propaganda of, 50–51, 55; as soldier, 20, 53, 123; translations of, 56, 76. *See also specific works*
Dante Alighieri, 20, 68; as adjudicator, 9, 17, 62, 89–90; and Cantwell, 5, 146, 180; circles in, 17; and the Fraudulent, 7, 123, 149; and Hemingway, 90; personality of, 54, 90, 120; and the Sullen and the Wrathful, 196, 203; and the Treacherous, 199. *See also specific works*
Danube River, 72
Death in the Afternoon (Hemingway, book), 16, 89, 90–91
Dedication of *ARIT*, 4, 94
De Gasperi, Alcide, 147
De la Mare, Walter, 116

Dese River, 31
De Vulgari Eloquentia (Dante Alighieri), 161
Dewey, Thomas E., 172
Dialogue in *ARIT*, 14, 18, 113–14, 119, 160, 163
Divine Comedy (Dante Alighieri), 23, 52, 90
Dolomites, 10, 14, 31, 66, 67
Domenico (Ico) in *ARIT*, 156, 157
Dominguin, Luis Miguel, 121
Donaldson, Scott, 39
Dorman-Smith, Chink: and Cantwell, 6, 8, 116; as chief of staff, 111; and Hemingway, 79, 112, 115, 122, 162, 167; and Shakespeare, 64
Dos Passos, John, 53, 88, 90, 174, 199
Douglas, Henry Kyd, 3, 206
Douglass, Frederick, 30
Duck hunting: and Cantwell, 10, 199, 201; as frame of novel, 5, 42, 196; guns used in, 92; and Hemingway, 14, 31, 52, 72, 105, 118, 125; methods of, 6, 196; timing of, 76, 118, 125; types of, 72
Dukakis, Michael, 141
Duse, Eleonora, 51, 54, 56, 101, 102n1
Dylan, Bob, 187

Early, J. A., 94
Eby, Carl P., 97, 105, 126, 130, 131, 137, 138
Eco, Umberto, 106–7
Einaudi, Luigi, 147
Eisenhower, Dwight D., 178; and Butcher, 45, 123, 176; and Cantwell and Hemingway, 114–15; home of, 120, 179; and Smith, 115, 172, 177
Eliot, T. S., 90, 112, 165, 168
Emily in *ARIT*, 81
Epworth League, 115, 178
Étoile, 121
Ettore in *ARIT*, 74, 75, 78
Euphemisms in *ARIT*, 56, 62, 141, 170
Eylau, 57

Fadiman, Clifton, 53
Falaise Pocket, 115, 121
Farewell to Arms, A (Hemingway, novel): and *ARIT*, 38, 111; Aymo, Bartolomeo, in, 69, 168; Barkley, Catherine, in, 73, 104; Bergamo in, 66; Caporetto in, 24, 30, 37, 183; composition of, 20–21, 89, 190; Cortina d'Ampezzo in, 14; death in, 168; Ettore in, 74; Greffi, Count, in, 201; irony in, 64; Mantegna in, 18; memory in, 183, 197, 201;

Farewell to Arms, A (cont.)
    Mestre in, 39; military decorations in, 24; multilingualism in, 7, 48; *pescecani* in, 43; priest in, 126; sexuality in, 131; title of, 53, 54, 195; Verona in, 66; Vicenza in, 66; victory in, 198; war in, 56, 176; wine in, 109; wounding in, 37

Fascism in *ARIT*, 47, 54, 143, 147, 151

Father, Hemingway as, 96

"Fathers and Sons" (Hemingway, short story), 130

Faulkner, William, 26, 56, 67, 87. See also specific works

Feltre, 50

Fifth Column, The (Hemingway, book), 21, 54

Fitzgerald, F. Scott, 72, 87, 112, 193. See also specific works

Fitzgerald, Zelda, 157

Five sons theme in *ARIT*, 97–98, 162, 173

Flanders, Battle of, 66, 182

Florence, 21, 42, 90

Florian, 136, 157, 158

Foch, Ferdinand, 33

Fonda, Henry, 53

Fondamente Nuove, 150, 172

Fornaci, 22

For Whom the Bell Tolls (Hemingway, novel), 87, 88; and *ARIT*, 40, 45, 102; audiobook of, 109; Brueghel in, 19, 154; civilian vs. soldier in, 73–74, 196; Custer, General, in, 138; death in, 173; euphemisms in, 56, 65; film of, 126; El Greco in, 154; Jordan, Robert, in, 122; Mantegna in, 18, 19, 154; Maria in, 73, 104, 105; metacognition in, 33; military orders in, 8; Montana in, 15, 41; multilingualism in, 7; sexuality in, 97, 131, 172; Velázquez in, 127

Fossalta, 21, 25

Framing technique in *ARIT*, 5, 42, 80

Franchetti, Afdera, 53, 96, 211

Franchetti, Nanuk, 205; and Alvarito, 53, 118, 125; and Hemingway, 14

Franco, Francisco, 141, 142n1

Frederick the Great, 122

Frye, Northrop, 45

Fuoco, Il (D'Annunzio), 50, 56

Gamelin, Maurice, 32–33

Garden of Eden, The (Hemingway, novel): alcohol in, 120; and *ARIT*, 108, 167; Bosch in, 184; Bourne in, 199; Boyle, Colonel, in, 10n2; Joan of Arc in, 137; mirrors in, 81; multilingualism in, 7; names in, 107; sexuality in, 130, 131, 172; violence in, 198

Gautier, Théophile, 112

Gellhorn, Martha: and children, 97, 194; and Cooper, 86; and Hemingway, 41, 75–76, 84, 164, 165, 171. See also specific works

Geneva Convention, 201

George in *ARIT*, 201

Gettysburg, Battle of, 183

Giorgio in *ARIT*, 62

"God Rest You Merry, Gentlemen" (Hemingway, short story), 76

Goebbels, Joseph, 88

"Good Lion, The" (Hemingway, short story), 43, 74

Gorizia, 51

Gorrell, Hank, 175

Gradoli, Marina, 154

Gran Maestro in *ARIT*, 58; and Cantwell, 51, 63, 110; health of, 124; mind-set of, 67; and Order, 65; professionalism of, 134, 192, salary of, 101; and Treviso, 25

Grant, Bud, 175

Grappa, 14, 50, 51, 63, 64, 110–11

Grave di Popodopoli, 28

Great Gatsby, The (Fitzgerald), 14, 39–40, 202

Greene, Philip, 43

Green Hills of Africa (Hemingway, book): and *ARIT*, 193; hunting in, 204; inspiration for, 69; Lewis, Sinclair, in, 88; manuscript of, 140; note to, 4

Gritti Palace Hotel: boat ride to, 164; and Cantwell, 71, 103, 129, 169; Hemingway at, 46, 74, 87; Jackson at, 62; location of, 46, 50, 78, 100, 150, 158; naming of, 156; Renata at, 133

Grosshau, 183, 185–86

Groton, 149

Guderian, Heinz, 174

Guevara, Che, 45

Guill, Stacey, 142n1

Habeck, Fritz, 175

Hall porter in *ARIT*, 6, 134, 152

Hamlet (Shakespeare), 131, 173

Hammond, Indiana, 40

Harris, Jed, 54

Harry's Bar: and *ARIT*, 46, 100, 129, 179; and Arnaldo, 137; and Cipriani, 58, 74; and Hemingway, 46, 75, 81; and Maxwell, 121

Havana, 26
Havre, 54
Hawthorne, Nathaniel, 148
Hazlitt, William Carew, 35
Heiachiro, Togo, 155
Hell: and *ARIT,* 42, 171; and Dante Alighieri, 5, 9, 17, 62, 90, 109, 180, 196, 199
Hemingway, Anson, 176
Hemingway, Ernest. *See specific headings and works*
Hemingway, Hadley Richardson, 14, 26, 87, 107, 109, 134
Hemingway, John, 112, 116, 201
Hemingway, Leicester, 112, 186
Hemingway, Mary Welsh: and *ARIT,* 4; Aspasia on, 75; Clark on, 178; and Dandolo, 52; and E. Hemingway, 8–9, 54, 65, 139, 157, 161, 186, 193, 199; Lewis on, 87; Maxwell on, 121; pregnancy of, 41, 97, 194; and Shaw, 123
Hemingway, Patrick, 96, 115, 149, 190
Hemingway, the Writer as Artist (Baker), 3, 50, 85, 128, 129
Henry IV, Part I (Shakespeare), 139
Henry IV, Part II (Shakespeare), 63–64
Henry VI, Part I (Shakespeare), 43
Henry VIII (Shakespeare), 192
"He Who Gets Slap-Happy: A Bimini Letter" (Hemingway), 138
Hill, Ambrose Powell, 206
"Hills Like White Elephants" (Hemingway, short story), 36n1
Hitler, Adolf, 111, 176
Hodges, Courtney, 181
Homer, 185; in *ARIT,* 93–94, 164
Horace, 159
Horwits, Al, 139
Hotchner, A. E., 41, 72, 89, 149, 175
Howard, Deborah, 35, 57, 78
Hugo, Victor, 49, 106
Hunting. *See* Duck hunting
Hurston, Zora Neale, 30
Hürtgen Forest, Battle of. *See* Battle of Hürtgen Forest

Illnesses, of Hemingway, 37, 44, 55, 68, 71, 158
"I love you" in *ARIT,* 82–83, 86, 94, 95
"In Another Country" (Hemingway, short story), 48, 157, 165
"Indian Camp" (Hemingway, short story), 197
"Indian Country and the White Army" (Hemingway), 88, 109, 163, 201

"In Harry's Bar in Venice" (Hemingway), 210–11; and *ARIT,* 75, 88; Byron in, 46, 53; Cipriani in, 74; Lewis in, 46, 53; Ruskin in, 53, 101; Venice in, 46
In Our Time (Hemingway, short story collection), 18, 39, 127
"Introduction, *In Sicily*" (Hemingway), 141
Irony in *ARIT,* 28, 40, 78, 122, 143, 183
Islands in the Stream (Hemingway, novel): and *ARIT,* 55, 78, 170, 186; audiobook of, 109; Dante Alighieri in, 90; ducks in, 14; enemies in, 38, 143; film of, 109; Hudson, Thomas, in, 13, 15; multilingualism in, 7; Togo, Admiral, in, 155; Tunney, Gene, in, 140; volunteers in, 112; vulgarity in, 170
Isonzo, Battles of the, 14, 55, 68, 116; and boatman, 51, 98; Cantwell on, 51, 64
Isonzo River, 51
Ivancich, Adriana: age of, 83, 97, 118; on *ARIT,* 102, 103–4, 130–31; background of, 96, 110, 112, 126, 133; characteristics of, 80, 105; and duck hunting, 6, 14, 52; and Hemingway, 105, 166, 199; memoirs of, 24, 74–75, 99n3, 140, 189; nickname of, 129; poetry of, 92, 96; and Renata, 4, 94; suicide of, 134, 164, 173; and White Tower, 65
Ivancich, Giacomo, 126
Ivancich-Biaggini, Gianfranco, 17, 52, 111, 126

Jackson, Ronald in *ARIT*: and Cantwell, 3, 6, 7, 19–20, 29, 33, 42, 57, 63, 135, 207; home of, 20; in manuscript, 62–63; military experience of, 21, 29–30; naming of, 19; narrative perspective of, 34; and Trieste, 16; and Venice, 17, 27
Jackson, Stonewall: final words of, 3, 21, 206; name of, 19, 101; wound of, 3, 85
Jacksonville, Florida, 41
James, Harry, 12
James, Henry, 112, 133, 179
James, Jesse, 189–90
Jeremiah Johnson (film), 21
Jewiss, Virginia, 54
Joan of Arc, 137
Johnston, John "Liver-Eating," 21
Johnston, Kenneth G., 18
Joyce, James: home of, 16; narrative techniques of, 26, 56; and Quinet, 193; and violence, 198. *See also specific works*
Julius Caesar (Shakespeare), 187

INDEX   225

Kansas City Country Club, 189
Kechler, Carlo, 14, 91
Kenya, 69
Keokuk, Iowa, 75–76
Kert, Bernice, 97
Ketchum, Idaho, 26
Key West, Florida, 26, 41
"Killers, The" (Hemingway, short story), 19
King Lear (Shakespeare), 80, 140
Kleinhau, 183
K-rations, 31

Languages in *ARIT*: Cantwell's errors, 20, 48; and Hemingway, 7, 48; Italian, 20, 91, 104, 123, 191; Spanish, 92, 104
Lanham, Buck: and Cantwell, 6; as correspondent, 6, 32, 65, 185; and Hemingway, 6, 32, 65, 182, 185, 201; in war, 152, 182, 183, 186, 200
Lanier, Sidney, 3
Latham, Aaron, 97
Latisana, 16, 17
Lauder, Mary, 140
Lawrence, D. H., 107
Le Buc, 125
Leclerc, Jacques-Philippe, 6, 119, 124, 125, 139
Lee, Robert E., 57
Leopoldina, 177
Les Paul Trio, 12
Lewis, Robert W., 99n4, 108n1
Lewis, Sinclair, 46, 53, 86–88, 112, 210
Lido, 47, 134
Light as theme in *ARIT*, 179
Light in August (Faulkner), 94
Lincoln, Abraham, 98
Lisca, Peter, 5, 16
Little Big Horn, Battle of the, 137
Lockridge, Ernest, 174
Longfellow, Henry Wadsworth, 90
Longhena, Baldassare, 17
Louis XVI, 124, 187
Lowry, Malcolm, 79
Lowry, Robert, 79
Lupino, Ida, 161
Lustig, Allen and Henry, 15
Lynn, Kenneth S., 87
Lyons, Leonard, 26

Macbeth (Shakespeare), 19
Madden, Thomas F., 40
Madrid, 40, 41

Maginot Line, 32
Malraux, André, 123
Manager in *ARIT*, 65
Mandel, Miriam, 22, 32, 58, 62, 145, 192
Mangin, Charles, 32
Mann, Thomas, 5, 10n1, 40, 47
Mannitol hexanitrate, 11
Manos, Aspasia, 74–75, 210
Mantua, 41, 68
Marano, 14
Marbot, Jean-Baptiste-Antoine-Marcelin de, 57
Marie Antoinette, 80, 124, 187
Marlowe, Christopher, 165
Marocchinate, 6
Marston, John, 112
Mathematics in *ARIT*, 22, 34, 67–68
Maupassant, Guy de, 140
Maxwell, Elsa, 121
McCarthy, Cormac, 186
McGeorge, Stephen, 31
McLaughlin, Robert L., 88
McLellan, Davis, 138
McManus, John C., 171
McNair, Lesley James, 183
Mellow, James R., 37
Melville, Herman, 140
Memphis, Tennessee, 41, 42
Men at War (Hemingway, book): Cambronne in, 49; cowardice vs. panic in, 165; Crane, Stephen, in, 70n2; Custer in, 137; immortality in, 38–39, 157; Italian front in, 64; Marbot in, 57; Shakespeare in, 63–64; soldier vs. writer in, 123; Togo, Admiral, in, 155; victory in, 198; wounds in, 64
"Mercenaries, The" (Hemingway, short story), 156
Merchant of Venice, The (Shakespeare), 76
Meredith, James H., 21, 34, 128n2
Mestre, 26, 39
Meyers, Benny, 149–50
Meyers, Jeffrey: and *ARIT*, 18, 86, 164; on Dorman-Smith, 8; on Hemingway, 13, 96–97
Middleton, Drew, 177, 198
Milan, 43, 50, 64, 91
Military awards: Croce al Merito di Guerra, 23, 58; Distinguished Service Cross, 24, 200; Medaglia d'Argento al Valore Militare, 23–24; Purple Heart, 29; Silver Stars, 200; Victoria Cross, 24
Military insignias, 7, 29, 32, 110, 121

Military units: Eighth Air Forces, 183; Eighty-Seventh Mortar Battalion, 185; First Infantry Division, 177, 181; Fourth Infantry Division, 115, 121, 169, 181, 182; Ninth Infantry Division, 181, 182; Second Armored Division, 177; Sixth Parachute Division, 171; Third Army, 182; Thirtieth Infantry Division, 177; Thirty-Sixth Division, 21; Twelfth Army, 181–82; Twenty-Eighth Division, 131, 182; Twenty-Second Infantry Regiment, 180, 182, 183, 185–86
Miller, Edward G., 182
Mirrors in *ARIT*, 81, 85, 106, 146
Missouri River, 190
Mizener, Arthur, 112
Monastier, 22
Mondadori, Alberto, 40
Monfalcone, 16
Monte Asolone, 110–11
Monte Grappa, Battle of, 50, 51, 54, 63, 110
Monte Pertica, 110–11
Monte Tomba, 110
Montgomery, Bernard, 81–82, 116, 122, 151, 170
Montrouge, 124
Mont.-St-Michel, 98, 189
"Monument, The" (Hemingway), 143
Moreira, Peter, 171
Moreland, Kim, 65
Moretto, 100, 102
Moriani, Gianni, 26, 48, 50, 55, 100, 150; as photo editor, 31, 34, 110, 125, 153, 157, 189
Moscow, 132
Mount Valérien, 125
Moveable Feast, A (Hemingway, book): and *ARIT*, 167; Cortina d'Ampezzo in, 14; Fitzgerald, F. Scott, in, 193; Fitzgerald, Zelda, in, 157; horse chestnuts in, 161; note to, 4; title of, 3, 49, 71–72; von Blixen, Baron, in, 193; wine in, 109
Muehlebach Hotel, 189
Murano, 35, 117
Museums: Accademia, 35, 48, 151; Pitti, 19, 20; Prado, 18, 127, 151, 154; Scuola Grande di San Rocco, 48, 151; Uffizi, 19, 20, 96
Mussolini, Benito, 44, 54

Napoleon, 57, 132, 164, 167, 175
Narrative perspective in *ARIT*: Cantwell, 10, 73, 81, 136; other characters, 34, 46, 192
"Natural History of the Dead, A" (Hemingway, short story), 27

Nervesa, 27
Newman, Steve, 182
New York, New York, 41
Ney, Michel, 131, 132
Night porter in *ARIT*, 58, 134, 147
Noghera, 31
Non-thinking in *ARIT*, 84, 131, 169, 173
Nordquist, Lawrence and Olive, 41
Normandy, Battle of. *See* Battle of Normandy
Nothingness as theme in *ARIT*, 128, 159
Notturno (D'Annunzio), 30, 52, 55, 57, 107
"Now I Lay Me" (Hemingway, short story), 17
Nuti, Elisabetta Zingoni, 44

Oak Park, Illinois, 41
Objective correlatives in *ARIT*, 50, 57, 69, 78, 130
Odessa, 91
O'Hara, John, 140
Old Man and the Sea, The (Hemingway, novel): and *ARIT*, 48; arm wrestling in, 197; dedication of, 4; defeat in, 61; enemies in, 38, 143; inspiration for, 4; metacognition in, 33; Santiago in, 63, 70n1; talking in, 135; wounds in, 70
Operation Overlord, 187
Order of the Brusadelli, 43, 57–58, 65, 69, 118
O'Shaughnessey, Margaret, 73, 127
Othello (Shakespeare), 28, 30, 42, 81, 102, 105, 112, 132, 174
Ovid, 159

Pacciardi, Randolfo, 24, 31, 44, 147
Padua, 17, 68, 87
Panunzio, Constantine Maria, 53–54
Paris, 26, 29, 40
Pasionaria, La, 45
Passchendaele, Battle of, 66, 182
Pasubio, 51, 63, 64
Patton, George, 109, 127, 182
Paul, Les, 12
Paul, Steve, 189
Père Lachaise, 172
Periodicals in *ARIT*, 125, 143, 167–68, 177
Perkins, Maxwell: death of, 72; and Hemingway, 23, 33, 87, 114, 126, 167; and *Old Man and the Sea*, 4
Pescecani, 6–7, 43, 47, 91, 123, 149
Peters, Harold, 177
Pfeiffer, Pauline, 69, 97, 166
Phlegyas, 5

INDEX   227

Piave, Battle of the, 22, 27, 37, 110, 116, 183
Piave River, 28, 31, 32, 44
Piazza San Marco, 17, 66, 133, 134, 136, 173
Piemonte, 62, 69
Pilottown, Louisiana, 31
Pius XII (pope), 117
Pivano, Fernanda: and *ARIT*, 104, 151, 159, 192; errors by, 80; husband of, 74
Platt, Frank, 176
Platte River, 31
Plimpton, George, 89, 90, 138, 140, 175
Pockmarked writer in *ARIT*, 74, 86–88, 89, 90; and Cantwell, 6, 63, 112–13; eating by, 116
"Poem to Mary (Second Poem)" (Hemingway, poetry), 155, 168, 207
Pola, 55
Poler in *ARIT*. *See* Boatman in *ARIT*
Polo in *ARIT*, 13, 189
Pony Express, 190
Porte d'Orleans, 124–25
Portogrande, 39
Pound, Ezra, 26, 75, 172
Powers, Katherine, 87, 88
Powers, Marcella, 87, 88
Proust, Marcel, 46, 49, 52
Punctuation in *ARIT*: errors in, 13, 131, 145, 147; exclamation points in, 162; idiosyncratic usage in, 30, 107; parentheses in, 54
Purgatorio (Dante Alighieri), 171

Quatre Bas, 132
Quesada, Pete, 171–72
Quinet, Edgar, 193–94, 199

Raab, David, 28
Rambouillet, 124, 125
Rapido River, 21
Rawlins, Wyoming, 20
Redford, Robert, 21
Red Lodge, Montana, 21, 41
Reed, Henry, 106
Reinhardt, Max, 85
Renata in *ARIT*: age difference with Cantwell, 4, 83, 197; animal compared to, 129; and Cantwell, 61–62, 84–85, 203; crying of, 91; entrance of, 80; family history of, 73, 92, 103, 111–12, 134; forcefulness of, 102; hair of, 104–5; marriage of, 117, 139, 164, 166, 178, 194; menstruation of, 92, 98, 105–6; naming of, 57, 107; poetry of, 92; portrait compared with, 146, 159, 186; pregnancy of, 105; retirement of, 117; and sailors, 197, 198; "transvestic hallucination" of, 126, 130, 131, 141; and Venice, 204
Renata, portrait of in *ARIT*: as character, 127, 141, 145; as gift, 30, 102; as interlocutor, 9, 134, 135, 147, 160, 186; painter of, 96; Renata compared with, 146, 159, 186; transporting of, 118; value of, 188
"Revolutionist, The" (Hemingway, short story), 18
Reynolds, Michael: on *ARIT*, 3, 101; and Hemingway, 11, 13, 22, 26, 37, 51, 53, 112, 125, 174
Rheims, 178
Rialto, 76, 112, 150, 153, 154
Richard II (Shakespeare), 177
Richard the Lion-Hearted, 73, 173
Rif War, 174
Riley, Fort, 189
Rimbaud, Arthur, 187
Rio Nuovo, 50
"Riparto d'Assalto" (Hemingway, poetry), 39
Ritz Hotel, 118
Robidoux, 190
Robilant, Carlo Di, 14, 74
Rolex, 124
Rome, 21, 133
Romeo and Juliet (Shakespeare), 66, 68, 145, 173
Rommel, Erwin, 14, 82, 111, 116, 143, 171, 198
Roosevelt, Franklin Delano, 149
Roosevelt, Theodore, 53
Ross, Lillian, and Hemingway, 13, 15, 19, 20, 72, 73, 89, 112, 116, 127, 145
Rostand, Edmond, 94, 141
Rotary Club, 115
Rush, Robert Sterling, 185
Ruskin, John, 48, 100–101, 102; in "In Harry's Bar in Venice," 46, 53, 101, 210
Russo, John Paul, 26, 51, 60

"Safari" (Hemingway), 41
Sailors in *ARIT*, 197, 198
Saint Lô, 115, 119, 183
Sanctuary (Faulkner), 55
San Donà di Piave, 21, 27
San Michele, 17, 55, 172
Santa Maria del Giglio, 54, 57, 78
Santa Maria della Salute, 17
Santa Maria Gloriosa dei Frari, 151
Sardi, Giuseppe, 57, 78

Sartarelli, Stephen, 57
Saxe, Maurice de, 122
Scafella, Frank, 128
Schio, 64, 134
Schnee-Eifel, 176–77
Scholes, Robert, 106, 108
Schultz, Carl H., 181
Scott, Campbell, 109
Scott, George C., 109
Scott's Bluff, Nebraska, 190
Scribner, Charles, 4; death of, 167; and Hemingway, 67, 75, 87, 112, 192
Scrovegni Chapel, 17
Season of *ARIT*, 5, 22, 23, 32, 37, 52
Serialization of *ARIT*, 88–89, 165, 177–78
Setting of *ARIT*, 5, 37, 194
Seward, William W., 72, 112
SHAEF, 120, 121, 124, 177; and Cantwell, 9, 115, 172; location of, 175, 178
Shakespeare, William, 20, 123, 139–40, 145. *See also specific works*
Shaw, Irwin, 123
Sheridan, Wyoming, 134, 190
Sherman, William Tecumseh, 171
Shoop, Duke, 177
"Short Happy Life of Francis Macomber, The" (Hemingway, short story): irony in, 78, 143–44; panic in, 165; Shakespeare in, 64; title of, 44; von Blixen, Baron, in, 192–93
Sicknesses, of Hemingway, 37, 44, 55, 68, 71, 158
Sigman, Joseph, 51
Sile Canal, 31, 67
Smith, Red, 135
Smith, Walter Bedell, and *ARIT*, 115, 172, 178, 180
"Snows of Kilimanjaro, The" (Hemingway, short story): alcohol in, 73; death in, 128, 168, 184; Harry in, 195; love in, 168; time in, 17, 26, 56, 197; war in, 38, 51, 111; writing in, 9
Solingen, 23
"Sonnet 61" (Shakespeare), 93
Sottsass, Ettore, 74
Sound and the Fury, The (Faulkner), 52, 96
Spanish Earth, The (Hemingway), 44
Stadtwald, 177
Stalin, Joseph, 147–48
Stein, Gertrude, 115, 172, 174
Steinbeck, John, 28, 68, 150, 168
Stevenson, Marcus O., 182
St. Joseph, Missouri, 189, 190
Stoneback, H. R., 169

Stones in *ARIT*, 100–101, 102, 152, 188
"Strange Country, The" (Hemingway, short story), 74
Strass, 183
Style in *ARIT*, 100, 103, 196
Styne, Jule, 12
Suicide, of Hemingway, 200
Sullivan, James, 170
Summersby, Kay, 114–15
Sun Also Rises, The (Hemingway, novel), 38, 73, 82, 165, 172, 178; Ashley, Brett, in, 84, 129; Burguete in, 45, 155; Cohn, Robert, in, 20, 49, 118; composition of, 72, 174; and courtly love, 94, 164; Flamands in, 66; impotence and wounds of Jake Barnes in, 85, 104, 146; language in, 7, 105, 129, 159; Mippipopolous in, 84, 129, 133; Montoya in, 58; Romero in, 118, 143; value in, 119; violence in, 197
Sun Tzu, 122
Sun Valley, Idaho, 126
Sweeny, Charlie, 6, 10n2, 174

Tagliamento River, 14, 17
Taming of the Shrew, The (Shakespeare), 68
Tanner, Stephen L., 39
Tender Is the Night (Fitzgerald), 153
Ten-in-One rations, 31
Thiess, Frank, 155
Thompson, Mark, 116
Three as theme in *ARIT*: battalions, 140–41; Cantwell's heart attacks, 38, 124, 206; decisions, 38; errors, 93; sexual activity, 129, 132; wives, 140–41
Time in *ARIT*: and defecation, 22, 24; and duck hunting, 5, 16, 76, 118, 206; and Venice, 26, 76, 78, 118, 136, 139
Tintner, Adeline R., 51, 57, 102n1
Title of *ARIT*: alternates, 3, 49; echoed in text, 3, 19, 60, 101, 195, 206; Hemingway's decision on, 71, 117
Tito, Josip Broz, 147–48
To Have and Have Not (Hemingway, novel), 85, 138
Toklas, Alice B., 115, 172
Tolstoy, Leo, 140
Torcello, 31
"Torcello Piece" (Hemingway, short story), 35–36
Torrents of Spring (Hemingway, novel), 33, 40, 88, 137, 174

Torrington, Wyoming, 19
Toussus le Noble, 125
Trade theme in *ARIT,* 7, 8–9, 84, 92, 93, 107, 133
"Treachery in Aragon" (Hemingway, short story), 198, 199
Trentino, 111
Treviso, 25, 27, 44
Trieste, 5, 9, 16, 21, 30, 54, 104
Truman, Harry S., 172
Truman, Margaret, 158
Tumbril in *ARIT,* 24, 124
Tunney, Gene, 140, 145
Turgenev, Ivan, 140, 197
Twain, Mark, 40. *See also specific works*
Two Gentlemen of Verona, The (Shakespeare), 66

Udet, Ernst, 111, 171
Ulysses (Joyce), 136–37
"Undefeated, The" (Hemingway, short story), 61
Under Kilimanjaro (Hemingway, novel), 75, 91, 149, 199; and *ARIT,* 72, 78–79, 94, 162; inspiration for, 69

Valhalla Express, 114, 170–71, 183
Vandenberg, Arthur H., 176
Vandenberg, Hoyt S., 176
Vasari, Giorgio, 59–60
Veliki, 55
Venice, 5, 16, 26, 31, 35, 126, 129, 204
Verdun, 89
Verlaine, Paul, 187
Verona, 66
Versailles, 178
"Veteran Visits the Old Front, A" (Hemingway), 43, 134
Vicenza, 66
Villon, François, 106–7
Virgil, 5, 68, 159
Viterbo, 117
Vittorini, Elio, 141
Vittorio Veneto, Battle of the, 21, 37, 49, 50, 51, 63, 110, 111

Von Blixen, Bror, 192–93
"Voyage to Victory" (Hemingway), 27, 149

Wagner, Richard, 89
Wagon Box Fight, 190
Waiter in *ARIT,* 58
Ward, Mike, 175
"War in the Siegfried Line" (Hemingway), 176–77, 182
Wassermann, Paul von, 141
Water, bodies of. *See specific bodies of water*
Waterloo, 49, 132
"Way You'll Never Be, A" (Hemingway, short story), 22, 38, 39
Wertenbaker, George, 201
Wes in *ARIT,* 12, 13, 15, 91
Westerbeke Corporation, 47
"Whatever that means" in *ARIT,* 95–96
White, E. B., 93, 116
Whitman, Walt, 98, 154, 164
"Who Murdered the Vets? A First-Hand Report on the Florida Hurricane" (Hemingway), 139
Wickes, George, 40
Williams, Tennessee, 107
Wilson, Margaret Woodrow, 158
Wine of Astonishment, The (Gellhorn), 186
"Wine of Wyoming" (Hemingway, short story), 190
Winner Take Nothing (Hemingway, novel), 22, 27, 38, 61, 76, 190
Wolfe, Tom, 167
Woolf, Virginia, 26
"Woppian Way, The" (Hemingway), 55, 171
Wounding, of Hemingway, 21, 22, 24, 76

Yellin, Emily, 88
Young, Philip, 124; on *ARIT,* 18, 86, 150

Zapata, Emiliano, 45
Zorzi, Rosella Mamoli, 48, 50–51, 55, 100, 150